Praise for *How to F*ck Up Your Startup*

"Entertaining and thought-provoking. Destined to be a classic in the field of entrepreneurship."

—Caroline Ahlefelt, CEO and Founder of TOMORROW,
and Former Board Member of LEGO

"Don't miss out on a humorous ride through the many reasons why companies fail, as well as how to avoid them. A mandatory read for everyone working with startups."

—Henrik Ernlund, Investor and Country Manager, SAS Institute

"A fantastic tour de force through the business failures that cause the vast majority of companies to crash—neatly accompanied by the remedies required to fix them. A no-brainer investment of your time."

—Peter Friis, VP Northern Europe, Google

"Success is hard to learn from. Failures are more generous in their inclination to point you to a handle. This book focuses on what to avoid, but it would be a failure to avoid reading it."

—Dr. Daniel Hjorth, Professor of Entrepreneurship,
Copenhagen Business School and Nottingham Business School

"I should have read this before I f*cked up my first startup and maybe things would have been different."

—Paul Clements, Investor, Founder, Creative and TEDx speaker

How to F*ck Up Your Startup

Kim Christian Hvidkjaer

How to F*ck Up Your Startup

*The Science Behind Why 90% of Companies Fail—and How You Can Avoid It

Matt Holt Books
An Imprint of BenBella Books, Inc.
Dallas, TX

This book is designed to provide accurate and authoritative information about entrepreneurship. Neither the author nor the publisher is engaged in rendering legal, accounting, or other professional services by publishing this book. If any such assistance is required, the services of a qualified financial professional should be sought. The author and publisher will not be responsible for any liability, loss, or risk incurred as a result of the use and application of any information contained in this book.

How to F*ck Up Your Startup copyright © 2022 by Kim Hvidkjaer

BenBella Books, Inc.
10440 N. Central Expressway
Suite 800
Dallas, TX 75231
benbellabooks.com
Send feedback to feedback@benbellabooks.com

BenBella and *Matt Holt* are federally registered trademarks.

Printed in the United States of America
10 9 8 7 6 5 4 3 2 1

Library of Congress Control Number: 2021034781
ISBN 9781637740590 (trade cloth)
ISBN 9781637740606 (ebook)

Editing by Katie Dickman
Copyediting by Michael Fedison
Proofreading by Sarah Vostok and Jenny Bridges
Indexing by Amy Murphy
Text design and composition by PerfecType, Nashville, TN
Cover design by Urgent.Agency
Illustrations by Kim Hvidkjaer
Printed by Lake Book Manufacturing

Dedicated with love to the two entrepreneurs before me, my mother and father, the entrepreneur at my side, Sofie, and the two entrepreneurs after (and outperforming) me, Katinka and Wilbert. Lucky guy, huh?

So, you have an idea for a startup?

Great!

You're not alone, however, as 63 percent of twenty-somethings either already own or want to start a business.

Already have a startup off the ground?

Congratulations!

You are still not alone.

In the US, 12,000 new companies are started each day. Every day of the year.

That equals 4,400,000 new companies annually, in case you don't want to do the math.

You're venture backed?

Oh wow! Impressive!

What is most likely to happen next?

You are going to f*ck up your startup!

Yes, the most likely scenario from here is your startup will fail.

It doesn't matter if you haven't founded it yet, if you've bootstrapped, or if you've already successfully pitched and received venture funding.

This is the general rule of startups: they fail.

- 90 percent of startups fail.
- 67 percent of startups stall at some point in the venture capital process and fail to exit or raise follow-on funding.
- 97 percent of hardware startups die (or become zombies).

Are you perhaps dreaming of becoming a startup unicorn?[1] The likelihood of that is less than .0001 percent. Best of luck—I sincerely doubt it will happen, and equally sincerely, of course, hope the best for you.

But, as you probably already know, hope is not a strategy.

---

1. A privately held startup company with a current valuation of US $1 billion or more.

Startups Suck

Launching a startup sounds sexy, but in reality it sucks.

The media enjoys portraying an entrepreneur with a hero narrative, but the rasping reality is building a startup is considerably closer to running a marathon through a minefield.[2] It's hell on earth with things blowing up around you, until you probably step on a mine yourself.

It's an awful, tiring, and long struggle of constant stress, often on the edge of a mental breakdown. And I'm not exaggerating even a tiny bit.

It takes a huge toll on your financial situation, your health, and your family. Even worse, an alarmingly large number of CEOs commit suicide when their companies crash.

And we could end the story right here. But—obviously—we won't. Instead, we will look at why 90 percent of companies fail and how you can avoid stepping on those mines while running your startup marathon.

With my motivational speech out of the way, let's get started.

---

2. Not to be confused with the Afghanistan Minefield Marathon run held at Bagram Air Base near Kabul.

CONTENTS

INTRODUCTION

I remember the day I realized I was a millionaire: New Year's Day 2007. It was the warmest January day Denmark had seen in years. My girlfriend; our beautiful one-year-old daughter, Katinka; and I had recently moved into a spacious 1896 brick manor house. The herringbone-patterned oak floors fit in perfectly for one of the most expensive areas in Denmark.

I sat at our kitchen table, looking out at the large terrace and picturesque garden. On the laptop in front of me, I studied the Excel spreadsheet which tracked the assets for all the businesses I'd started in the last ten years. When I registered the total sum in the final box, I stopped and double-checked the math. Yes, it was true . . . I'd finally done it. I was a millionaire! My assets, real estate investments, stocks, private equity, and cash added up to well over the equivalent of $2 million. In those days, $2 million could support my family for the rest of our lives if converted to cash and invested.

I had no such plans. My career was ramping up. After completing my Executive MBA at Copenhagen Business School, I sold a large chunk of my startup, Shockwaved, a marketing company that made online games, to one of the top three advertising agencies worldwide, TBWA. If all went well, the company would soon announce me as the new CEO of their Danish division. I'd get to run the new digital leg of the Danish business, as well as the other companies in that group. Meanwhile, Denmark's leading business magazine, *Børsen*, slated me in a front-page feature on

1

"Denmark's Six Rising Stars." My life was 100 percent on track; I was exactly where I wanted to be. I had become a proud member of the cult of success (more on that in a bit).

Fast-forward two years—and I was basically broke.

WTF just happened? The deal with TBWA went through according to plan. I was the CEO of TBWA\Denmark, the parent of TBWA\PLAY, which had absorbed Shockwaved.

Unfortunately, the Great Recession and poor managerial decisions (mine included) sent the company's valuation plummeting. Not to mention, the real estate market was in free fall. The value of apartments I'd purchased through my real estate investment startup (the one that helped tip me into millionaire status a few years earlier) threatened to bankrupt me.

In the period between 2007 and 2009, I'd lost more money than the average American earned in a lifetime. And certainly more money than my fairly entrepreneurial parents ever dreamed of with their mix of day jobs and small laundromat businesses.

I was now a broke thirty-one-year-old with a young family to support and a sizable mortgage now beyond my means. The worst part? I'd seen much of my misfortune coming and failed to act. Several years earlier, well before discovering that I was a millionaire on paper, I'd even written a report predicting the real estate market crash. I'd meant to sell my real estate holdings shortly after completing the report, but the truth was, I got too busy. I'd let things fall through the cracks.

Though I didn't know it yet, my first business failure was that I'd overextended myself (you'll read all about it in the section on plate-spinning in chapter 1). Every weekend, I intended to address the mounting problems in my various startups and investments. But twenty-four hours weren't enough in the day. Overwhelmed, I'd let the plates drop, one by one. I even ended up in jail. Unable to fix it, my focus became, "How do I get out of this alive?"

I wasn't alone in my misery, of course. Failed startups littered the business landscape all around me, thanks to the Great Recession. Still, I chose one of the riskiest career paths known to humankind. Entrepreneurship lived in my soul. I'd heard the statistic a thousand times in business school: as many as 90 percent of startups crash and burn—and that's not even during recessions. Let's quickly illustrate it. Hold up both of your hands and then fold down all but one finger (feel free to make it the middle finger, if you like)—that's what your odds look like. What's more, those startups that do make it very rarely make their founders wealthy. The number one lesson I'd taken away from my years (so far) in the entrepreneurial trenches: startup life is not for the faint of heart. Startups suck, as I believe I mentioned once already.

Yet, for me, the risks were well worth the potential rewards. I'd been a lousy founder, but it didn't change the fact that I loved what I did. I'd tasted the thrill and freedom of the entrepreneurial life, and there was no way I was going to shift to a nine-to-five job. That wasn't the answer. Once I finished licking my wounds and saved my house from foreclosure, I needed to understand how things went so wrong to avoid f*cking up my next startup (and the one after that, and the one after that . . .).

As I regained focus, I looked inward at my practices. Then I focused outward, analyzing once-promising companies who also lost their way. Most entrepreneurs blamed their failed businesses on the market crash. "The money dried up," they'd say with a shrug.

The more I studied failed businesses, though, the more I realized startups were only at the mercy of the market's boom-bust cycle when they lacked proper foundations. And no, it's never as simple as running out of cash. Bankruptcy is a symptom, not a disease. I realized that we founders wasted so much time and energy trying to project a "crushing it" image. We instead needed to spend more time examining and being transparent about our struggles and failures. Then we'd be better equipped to correct course when bad weather loomed.

Over the next decade, as I clawed myself from the wreckage of my failed business ventures, I remained an avid student of failures—not only in startups but also in how we screw up our health and other life aspects as well. As a founder, though, studying startup failures became a passion project. I became obsessed with examining every detail of how promising and well-funded companies failed. What were the red flags along their journey from blockbuster to bankruptcy? Over time, I added a team of several researchers to help. I interviewed dozens of founders, dissected the business plans of a myriad of failed companies (including my own), and gathered as much intelligence as was available on the finances and day-to-day operations of struggling startups. We compiled this information in a database. My team and I analyzed the strategic and operational mistakes shared by most failed businesses.

It's thanks to my morbid interest in failure that I've been able to succeed in business since my rock-bottom year in 2009. This is not to say I haven't experienced small (and some not-so-small) failures along the way. But I've been able to recognize and head off the catastrophic ones, the unequivocal failures. I'm happy to report I not only managed to save our house but also launched multiple successful companies in a wide range of industries. I've also invested in several startups and now sit on the boards of many of them. At this point in my life, with two children—my equally beautiful son, Wilbert, was born in 2011—and twenty years of working like a maniac behind me, I'm enjoying the slightly more balanced lifestyle that entrepreneurship allows me to have. Once again, I have reached the goal I'd briefly met at age twenty-nine: If I wanted to retire today, I could. I don't want to, of course! I'll be starting new businesses when I'm eighty, just for fun. Just don't tell my girlfriend that.

Often, when the kids are in bed, I sit down to analyze and write about failure. Why do I do this? Because I want to share what I and others have had to learn the hard way. In the chapters ahead, I'll reveal the statistically likely patterns that destroy young companies time and time again so that you can redraw these patterns in yours. These patterns are derived from the long-term study and structured analysis of over 160,000 failed companies, as well as founder interviews, startup postmortems, and several other data sources. I'll show you, at every step, how to identify, avoid, and fix the most lethal attitude, business model, market research, funding, product development, organizational, sales, and growth failures known to startup-kind.

You'll still f*ck up once in a while, of course. It's a failure-minefield out there, no doubt. And our fundamental goal, what I've called the Rule Zero of Startups, is "Don't die." The point is that knowing the biggest potential problems will help you avoid them. Minefields are much easier to navigate when you can see the mines and know how to detonate them.

Because, let's face it: you need all the help you can get. When else in your life have you taken a bet with 10 percent odds? When else have you sacrificed (or considered sacrificing) the amount of cash and sweat and tears you have now? When else have you tested the patience of your friendships and family the way you have or will for your business? Probably never. But here you are. You've decided the risk is worth the reward. You're going for it. And as much as I appreciate a good failure story, I love a good exit story, and I'm a sucker for happy endings. Ready to write one for your startup?

What Is a F*ckup and Why Should You Care?

Before we dive in, let's agree on what a f*ckup actually is and is not.

It is *not* selecting the wrong paper type for your business cards or too-expensive computers for your new office. It is also not being hit by lightning on your way to work (as you could not really see that coming). It *is*, however, failing to make a solid business model for your business before investing all of your life savings.

Definition of a f*ckup:

> **NEGLECT OF ACTION RESULTING IN A SIGNIFICANT AND PREVENTABLE MISTAKE.**

A f*ckup is something you neglected to do which has a significant (negative) impact that could have been prevented had you handled the situation differently.

For most startups, it's often multiple f*ckups in combination that lead to their downfalls.

Why Are F*ckups Important?

Most of us *are* living in the cult of success, which I so happily joined back in 2007. We all want to present ourselves in our best light—showcase our exciting careers, great relationships, funny and creative kids, and our healthy eating and exercising habits. When I see updates from friends on Instagram or Facebook, I see smiling, happy people somehow always on vacations. The same is true for many of my updates. It never rains, kids are always happy, and dinner always looks amazing. Take this book: It's my first, so by definition it is the best-selling book I have written to date. And, of course, the worst. Why not slap one of those fantastic facts on the front cover?[1] "Fake it till you make it" is important, as we will discuss under the Impostor Syndrome. Reality, of course, has a much wider range of fantastic and terrible situations.

The cult of success mindset often works against us. Multiple research projects have connected it to mental health issues, depression, loneliness, unhealthy ideas about our bodies, and overall low self-esteem. What's more, it is also affecting our judgment.

The media's favorite description of startups can give a false impression of what it takes to find success. Believing that you have to be a twenty-three-year-old college dropout armed mainly with passion and a do-or-die attitude toward his (not hers, since the studies always seem to neglect the female entrepreneurs, as we shall get back to later) first unicorn-sized company is today's norm of a (potentially) successful entrepreneur.

One in eight billionaires on the *Forbes* ranking of the four hundred wealthiest people in America was a college dropout. Batuli Lamichhane, a notorious chain-smoker, lived to the age of 118 despite her habit of smoking thirty cigarettes per day.

Oracle founder Larry Ellison; Microsoft's Bill Gates; Facebook's Mark Zuckerberg; Uber co-founder Travis Kalanick; fashion designer Ralph Lauren; WhatsApp co-founder and former CEO Jan Koum; CNN founder Ted Turner; Ty Warner, the creator of Beanie Babies; Dell founder Michael Dell. Apart from being billionaires, one thing they all share is that they didn't graduate college. Heck, the brilliant (and of course billionaire) entrepreneur Peter Thiel even launched a $100,000 grant for young entrepreneurs who want to drop out of school. And I'm just getting warmed up. It would be easy to write a piece on how it seems college dropouts have greater success.

---

1. This is an idea stolen directly from the cover of advertising guru Paul Arden's first book, *It's Not How Good You Are, It's How Good You Want to Be*, which I was lucky enough to have recommended to me back in my days at TBWA by the brilliant Nick Baum, VP of TBWA\Europe, who knew Paul. I now highly recommend it to everyone.

The problem? This representation of startup success is both wrong and directly dangerous.

When we focus on those who survive or succeed, we ignore the vast majority of those who didn't. Instead, if we look at all the people who dropped out of college, we see the greater percentage not only don't become millionaires, but they also tend to stay stuck in lower-middle to middle-class jobs for their entire careers. They earn less in a lifetime than their peers who did graduate college. They die earlier. Once you take a step back, you can see the whole picture. The newfound viewpoint shows you the most accurate representation of the facts.

While studying these success stories *is* important, merely trying to duplicate them would be a huge disservice to both you and your startup.

Making decisions based on the successes of outliers is a logical error called *survivorship bias*. It is a distorted logic, concentrating on the people or things that survive and succeed while ignoring the others.

Below is my sketch of a combat airplane used by the US Air Force during WWII.

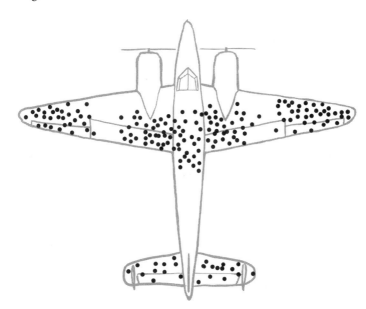

The dots represent data collected on the planes returning from combat. Can you guess what they are?

If you guessed bullet holes, you are correct.

Abraham Wald, a Hungarian mathematician, was tasked with studying the location of these holes to determine how to better strengthen the plane with armor.

Based on the image and bullet holes, where would you recommend the designers add more reinforcement? Remember, armor adds weight to planes and we still need them to fly long distances with the same fuel load, weapon load, and pilot weights.

Are you considering the wings or central part of the fuselage? What about the tail fins? If so, then you'd be on target with what Wald thought, at least at first. Once he stepped back, he realized that the planes he *wasn't* examining were in fact the most vulnerable. Why? Because those planes never returned home to be part of the study. His initial focus on those planes that returned is a classic example of survivorship bias. Switching his perspective gave more concrete data on how to help a plane survive a combat mission. Hit in the wings or tail, the plane could still fly. Hit near the engines, cockpit, or the rear part of the fuselage meant not only the plane, but also the pilot, wouldn't be returning.

Consider also the Brodie helmets introduced during WWI. Field hospitals became overrun with wounded soldiers suffering from head wounds. The number of injured soldiers rose above any previously recorded. Commanding officers believed the helmets to be a reason why there were so many injuries. Until they stepped back and considered all the head wounds previously fatal without a helmet and those soldiers who had removed their helmets and died from the same injury as another wounded man treated in the field hospitals. Once they stopped counting the injured and instead counted the dead, they realized that the helmets were protecting the men as designed and reducing the death toll.

What Can Failure Do for You?

When you ask people what failure can do for them, they will likely give you a side-eye. After devoting years of my life to evaluating failures from a multitude of perspectives, I can say there is a lot to be gained by understanding failure. It's not such a ridiculous question after all.

What began as a hobby has grown into an extensive, long-term study of failure. In the last fifteen years, I've analyzed, compared, and studied more than 160,000 failed companies. It started as more of a hobby, but in the last several years, I have researched, studied, compared, and analyzed thousands more all in my quest to understand the startup market (and then share what I learned). While to some this deep dive into business and startup failures may seem morbid, it's become a labor of love dedicated to helping unravel the realities of how to use failure as both a learning tool and how to spot it from a distance to avoid or negate it. Oh, and I did something similar on why people die before they potentially should—now, that is actually morbid.

In this book, we take a wide-angle view of the multitude of common failures founders make. The ones that either individually can be enough to take down a company or, once mixed with a few others, can shut 90 percent of companies down.

A word on the failure rate of startups: I learned the popularly referenced failure rate mentioned above while taking my Executive MBA—all the way back in those days when Amazon only sold books. A bit more recently, the Startup Genome project in their 2019 report said that 11 out of 12 failed. But please consider these as very, very broad strokes. My own calculations, as an example, show that just one year after launch, 54 percent of all companies within the agriculture, forestry, and fishing industry had closed. Bam. Then compare this to only 41 percent for a five-year period within real estate and rentals. In Lithuania an average of approximately 40 percent of startups from across all industries die within the first year alone. In the United Kingdom the same number is only around 10 percent. Where would you rather be?

The point here, of course, is that the failure rate greatly depends on your perspective—industry, geography, time period, and other variables affect the actual number. Add to this that there isn't even a universally accepted definition of what a startup is anyway.

Accept that your startup is more likely to fail than succeed. But increase your chance of survival greatly by learning about each of the types of failures you will potentially encounter in your run through our minefield.

Far be it from me to tell you how to read this book. If you feel compelled to flip ahead to a chapter topic that speaks to you, OK. I'm not going to stop you or quiz you. But don't forget to go back to the other sections as well because having a road map through this minefield marathon of startups can save your hide. I have strategically laid out the contents of the book to take your startup from idea conception to exit strategy if you follow along my well-lit path.

My goal is to help you foresee, overcome, and plan for the most likely and massive failures the startup world will throw your way. So learn from the mistakes I and many others have made so you can do better. When (not if) you make mistakes of your own, take note, share them, and learn from them so you're able to avoid those and similar mistakes the next time. Then you, too, will be able to nod knowingly when asked what failure can do for you, because you'll be an insider with other elite failure experts.

Chapter 1

Attitude F*ckups

The year was 2009. Digital media was still relatively young and very much on the rise, throwing the world of journalism into tumult. As the distribution and billing models behind news content increasingly shifted from print to online media, journalists worldwide sought new ways to interact with their readers and make a living off their work.

Enter Paul Biggar and Nathan Chong. The two computer scientists saw an opportunity in this shifting media landscape. Founded in October 2009, their startup, NewsTilt, aimed to help journalists become entrepreneurs who sold their work online. The computer duo figured if they could find a way to capitalize on reporting the news by offering a platform for independent journalists, they could build a platform with online staying power. NewsTilt would keep 20 percent of ad revenue while the rest went to the writers. Their revenue model included hosting and selling ads on branded niche sites. The market potential was sizable due to pressure on traditional media (with millions of journalists feeling the same pressure on their jobs) from a multitude of emerging digital platforms. Biggar and Chong wooed Y Combinator—the famed seed money startup accelerator known for funding massive successes like Airbnb, Stripe, and Dropbox—with a strong pitch.

TechCrunch, the leading tech industry journal, announced the launch in April of 2010. They called NewsTilt "compelling" and predicted a "promising future for the company."

Two months later, NewsTilt's doors closed for good.

As someone with a stake in the news industry (I had clients in the industry in my own company at the time), I followed the meteoric rise and fall of NewsTilt with great interest. Later, while I and the rest of the team had managed to take the media company Aller from the red to the black during my tenure as Chief Commercial Officer, I also learned first-hand it was no easy task to capitalize on journalistic content. But how had Biggar and Chong failed so soon back then?

I've interviewed Paul Biggar and I'll tell you the full story in Attitude F*ckup #3: The Passion Pinch. But first, let's talk about why attitude failures matter so much.

No one today hires only for skill. And no founder today runs a successful business on the backs of their talent and a solid business model alone.

As cliché as it sounds, attitude is everything.

Why? Because startups are like marathons—they're agonizingly hard and demand the right mindset to push through the toughest parts.

While trying to get a startup off the ground, you'll take blows from all angles. You'll face cutthroat competitors, unfit partners, and skeptical family members. Oh yes, and even sometimes angry employees. And ditto customers. Perhaps even a pandemic. You'll need to be able to recover quickly each time you face a challenge. Many founders, in a temporary fit of vulnerability, confess the startup life comes with significant mental health challenges. Depression and anxiety can understandably arise for even the most well-adjusted entrepreneur—even one who's been living for years under constant self-applied pressure to perform, mixed with a constant fear of failure and bankruptcy. It doesn't help that the fear is valid. The numbers are against you. As I've already pointed out, up to 90 percent of businesses fail within the first year.

To thrive in the shadow of these odds, you must get into the right headspace before you launch your startup. So, without further ado, here are the most lethal attitude failures you can make—and how to fix them.

Attitude F*ckup #1:

Not starting

You can't win the race you don't start. Don't let your startup go stagnant on the starting block. Get set. Take a breath. Run.

We're starting out with a problem that may seem simple enough: not starting.

I can think of a million reasons *not* to start a new company. To name a few:

- I have a great job.
- I like my steady income.
- I have a family.
- I'm too young.
- I'm too old.
- I need to save for retirement.
- I want to spend more time with my family.

On the flip side, there are all the compelling reasons to start your own business:

- I love working for myself.
- I want to control my financial future.
- I want more time with my family.
- I love innovating.
- I have an idea that I believe the world needs now.
- I love being in charge of my destiny.
- I hate working for "the man."

Honestly, it's not my place to judge your reasoning either way.

There are a ton of theories floating around the startup community that say you have to start young as an entrepreneur. While there may be some benefits to being young and hungry when you launch your first venture, it's not necessary. Although, if you are already used to eating Ramen noodles, not having to pay for diapers or childcare, and not having a spouse to support, you may have what others view as an advantage.

Sure, you'll likely hear the jokes that internet entrepreneurs are like professional basketball players: they peak at twenty-five and are finished by thirty.

I, myself, started out around nineteen years old (eighteen being the earliest age it's possible to form a company in Denmark). Elon Musk was twenty-four when he co-founded Zip2, the city guide software company that would kick-start his serial entrepreneurial life. Bill Gates was only twenty-one when he co-founded Microsoft. Same for Steve Jobs when he and Steve Wozniak founded Apple. Mark Zuckerberg was nineteen years old when he launched Facebook, and he became a billionaire by age twenty-three. I'm thinking that by now you sort of get the picture.

Success at a young age is obviously very impressive, but also equally misleading. Age really is just a number. In fact, founders with other business experience under their belt are just as likely to succeed when they launch a company. Take these classic examples of older founders: Mark Pincus started Zynga at age forty-one, Evan Williams began Twitter at age thirty-four, Arianna Huffington was fifty-four when she founded Huffington Post in 2005, and Colonel Harland David Sanders was sixty-two before having success with KFC. I had the pleasure of meeting the prolific inventor Dean Kamen in 2016 as he gave a riveting talk on, well, inventing stuff: he was forty-nine when he launched Segway and before he later launched iBOT.

My analysis of hard data from the last twenty years also supports this age-is-just-a-number argument, as startup CEOs are actually getting older. Add to this that their education level is also rising, while their experience is less affected.

The idea of not starting because of age or any other excuse is an example of entrepreneurs buying into loss aversion. But don't worry about that yet. We'll take a deep dive into the minefield of decision-making problems in chapter 8.

In conjunction with not starting, people often allow a fear of failure to keep them stagnant. Being scared of failure is a lousy way to flake on your dreams. The stigma that failure is shameful keeps a lot of talented people from ever taking the first steps toward achieving greatness. Don't let that happen to you.

The Fix: Act to Achieve

Here's the honest truth. If you've been thinking about starting a company, now is the perfect time. Seriously, I don't need to tout platitudes like "the future is now" or "there's no time like the present." Why? Because you already know it. Deep down, you know the time to start your company is now. So read through this book to get yourself prepared. Avoid the stupid stuff that will likely crop up along the way (because we will look at how to avoid and overcome most of it in this book) and get to work.

Let go of the notion that failure is shameful. The reality is that failure is brave. Taking the initiative to do something new, follow one's dreams, or take an educated leap into a new market is brave. Even if you fail, the journey is one worth celebrating rather than hiding in shame. To up the ante, add some social pressure to hold you to your goals. Tell people your plans to start a company. In the event you fail, share what you learned from the experience and how you plan to do something different the next time around. Then do it.

If you still don't believe me, think back on your life. Do you have any regrets? Anything you'd do differently given the chance? Don't let not starting your business be a regret five, ten, or twenty years from now.

Not sure if you should act on your startup idea or not? I have a quick process of elimination with my Toilet Test.

The Toilet Test

Attitude and mindset go hand in hand, so bear with me for a minute.

If you're still not sure the startup life is right for you or if the idea that has you considering a startup is the "right" one, let's put it to what I call the "Toilet Test." This simple test has helped me and other entrepreneurs I've worked with determine if an idea is worth pursuing—or should get flushed.

Think about the burning idea in your head that made you consider a startup. How often does it cross your mind? And we're not talking about vague passing inklings of something generic here. I mean, how often does the new solution you have for whatever problem you plan to fix in the world pop into your head? Does it send your pulse skittering? Does everything else in your world fade away, even if only for a few moments, when it crosses your mind?

Would you say you think about it at least as often as you go to the toilet each day? Whether you're at work, relaxing on vacation, or spending time with friends and family, is it on your mind? Does the idea of going a day without thinking about it sound absurd? If you answered with a chorus of resounding "yeses," my guess is you're exactly where you're meant to be reading this book.

If you answered "No," then you likely have a passing, fleeting idea. These fleeting ideas won't get you up out of your chair and running to jot down a note, doodle a logo design, or flesh out a marketing and business plan. So flush this idea and move on to the next one. If your idea isn't catching your attention at least once every twenty-four hours, it isn't the one to drop everything for to start a business.

That doesn't mean you aren't meant to be a startup founder. It just might be that you haven't landed on the right idea yet. Entrepreneurs are creative and have more ideas than time to focus on them. So put your idea to the Toilet Test and if it's worth keeping around, let's take care of business.

Impostor Syndrome

That momentary worry about not being qualified or enough of an expert to do something can be healthy. Letting it consume you to the point of inaction isn't.

As the English mathematician and philosopher Bertrand Russell said, "One of the painful things about our time is that those who feel certainty are stupid, and those with any imagination and understanding are filled with doubt and indecision."

This attitude f*ckup is actually quite simple: if you don't believe you can do it, then you can't.

Further, if you keep telling yourself you're an impostor, you will believe it, even if you aren't. This means you're allowing doubt to drive the bus.

All too often, I see a flicker of doubt in a founder's eyes when I ask them point-blank if they have what it takes to endure the low points of startup life. I hear struggling entrepreneurs lament, "Maybe I'm just not cut out for this." This response drives me crazy. It makes me think twice about investing in even the most promising venture. Most likely, I won't invest if the founder has doubts. Why do founders write themselves off, rather than questioning their strategy or execution, as soon as the going gets tough? Why jump to the conclusion that the problem lies within their personality or intelligence? That's doubt at the wheel, and it's downright dangerous.

You already know doubt. Everyone's experienced it frequently in their life, whether you felt it ice skating for the first time, selecting which college to attend, or choosing the right outfit for an important meeting. Doubt is normal and to be expected.

Remember how I compared your startup to running a marathon? If you doubt yourself all the way, you'll never make it to the finish line.

I'm a runner, and every time I take on a race, I'm plagued by some element of doubt. I don't doubt I can go the distance, as I've done my share of marathons and have even completed an Ironman. I do doubt that I'll be able to do it well enough, fast enough.

There was a time when running a mile in less than four minutes was beyond the limits of human speed. Whether an impossible accomplishment or maybe fatally dangerous, no one thought it possible. Ah, the slippery holy grail. In 1926, fitness expert R. M. Sargent built on the work of the British physiologist and Nobel laureate Archibald Hill. He proved through calculations that breaking the four-minute barrier was impossible. He cited factors such as energy expenditure and oxygen requirements.

In his book *The Perfect Mile*, Neal Bascomb shares that Archibald Hill wrote a year later, "It's not unusual for an athlete to tear a tendon, or to strain a muscle, and not unknown even for him to pull off a piece of a bone by an exceedingly violent effort. We are obviously not far from our limit of safety . . . athletics would become a highly dangerous pastime."

You, too, Brutus? Yes, even Brutus Hamilton, the American track and field Olympian, coach, and athletics administrator, argued against the plausibility of such a feat. In his list of "ultimates of human effort," he described some of the perfect records beyond which man could never go, including the four-minute mile.

As the astute reader (yes, you) has guessed by now, Hamilton would later turn out to be wrong.

Meet Roger Bannister, a young English medical student and an avid *amateur* runner. Motivated by the pursuit of breaking the four-minute mile, he set to training.

Many before him had tried and failed. But at Iffley Road Sports Centre in Oxford on May 6, 1954, Bannister broke both the tape and the world record. He then collapsed as his time of 3.59.4 seconds was confirmed. It stood an impressive 1.4 seconds faster than the world record.

Granted, Bannister wasn't running the minefield marathon startup founders endure to achieve his goal, but he did need to prepare for any potential pitfalls along the way.

You can see where I'm going with this argument, can't you? Anything seems impossible until it's achieved the first time.

Moreover, I'm pointing out the difference it makes when doubt is no longer in the driver's seat. Once Roger Bannister had proven that breaking the four-minute mile was possible, the world's doubt disappeared for good.

Now, the previously insurmountable barrier was a beacon, calling others to rise to it.

Bannister later became a leading neurologist, contributing to significant breakthroughs in autonomic nervous system studies. His running success put him in the record books, where he'll live in perpetuity, even though on June 21, 1954, a mere forty-six days after his milestone time, a Finnish rival broke Bannister's record. Shaving seconds off Bannister's time, John Landy ran a mile nearly three whole seconds (an eternity in runners' time) faster than the previously "unbreakable" world record. And many others would follow shortly after.

Interestingly enough, the Dunning-Kruger effect shows that people who are unskilled and unaware of their deficits are actually more confident than people with skills and experience. Therefore, people who can't see their own incompetence for what it is have an overinflated sense of abilities when assessed in the study, while those who are quite intelligent, skilled, and experienced undervalue their abilities more than anything.

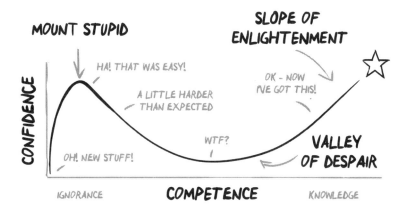

Traveling from Mount Stupid (high confidence, low wisdom) through the Valley of Despair (lower confidence from increased wisdom) to the Slope of Enlightenment (high wisdom and high confidence).

So if you doubt that you can do it, the odds are stacked against you on the failure scale.

The Fix: Fake It Till You Make It

When I first took up running, I had to prod myself to get out there each time. "I should really go take a run now," I'd groan to myself. It wasn't until I began saying to myself, "I'm the kind of person who wants to run because I'm a great runner. Running is easy for me!" that my game started to shift, and I overcame my self-doubt. I started identifying myself as a runner versus someone who was "just running." Much like a musician versus someone who plays around on the guitar, or a startup founder versus someone who happened to start a company.

But I'll admit the "fake it till you make it" technique isn't for everyone. Indeed, it can backfire spectacularly if you can't quite tap into your Superman, Superwoman, or other super persona.

If telling yourself that you're a born entrepreneur doesn't have you bursting to move your project forward, you should regroup and rethink your perspective. Approach the idea again in six months. Take as long as you need to get to the point where you're thinking, "Heck yeah, this is what I was born to do." Then get back into the game.

After all, you could find yourself becoming a much more confident person in six months. For the naysayers who believe we can't change? That's bollocks. I'm a firm believer that no one is set in stone. If we work hard to develop ourselves, we will change and we will evolve.

A few quick tips to overwrite the impostor inside:

- Celebrate all victories! Big and small. It may increase your champagne budget, but remember that champagne is healthy.
- Strike a Superman or Superwoman pose with a verbal mantra reaffirming your awesomeness.
- Share your doubt with a friend or a mental health professional.

- Keep an accomplishment journal.
- Wear things that make you feel confident.
- Make a list of your strengths and read it every morning.
- Journal what you want your successful life to look like in one year, three years, five, ten, and twenty years.
- Set an alarm for three times a day with a positive affirmation.

Let's pause here for just a moment to acknowledge these tips may sound cliché, cheesy, and quite possibly eye-roll worthy. However, give it a go and try a few. Once you get over the original feeling, you'll find they are cliché for a reason: they work.

The Passion Pinch

Following your passion is not enough to achieve success in today's highly competitive business environment but without it, you're completely screwed.

Passion **is a word** often misused by popular psychology and management consultants.

"Have passion, and everything will fall into place," they claim. You probably already know this is untrue. Passion counts, of course. But it's only part of the equation when it comes to successfully launching a business.

Before we dive into the rest of that equation, let's talk about what passion is and how it applies to startups.

The early philosophers introduced us to two different types of passion.

The first kind of passion is a loss of reason and control. It was defined this way originally by the Greek philosopher Plato some 2,400 years ago, and more recently by the Dutch philosopher Spinoza. Plato and Spinoza embraced the Latin etymology of the word *passio*, which means suffering. These philosophers spoke of passion as a dangerous force that superseded human logic and ruined lives. This is quite far from the widespread use of the word today. As the astute Nigel Warburton points out, Plato was—in addition to being brilliant—of course also completely whacked, as he believed that philosophers should rule the world, that only certain people were allowed to breed, and that "defective" offspring should be killed, but I'm getting sidetracked.

The second kind of passion, espoused by the famed French philosopher Descartes, described human passions as "the perceptions, sensations, or commotions of the soul" (aka emotions). Descartes saw them, overall, as a constructive force—when balanced by reason.

Though Spinoza disputed this idea in his posthumous and somewhat strange book, *The Ethics*, Descartes's famous dualist theory of emotion balanced with reason is the one you've perhaps heard about. It's the definition that's shaped modern philosophy.

The German philosopher Hegel was another grand champion of the idea that passion could be productive. Hegel went so far as to argue that passion was required to reach the highest level of achievement. "Nothing great has been accomplished in the world without passion," as he put it.

Understanding passion, we circle back to the story about NewsTilt. A company backed with an up-and-coming business model and Y Combinator funding managed to crash and burn after only two short months. Among the reasons why the company failed are the following:

- Journalists had little faith in the platform and didn't post on it often.
- Readership never took off.
- The founders disagreed on how to produce and deliver promised platform updates.

But at the heart of NewsTilt's failure, I believe, was the fact that its founders weren't passionate about the news industry. When talking recently with Biggar, he admitted as much, saying: "I think it's fair to say that we didn't really care about journalism." For Biggar and Chong, journalism wasn't a core part of their identities. They had no interest in spending every waking hour that they weren't using to manage the company's day-to-day operations to learn about their new industry. They didn't even read their own publication. As Biggar summed up: "But even when we had NewsTilt, it wasn't my go-to place to be entertained—that was still Hacker News and Reddit. And how could we build a product that we were only interested in from a business perspective?"

Biggar and Chong treated their roles at NewsTilt like nine-to-five jobs, which is not how a startup gets built. On top of this, Biggar wrote: "When Nathan and I signed up together, we had not spent any time working together, and that was a big mistake." We'll cover this type of mistake more in chapter 6, where we talk about operational failures. Without a shared passion for their industry to unite them, the founders failed to rise above their setbacks and differences.

Again, I'm not saying that I subscribe to the big fat myth that all you have to do is "find your passion" and "follow your passion," and you'll be a huge success! As many entrepreneurs have learned the hard way, that's not true.

Don Charlton, co-founder of JoinSources, a file management platform akin to Dropbox and Box, is a worthy example. Charlton, a web designer, had a genuine passion for the industry. He identified the market potential in cloud storage and backup services. He launched JoinSources when Box came onto the scene with great fanfare. Fearing he couldn't beat the competition, Charlton pivoted to the content management systems (CMS) market.

CMS was also a niche Charlton felt passionate about and in which he saw room for improvement. As he himself wrote in an article on *Inc.*: "I was passionate about building custom, CMS-driven websites . . . The world needed a solution, and I was going to give it to them. The only problem was there were at least five hundred other people out there with a passion for building custom, CMS-driven websites. They too believed the world needed a solution, and they were going to give it to them."

The result was that Charlton's passion led him in the wrong direction. Unfortunately, it happened not once, but twice. Despite his skill and energy, he ran headlong into a crowded space dominated by giants like Weebly, Squarespace, and eventually WordPress. Charlton's CMS platform never made it off the ground.

Just because you have the passion doesn't mean you're bound to strike gold if you follow it.

But if you don't have the passion, then you will definitely not strike gold. If you're starting this business only to get rich, that is a significant f*ckup.

The Fix: Merge with Your Mission

We're only in the first chapter, and already you've stumbled upon a genuine quick-fix:

Make sure you're building your startup within a field for which you have passion. Not the obsessive kind, but the harmonious, energy-giving kind. That's it.

Doing work you're passionate about is one of the shortcuts to success, and doing the opposite is a complete, first-rate failure.

If NewsTilt's founders had possessed a passion for their field, their company could have found its footing. While it wouldn't have been a complete fix, had they brought an experienced, passionate editor on as a partner (or even a board member from the get-go), their company may have found success.

On top of this, Biggar and Chong should have tried thinking like journalists themselves. As any good reporter will tell you, good journalism requires deep-diving into one's subject matter, understanding it from the inside out. What a different outcome they might have seen had Biggar and Chong spent even one month immersing themselves in their prospective field through research and interviews with editors, publishers, and writers. Not only would they have been better equipped to deal with the challenges facing NewsTilt, but they might also have had a chance to fall in love with their field before marrying into it. If their passion had still been elusive upon more in-depth examination, well, my advice to them would have been to cut their losses and end it there. Better to lose a month than all their energy, millions of dollars, and much goodwill and respect.

Since then, Paul Biggar has co-founded impressive companies within tech that align with his passions, namely the highly successful CircleCI (a solid CI/CD platform for those close to tech, used by Facebook and Spotify among others) and then the very ambitious Dark, a new approach to building serverless backends. A perfect merge of passion and prowess.

If you don't have passion for your industry, your project, and your setup, then wait it out and find the next project with the right fit. Otherwise, you'll be pouring gallons of energy into a bottomless pit. Founders who lack passion for their industry are off-strategy.

And what if you don't have passion for anything other than being an entrepreneur? What if you can't find an intense, all-consuming, burning flame inside you? Consider the following:

1. **Passion isn't always a burning flame.**
    We're told passionate people jump out of bed at 5:00 every morning, exercise, enjoy the problems of their passionate brainchild startup for twelve hours, perform some yoga, and then hit the sack. Well, these boundlessly energetic people may exist, but we all experience passion differently.

    Maybe you have a more reserved personality. Imagine you don't feel consumed with a burning fire of excitement when you think about fintech. But all the same, this area of business is interesting to you and, in fact, not a day goes by when you're not thinking about it. For you, the fintech space elicits a steady, warm glow of interest. Bingo, that's your passion.

    Passion does not have to burn to be efficient. Descartes's harmonious brand of passion balanced with reason is the clear winner. It gives energy and motivates action. It does not suck out all your lifeblood. But, to Plato's credit, there will likely be a considerable amount of suffering along the way as you pursue your passion. So gear up, get your head in the game, and make it happen.

2. **Make sure it's *your* passion.**
    You don't have to tailor your passions to impress others. The passion should be yours. If you believe in an idea enough to give it enormous amounts of your time and energy, your passions will catch on with others.

    No, you don't have to cure cancer through AI—even though millions of people would appreciate the effort. Something less sexy that you're passionate about will do the job, and likely much better.

3. **Don't follow a fleeting passion.**
    I often see people following a fleeting passion, so kindly be aware: not all passions should become startups. Sure, some bizarre ones can be if you're able to position them in a way that they find an audience. But that doesn't mean that any passionate football player

should turn pro or that any passionate painter should quit their day job to become a full-time artist. I'm not suggesting you can't make a superb living as a professional painter. I'm asking you to be realistic. Methodically consider it, using a business plan and spreadsheets in combination with your passion. Or, if you love flowers, be realistic about how hard it is to make it as a florist. We'll get back to why I believe the floral business is f*cked up in chapter 2 when we talk about business model failures.

Also, remember you don't have to follow all your passions. I have many myself, but I've learned I can't be everywhere at once and have to kill some darlings every so often.

Luckily for us entrepreneurs, once we're invested in one venture, other passions can wait on the back burner. Many ideas can keep warm surprisingly long, until you're ready to chase after them in a version that fits the market at that time.

The bottom line: you've got to find this startup business absolutely fascinating. Do you? Or do you find the idea of getting a PhD far more interesting? If that's what you're thirsting for, by all means, go and do the PhD!

Attitude F*ckup #4:

Plate-Spinning

Imagine the circus act where a performer sets multiple plates spinning on their hands, shoulders, head, and knees. It's fun to watch but hard to do.

A common offshoot of the passion pinch is plate-spinning. If you're pursuing too many things at once, your most important project is suffering for it.

My father used to lecture me about what he called my "plate-spinning startups." And while I called myself a parallel entrepreneur with pride (serial entrepreneur was cliché), I realized he had a valid point.

To make things worse, you'll see exactly how my plate-spinning tendencies landed me in jail. Yes, the police-dragged-me-away-in-the-middle-of-the-night type jail. Not only was I juggling too many things, but I also made a major organizational failure. It's my least favorite story, but I'll tell you about it in chapter 6.

I'll give the "Most Notable Plate-Spinning Award" to NewsTilt's co-founder Paul Biggar, who can explain better than me how his startup's failure was both the result of the Passion Pinch and also Plate-Spinning. From his blog:

> I finished and submitted my PhD thesis a week before the Y Combinator application deadline. Three days later, I gave a talk to 900 people at StackOverflow London. When I moved to California in January to do Y Combinator, I had still to organize my wedding in May, and I had a paper to write in between. My PhD defense in April was four hours after we launched NewsTilt. In May, I got married and went on honeymoon.

Paul is a bright guy but was spinning too many plates at the same time. The rule is: no matter how small or how big you get, you need to focus. Do as my dad says and say "no" to plate-spinning startups.

The Fix: Accomplish More By Doing Less

I may not know you, but I can guess you're doing too much. In any case, this is true for most ambitious people I know. It's even more accurate for those of us interested in startups.

So get real and honest with yourself. Do you have too much to do? If so, then get real. Do less. Simplify. How? Prioritize with a not-to-do list.

I have one, and it's fantastic. This is where I place all the ideas that pop into my head every day for safekeeping. Not only is it satisfying to get them down on paper, but it's also a great way to acknowledge every idea without having to run with it. Only about 20 percent of the ideas I write down for consideration are ones I come back to. The other 80 percent are still pretty good, if I do say so myself, but they're not the right ideas for me to pursue. I'd be happy to share them with anyone who needs some inspiration! Send me an email if you want me to share an idea or two! Know that I'll ask you to promise to do your best to avoid the failures in this book before you run with one of them.

Lone-Wolf Syndrome

As a solo founder, you have full control and all the profits, but also all the problems, losses, hardship, investments, footwork, and anxiety— and an increased risk of failure.

When I was twenty-three, I had the idea to launch a digital marketing company that used games to promote products. While I had a passion for online gaming and understood that aspect of the business model, I knew nothing about marketing. But I was young and feisty and most definitely suffering from Lone-Wolf Syndrome: the belief that I could be successful all on my own. Instead of seeking a knowledgeable partner or partners, I launched my business solo and hired other passionate people. My client acquisition strategy? Charge rock-bottom rates to get clients in the door and worry later about how to earn real money.

It wasn't until Mads Rydahl, the clever founder of a competing gaming company (and later one of the key people behind Siri, the now world-famous product bought by Apple), reached out to me and said, "Kim, what are you thinking? You're not only undercutting the rest of us in the digital marketing space; you're cheating yourself. You could double your rates and still reach more clients than you'd have time to serve. Do yourself a favor and think three months into the future. The rates you're charging are damaging to the industry and unsustainable." It was a wake-up call I wouldn't have needed had I taken the time to learn about the financial realities of running a digital marketing agency before blindly launching.

The Fix: Find Your Pack

Of course, it's not only about aligning and focusing on your product. It's about knowing that product, and your industry, inside and out. Often, enthusiastic founders choose to operate in lone-wolf mode, believing we can figure everything out as we go. The problem is, we humans have a tough time recognizing our lack of ability. In psychology, the Dunning-Kruger effect is a cognitive bias where people judge themselves to be more knowledgeable than they are.

This is why I suggest getting experience in your field before you try to go it alone. Sure, Lone Wolf, you might subscribe to all the right newsletters, read all the right books, and take all the right webinars, but every industry looks vastly different from the outside than the inside. And it's often only from the inside that you can know your industry at least well enough to challenge its existing players. You need to understand what your competitors are doing—again, not only from an outsider's perspective.

If you're a recent college graduate with an accounting degree, for example, you probably shouldn't attempt to start a solo practice fresh out of school. You should go to work as an intern or a junior employee for a future competitor. I am not suggesting a lifetime of working for the competitor, complaining about their lousy lunchroom. But a short stint there could easily earn you valuable insights. Observing and training beside your colleagues for three months will prove that consulting is a more profitable revenue stream for accountants—much more than creating annual reports all day long. If you'd gone straight out on your own, it might have taken you three years to learn that.

Another great way to develop your skills is through mentorship. There's nothing like being mentored by someone more experienced (or just plain smarter) to keep your humility in check—a critical prerequisite for growth.

One of the mentors I found early in life (who was and still is both more experienced and smarter) was entrepreneur extraordinaire Caroline Søeborg Ahlefeldt. I met her when applying for *Space Invaders*, a digital design education she created, and have had the pleasure and benefit of her sharp wit in support of work-life balance, business, and boardwork.

To find your mentor, you might start with your LinkedIn connections. Learn all you can about a prospective mentor, then approach them with a positive note to the effect of: "Hey, I know you're really great at X, which I want to learn about. Would you be willing to share your wisdom with me?" If they say they don't have time, your next question should be: "Would you be willing to recommend another expert for me to talk to?" Sending an email may be the easiest route, but then again, sometimes "easy is evil." I always find a phone call to be the most effective way to reach out. Eventually, you'll find someone with in-depth knowledge in your field who is willing to share that knowledge with you.

You might be asking, "Why should this person answer more than a couple of my questions if they don't know me?" Good question. Perhaps this person is nearing retirement, has time to spare, and wants to stay engaged in their field. They might see mentoring as an opportunity to make some extra income, which is acceptable. I don't recommend hiring a mentor or coach by the hour. Although, you might offer your prospective mentor a seat on your company's board (with eventual compensation) or a fair amount of stock in your business.

In the long run, you'll save valuable time by taking the time to learn from others in the business.

The Last Word on Attitude Failures

Here's the bottom line: it's not enough to recognize that your attitude is f*cked up; you've got to want to change your thinking, and that takes work—inner work. Please feel free to give this book to someone more interested if you don't care about inner work. Everyone and their brother wants to do a startup. I applaud you for knowing yourself well enough to decide if it's not for you.

If you want to dig deep and do the inner work it takes to be a successful founder, you're in the right place. Leave doubt at the door, find your passion, focus on only one thing at a time, and, for the love of everything good, connect with people who are willing to mentor you. If you start there, you will be on more solid footing than over half the people who "want to start a business someday."

With this out of the way, we are now getting to the good stuff. If you haven't been to business school, the next section will give you the highlights you need to know. And for those of you chomping at the bit to hear how both a tea brewing startup and a juice-making startup could snag a ton of investor support (the way only Silicon Valley startups can) only to both go belly-up in less than a year, keep reading. You are in for a treat.

Chapter 2

Business Model F*ckups

I've always been a fan of *Starship Troopers*, the highly underrated (and full-blown satirical) movie released in 1997, a time when I was also working with visual effects and met some of the creators at a conference in London. It is based on the eponymous book by Robert Heinlein, who later in life said: "Never attempt to teach a pig to sing; it wastes your time and annoys the pig." He did not specifically intend this to apply to business model failures, but it sums those failures up perfectly. This chapter will touch on the top failures common in startup culture once you get past the abundance of attitude issues.

You have your attitude in check, and you're ready to go. Right?

I thought I did. To be fair, if someone developed a time machine and went back to interview twenty-three-year-old me, I would've told you my first *real* startup, Shockwaved, was destined to be a hit. I had a great idea, the zeal of youth, and enough education to be dangerous. Looking back, I can see the attitude failures I made. Still, the most detrimental failure was less about my attitude and more about my business model, which leads me to the failure that ultimately made me sell Shockwaved for far less than I could have. If only I hadn't made the number one business model mistake: failing to have one.

A simple Google search will back me up here when I tell you the number one mistake startups make is not making a plan and having a business model. This chapter highlights the most common business model mistakes a founder can make. But imagine if Steve Jobs, Ronald Wayne, and Steve Wozniak hadn't developed a sufficiently strong business model before founding Apple. The 1.4 billion people using Apple devices worldwide today would be stuck with the alternatives. (To the Apple lovers in the crowd, imagine the horror!) Had they been content to just throw together ideas without an adequately strong plan for implementation or the market of their consumers, we'd be without a whole host of products so many of us rely on daily.

What if Jeff Bezos hadn't planned to strategically grow Amazon into more than an online bookseller? I'm betting a significant number of you purchased this book through Amazon in either print or digital form. And a sincere thank-you for doing so—even more so if you find time to leave an honest review there also! Without Amazon, where would you get your resources? How would you learn the most common startup failures and how to avoid or fix them? It could easily be argued that bookstores haven't kept up and adapted over the years. Waldenbooks closed. Crown Books was bought by Borders, and then Borders closed, and so on. I'm a believer that had Jeff (no, I've never met the guy, but he sounds more down-to-earth as just "Jeff") not built Amazon and created a platform to allow us to spend this time together, then we'd be talking about another person who would've come up with the idea and run with it. This is true for many business ideas.

I don't know about you, but I'd rather have an Apple- or Amazon-esque company than one the likes of Teaforia, Lookery, Boo.com, or the Poultry Exchange. If those names don't ring a bell yet, they will soon.

Business Model F*ckup #1:

A Poor Business Plan

A surprising number of businesses fail simply because they fail to produce a meaningful business plan.

At twenty-three, I was an enthusiastic freelancer designing online games (mainly because it sounded—and was—fun). At the time, I believed game advertising would be a marketplace that would grow (which it did) so I slipped into the business of owning a company rather than being a gig worker or freelancer, all because I followed my passion and had good instincts. Until it came to naming the company, of course. Because the platform I had used to build my games was called Shockwave, I titled my Shockwaved portfolio Shockwaved.com. Not only did people confuse my company with the gaming platform, it was a word Danes didn't know how to spell. This meant I spent an inordinate amount of time spelling out my email over the phone each day. Thanks to my boundless enthusiasm and ability to sell others on my ideas, I had the initial good luck to work with some great advertising agencies. They contracted my services for prime clients like Nike, LEGO, Motorola, Disney, and PlayStation.

While I had a good idea and some initial good fortune, Shockwaved lacked any inkling of a strategic revenue plan. Oh, and a strong core business plan? Nope. This meant that the only way to keep the venture afloat was to work my ass off and hope for the best. Because I lacked a core business model, I worked with my feet, not with my head. I was all brawn and no brains. Whenever a problem would arise, I'd scramble to fix it on the spot. For example, I didn't consider how I would create and sustain ongoing relationships with my clients in advance. I pitched my clients à la carte services, delivered the goods, and started from scratch with new pitches every month.

Further complicating matters was that the agencies who contracted my services for their clients were adding hefty margins on top of my fees. It worked out that they charged their clients around three times what I charged. This made my product more expensive than it should have been, making it difficult for the agencies to repeat-sell to their clients. By the time I figured out this major problem, it was too late. I couldn't circumvent the agencies and sell direct to the brands without alienating the agencies.

Along the way with Shockwaved, I did find some lucky successes. The most money we ever made was through providing streaming services to host an app we'd created for one client, a national radio station. This surprise revenue stream might have been one we'd started with had I taken the time to think through my cost structure and write a business plan for the company from the get-go. Unfortunately, this unforeseen revenue came too late to really save Shockwaved. With no repeat sales to count on, the venture quickly outgrew the resources I'd earmarked for it, and I later sold it (also too cheaply).

Another more recognizable venture fell into a similar trap a few years later. Are you familiar with the viral sensation Vine? In 2012, Dom Hofmann, Rus Yusupov, and Colin Kroll founded the six-second video hosting service sensation. Its popularity soared, as it was a video snippet version of Twitter. Sounds fantastic, right? Yeah. Too bad the creators of an innovative way to express oneself online didn't settle on a working business model. Yikes!

In true Silicon Valley fashion, the company launched hard. Vine gained immense popularity and hit its first roadblock when its still photography competitor, Instagram, offered users the ability to create and share fifteen-second video clips. Instagram already had two years of market growth behind them, so users stayed with the platform they already used rather than adopting a new one.

When it came to finding advertisers to use Vine, many found it hard to create a six-second ad. User issues soared. Users struggled to achieve brand partnerships yielding little to no return for creators to use the platform. While Vine's concept felt new and fresh, there was nothing new or innovative about the app to draw in new users or keep initial users once Instagram offered competition. Any time users made suggestions or complaints, they seemed to fall into an abyss. This left the end-user dissatisfied until they deleted their account.

Despite Twitter buying Vine and keeping it as a stand-alone service, eventually Twitter announced its new video feature while the app waned.

"I'll be back" is more than a line from a movie. It is quite common for founders to revisit industries they've been in. After Vine closed its doors, Dom Hofmann, one of Vine's three founders, announced Byte, a new video app launched in 2020. While Byte features new options that Vine never did, it still lacks many features available on other platforms like TikTok and Instagram. Did you just get déjà vu? Yeah, me too.

While Dom Hofmann had a new plan this time, more focused on being sponsor-friendly, he still did not focus on helping the users make money. In 2021, Brendon McNerney, a former Vine star, and founder of another short-form video app Clash, acquired Byte, this time focusing more on allowing creators to monetize their content. This time they avoided at least one classic problem: failing to have a business plan.

The Fix: Put Your Plan on Paper

Any business plan is better than no plan at all. I think it's fair to say that the only bad business plan is the one that exists solely in your head—as mine did when I founded Shockwaved.

It should go without saying that writing a business plan is vital. This book's scope doesn't include the how-to aspect of writing a plan, nor should it since hundreds of resources are available online and in bookstores. But I'll offer a bit here to get you started.

Rather than create a full-blown fifty-page business plan, let's start with the basic steps of successful planning. Alexander Osterwalder and a lot of other smart people have developed an approach called the "Business Model Canvas," which will ensure your startup has legs. The Business Model Canvas is a visual (yay!) tool used to map out the business concept to articulate it for easy understanding, assessment, and improvement. It's a single-page document with nine parts that can be sketched anywhere—a whiteboard, notepad, or napkin! If you have an idea in mind, then you can have a first draft done in fifteen to thirty minutes. As you can see, the left side is mainly about the inner workings of your startup (partners, activities, resources, cost), and the right side is about the external part (value propositions, customer relationships, channels, customer segments, and revenue streams).

BUSINESS MODEL CANVAS

KEY PARTNERS	KEY ACTIVITIES	VALUE PROPOSITION	CUSTOMER RELATIONSHIPS	CUSTOMER SEGMENTS
	KEY RESOURCES		CHANNELS	
COST STRUCTURE			REVENUE STREAM	

Every business plan I write or consider for investment purposes focuses on seeing patterns and weaknesses before diving too deep into a new business venture.

Here's my step-by-step planning tool (and approximately how long each step takes):

1. Develop your business model canvas (15–30 minutes).
2. Expand this business model canvas with a one-page business plan (15–30 minutes).
3. Make a budget (2–4 hours).
4. Make a project plan (2–4 hours).
5. Wrap the above up into a business plan (1 day).

By doing these tasks—and in this specific order—you approach the job in an iterative manner, tackling the most important items first. If, or rather when, you get to a point where the current business idea does not make sense or requires some tweaking, you will have saved yourself a lot of time. As you progress, you will gradually invest more energy in the plan. Taking this approach is especially effective because, as time goes on, you will simply revisit and reclimb the ladder to correct or adjust any fundamental issues rather than needing to revise a whole section of your fifty-page plan. Most people need to take a few runs at this to iron out all the kinks before they wind up with a plan they can take further.

Business models are a fluid document. No billion-dollar business reached their level of success by limiting themselves to one initial plan. Giants like McDonald's, Amazon, and Walmart, to name a few, pull that bad boy out, dust it off, revise, and resubmit all the time. Besides, staying relevant in your marketplace means being aware of changing needs (aka problems) and creating new and improved solutions or products.

To make it easy for you, both the Business Model Canvas and the associated one-page template are available for free download at kimhvidkjaer.com. The same goes for the sample budget, project plan, and final business plan templates. The budget is (of course) quite import-ant for the realism of your plan, but we'll discuss that more in depth in chapter 4 when we talk about the "bad budgeting" funding f*ckup.

Business Model F*ckup #2:

Idiot Industry

Your choice of industry directly affects your outcome. It's better to be an idiot in an intelligent industry, than intelligent in an idiot industry.

Michael Porter's book *Competitive Strategy* was first published in 1980 and has since been reprinted sixty times in nineteen languages worldwide. Not to mention, it's been voted the most influential management book of the twentieth century—it's worth a read.

At the core of his teaching, Porter describes the Five Forces Framework (alliteration, anyone?), which models a method to identify how attractive an industry is. This is the most simplistic way to ensure you aren't choosing an idiot industry for your startup. If you've done the business school thing, the five forces will be familiar when analyzing industry attractiveness.

That leads us to the question: Is there such a thing as "good" and "bad" when it comes to the industry you choose? How important is industry attractiveness, really? There are differing opinions on this topic, but let's cut the crap and answer—yes, our data here is clear and to the point. For most startups there are good and bad industries, and it is *highly* important to consider their attractiveness. To avoid landing in an idiot industry, you should look at the data on your industry before making the leap to launch. This isn't to say all low-performing industries have to be avoided or that high-performing industries are worthy of your time and energy. Remember, there are other arguments than money. If you are building a startup, then you are also essentially shaping how tomorrow will look. Please make products that will make the world a better place, even if only by a little. Create something appealing, and not appalling.

On the other hand, some industries might be great fits for your skills and interests, but have terrible EBIDA (Earnings Before Interest, Depreciation, and Amortization, i.e., earnings before the boring stuff that is less directly controlled in your business) scores.

In Porter's framework, you look at the competition in an industry through the lens of five primary forces (the market environment): 1) threat of new entrants, 2) the threat of substitutes, 3) bargaining power of customers, 4) bargaining power of suppliers, and 5) the competitive rivalry in the industry. By assessing these five factors, you'll gain a better picture of your industry.

In the grand scheme of things, one example of idiot industry still has me shaking my head. Literally, my son walked into my office while I was writing this and asked what was wrong. I'm confident he thinks I've lost it. This example will quite likely leave you feeling just as flummoxed: The Poultry Exchange—a startup launched in January 2016 by Janette Barnard with the idea of being a meat market for chicken. It aimed to address the leftover processed chicken from suppliers that hadn't already been sold to buyers. Regardless of the presold amount of poultry, all the ready chickens were slaughtered. Only the agreed-upon parts went to contracted distributors, thus leaving the excess chicken in need of a buyer. Quick. Keep in mind that anytime you need to convince an industry they need to change an integral component of the way business gets done, there will be pushback. Despite raising seed funding from an angel investor (we'll talk more about those later in chapter 4), who not only believed in the solution Barnard offered to the market but was intimately familiar with the agriculture industry's way of working, by mid-2017, The Poultry Exchange had closed its doors. The reality was, the industry was content with the way business was being conducted and saw no need to change things. This wasn't the only thing to bring down The Poultry Exchange. They also fell victim to another unfortunate failure we'll discuss later in the chapter: terrible timing.

If you've always dreamed of opening your flower shop, for example, you should know, it is a famously unprofitable sector. Your dream may not be impossible, but you should at least have a strong strategy for outperforming your competitors at every step. You need to have an advance plan for how you'll offset the short supply of flowers on Mother's Day and Valentine's Day. And deal with a product that has an incredibly short shelf life. And that's only the beginning. You'll also need to have a clear plan for how you'll be the very best in your industry. Maybe you already work at a florist and have personal connections with rich and famous clients who insist that you and only you arrange their alyssum. In this case, your reputation will precede you and pave the way for the best chance at success.

Similarly, cafes and coffee shops always sound like a romantic business, but they are highly competitive, offer super-small profit margins on the small cafe scale, and require a ton of work. I'm not saying you should give up on a dream to have an awesome cafe. It is advisable, however, to try your best to stand out from the crowd in a significant way.

The Fix: Select an Attractive Industry

To establish a startup with a sustainable competitive advantage that allows you to be profitable for years to come, you need to gain the upper hand over your competition. Porter's five forces determine the state of competition and the long-term profitability within any one industry:

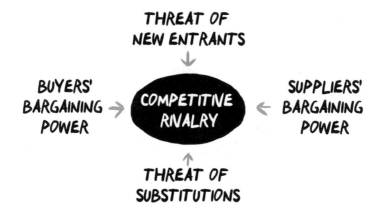

- **The threat of entry:** All industries have an entry barrier. What determines how high or low that barrier stands is how difficult or easy it is to enter the industry. If you were to start a housecleaning service for private homes, you'd need little capital, education, or assets. This industry could be accessible to a teenager as well as someone middle-aged. This entry barrier is low. That may seem good if you are starting out, but it is terrible once you're established in the industry. If you instead were looking to start a law firm, you'd need a certain level of education, licensure, capital, and experience. Those components make that industry's entry barrier high. The higher the entry barrier to your chosen industry, the less the threat of competition. And when you are already there, then consider raising it to make it harder for competitors!

- **The threat of substitution:** Substitute products do not belong to the same industries but meet a similar need. A smartphone is a substitution for a traditional landline, a tablet, e-reader, computer, and other things. Social media is similar to being a substitute for newspapers and magazines. Put more simply, a train is a substitute for a car, but they don't directly belong in the same industry. Porter warns the two substitutes a business owner should watch for are those that become cheaper relative to their performance and those that accrue higher returns on capital.

- **Bargaining power of suppliers:** As suppliers and buyers are mirrors of one another, it's important to consider them together. Stronger suppliers make the industry less attractive overall. Example: Airbus and Boeing pretty much dominate the airline supply as the only major large passenger aircraft manufacturers. Problems arise if the suppliers stop providing the product, reduce the product's quality, or raise the prices.

- **Bargaining power of buyers:** On the flip side of this coin, the buyer can stop buying the product or demand lower price points or better quality. Whoops! Creating your startup within an industry that is winning this power struggle against both its suppliers and customers gives you an obvious but strong advantage.

- **The intensity of rivalry:** This boils down to the simple question—how tough is the competition? The players already in the game will always have a leg up on a new entity in any given industry. They can use tools like price-cutting, ad battles, new products/services, and exemplary customer service as a means to cut the competition. It makes sense to consider an industry with low competition. Mapping out the competition to determine how many players exist, the industry growth margin's height, and if the fixed costs are low can help determine the industry rivalry.

Looking back at the flower industry, say you don't yet have a foothold in your low-performing industry—then what? Then you'd better have a plan for disrupting that industry, for f*cking up the flower world, if I may. The concept of disruption might seem a bit worn by now, but it's still equally valid. It was originally coined back in 1992 by Jean-Marie Dru, the chairman of TBWA—and probably the smartest adman I've ever talked to. That's right: if you can't beat them, disrupt them; if you can innovate in your category, you've got a shot. Maybe you do this by patenting a shipping method that keeps cut flowers fresher longer than anyone else. Or suppose you devise a winning strategy to shake up the wholesale flower market. This kind of disruption is what it will take to make a decent living in a poor-performing industry. You'll never get rich as a florist, but if you're okay with that, go ahead and follow your dream.

Better yet, though, try implementing this fix in a high-performing industry. A cheap trick I've used is to disrupt a slow-moving, established, but profitable industry by doing things faster. Speed kills the competition. In 2007, I, with three other partners, founded Nature Energy, the first utility company in Denmark to be focused on delivering renewable energy. It was a big thing for all of us back then. We knew the need was there, and we knew there was money in it because the existing suppliers were earning bucketloads of it. These competitors—the old monopolies—were big but also slow, which gave my partners and me several years to build up our own company without them noticing and reacting. Even better, we had a structurally related industry—telecommunications—that had experienced a similar shake-up at the time, which we could model our approach after.

To reiterate, choose a non-idiot industry to get your startup off on the right foot.

As the astute reader (yes, you) may have noticed, I am still a Porter's 5F fanboy,[1] despite it originating in another millennium. It's old, and there have been both critiques and creative contributions since then. Adam Brandenburger and Barry Nalebuff, in the 1990s, added the idea of "Complementors" as a sixth force. This theory is a fine addition you should keep in mind along with other factors such as government, innovation, and, of course, all the resources you and your startup would bring to your target industry. You get the point.

Warren Buffett (who, of course, is one of the best-performing investors of all time) simplifies Porter's five forces as a "moat" surrounding a castle. Well-performing companies face attacks from all sides. With a deep and wide enough moat surrounding their castle, possibly filled with hungry sharks, they can fend off their adversaries and keep control over their position in the market. It's the rivalry between competitors in the marketplace that is the most powerful of the five forces.

---

1. Porter's work, with its focus on strategies as fundamentally generic and identifiable positioning of companies in the market, belongs to the "Positioning school" of strategy, as later described alongside other schools of strategy in the book called *Strategy Safari* by Henry Mintzberg et al. If you like business strategy (as I do), then you should grab a copy of that for both entertaining and enlightening reading. After you're done with this book, obviously.

The Problem-Less Solution

Starting with the solution instead of the actual problem is a real problem. No problems to be solved equals no profits to be gained.

Be careful if your business idea hinges on changing people's habits. If you're solving an obvious problem in a new way, that's great. But if you're trying to change a problem that most people don't think of as a problem, you're in for an uphill battle.

In the digital age, an all-too-common example of the Problem-Less Solution is when a startup attempts to digitize something that's better done by hand, the old-fashioned way. One company, Teaforia, tried to disrupt the age-old tradition of boiling a kettle for tea. They produced a Wi-Fi- and Bluetooth-enabled $1,000 tea infuser that would do the job itself. Ignoring the hefty price tag, the tea brewed in the machine failed to exceed traditionally brewed tea's quality. Plus, the specialty drinkware for the device needed to be handwashed and meticulously maintained. Nothing about this venture actually fixed a problem. Heck, I'd suggest it wound up causing more problems. When it turned out that tea drinkers preferred to boil the water for their cups of tea, thank you very much, the product bombed. Did its founder learn from the experience? I'm afraid not. Rather than considering that his product was totally unnecessary to anyone, he reflected in a company statement that success would have required "a lot more money and time to educate the market, and we simply couldn't raise funds required in what is a very difficult time for hardware companies in the smart kitchen space."

The digital pioneer and highly successful serial entrepreneur Tim Frank Andersen once advised me something along these lines: if you're ever approached to invest in a startup that requires "educating" consumers on its necessity, keep your money and run.

Remember Juicero, the at-home juice appliance? Founded by Doug Evans and Jeff Dunn, the make-your-own-organic-juice-at-home product aimed to rival any down-the-block juice bar with a fancy Wi-Fi-connected appliance that lived on your kitchen counter. Initially priced at almost $700, the customer base was exclusive (read: limited). The device only worked with their custom pouches (priced at another $5–$7 per pouch, mind you) with printed QR codes for the machine to read. Guess what happened when a QR code was unreadable by the machine? You've got it. Absolutely nothing. No delicious organic freshly made juice—just the sting of aggravation. Oh, and Bloomberg later had fun mocking the company, noting how anyone could easily just squeeze the pouches by hand—in practice rendering the hardware thingie worthless. Einstein (Ben Einstein, the venture capitalist, not the theoretical physicist) even did my favorite hobby of deconstructing the press, only to conclude that it was overly complicated, which also inflated the price tag. So after floundering on the market for a few more months, this Silicon Valley startup went bankrupt. Why? Because the product didn't actually solve a problem. And for those organic juice–loving people in the crowd, it was faster and cheaper to stop at their local juice bar down the street.

The Fix: Focus on the Problem

Even Einstein (yes, now I'm referring to the physicist) agreed that focusing on the problem required more time and energy than a solution.[2] In fact, when presented with the concept of having one hour to solve a problem, he declared he'd spend fifty-five minutes thinking about the problem and only five on solutions. He remarked that the more time spent considering the problem, the more quality solutions one will find. Only when one can home in on the issue at hand and all the components entrenched in what makes a problem an actual problem can someone develop an excellent solution that holds value.

---

2. Speaking of problems, Einstein also married his cousin, which I imagine as a great source of *more* problems and really don't recommend, as well as taking part in a ton of other failures, such as erring in the "proof" of his most famous equation, $E = mc^2$. Ignoring that, he obviously did have a ton of seriously clever ideas.

So how can we fix this? In five simple steps:

1. Write down the problem, not a specific solution (visualize the blank paper Teaforia and Juicero must have had).
2. Determine if it's what BigCommerce co-founder Mitchell Harper calls a Tier 1 problem (i.e., painful enough for the target audience to care enough). Think headache pills, not vitamin pills. If it's not, keep writing problems until you land on a Tier 1 problem.
3. Correctly determine the currently existing solutions, and look for pain points.
4. Verify there's a budget for a solution.
5. Use your prospects to define your road map.

Remember, Tier 1 problems affect the largest possible market share for your product or solution. If you're struggling to find the right problem to solve, start with an issue you've personally encountered. This personal experience and relatability is a starting point to test if a problem applies to enough other people to develop a solution.

Business Model F*ckup #4:

Co-Dependency Collapse

In any other aspect of life, true co-dependency can be a hindrance to personal growth and development. The same is true in the business world.

Does your startup rely on relationships within a single industry, or worse yet, a single client, in order to succeed? If so, you've got a problem. For a hypothetical example, let's say you're making video games that only work on the PlayStation platform. This might be great in some respects. PlayStation, for now, is a successful company with deep pockets. They're already educated about what their consumers want. And without a doubt, they have established systems for working with suppliers like you. The problem you face when you make PlayStation your only client is that you're reliant on an ecosystem that could someday collapse. As unlikely as it seems, PlayStation could go bankrupt, leaving you out in the cold. Or, more likely, some structural change (business, technology, or otherwise) could hinder your access to the platform.

Take what used to be my son's favorite drug, the megahit game *Fortnite,* for example. Back in 2020, Epic, the game's creator, took Apple to court after Apple kicked the game off its App Store. Epic had launched a new direct payment system in the app that bypassed Apple's cut, thus breaking their rules. Epic alleged that Apple violated antitrust law. Had Epic only offered their blockbuster game on Apple's App Store platform, they would be sunk. Especially once the judge ruled that Apple couldn't remove Epic's developer account, but Apple was also under no obligation to reinstate the game on the App Store.

I've experienced Co-Dependency Collapse more than once. At the beginning of this chapter, I told you about my company Shockwaved, which suffered because I made the mistake of relying on advertising agencies to connect me with my endgame clients. If I'd broadened my client base to encompass the agencies and the brands I ultimately created games for, I would have retained more control of my pricing structure, kept a greater percentage of my fees, and forged relationships in multiple industries—not only within the advertising world. I should've known better than to commit this failure. Years earlier, I'd had a job creating special effects for advertising agencies. I loved the work, but it didn't last. Because the company that employed me, Sonne Film, only created special effects for commercials, their revenue nose-dived when the advertising market collapsed. This was my first experience with co-dependency f*ckup. The head of product at Sonne Film at the time, Ulla Rørdam, explained to me how Sonne was caught in the co-dependency trap as a sub-supplier to the advertising industry. With only a limited number of avenues to utilize for clients, if the advertising budgets plummeted, so did Sonne's workforce, budget, and market share. In a similar manner, the tremendously skilled television producer Thomas Heurlin, owner of Impact TV and a very dear friend, only has a handful of direct customers as there are not that many Danish broadcasters to approach with each new television format. This requires a massive balancing act. It wasn't actually until I founded my first company that I truly understood the pain points of being stuck in a co-dependency situation.

Those familiar with the tech industry likely know what a single point of failure (SPOF) is. It's that part of a system that, if it fails, will halt the workings of the entire system. Think back before cloud mirroring of a hard drive. If that hard drive failed, the entire machine stopped working and everything on the drive was lost. Looking at Epic and Apple, it's easy to see that had Apple's App Store been the main distribution point for *Fortnite*, the whole operation would've fallen apart.

To better understand this SPOF concept, take Lookery, an information farming service that provided "statistic showcasing services to large social media sites." Founded by Scott Rafer, David Cancel, Rex Dixon, and Todd Sawicki in 2007, Lookery received two funding rounds from over twenty investors. At the core, Lookery had a major vulnerability. Built as a "no-frills banner network for Facebook app publishers," Lookery failed to consider any future design changes the social media giant might roll out. When Facebook did it in 2008, Lookery was forced into playing catch-up to stay viable. Rather than look for an exit solution, Lookery attempted to rethink their strategy and solution without success. It was closed and purchased by Adknowledge later that year.

Similarly, in 2007, the four management consultants Ariel Diaz, Jeff Hebert, Matt Hodgson, and Brad Johnson founded YouCastr, a video platform that aimed to sell video content online. The platform offered a new way for video broadcasters and online content producers to make money by selling live broadcasts, on-demand videos, and video downloads found nowhere else online. The company's initial success came by way of partnerships with high schools and colleges. They produced live and on-demand offerings for school sporting events that wouldn't otherwise be televised on traditional television networks. As the market focus shifted to include an open market of video content producers looking to sell live and prerecorded products to consumers, the company was hesitant to pivot. The founders feared alienating their loyal customer base, but when the business model finally changed focus, they realized the market was nonexistent.

The founders spent countless working hours attempting to acquire fundraising to carry the company through, but within two years, the economic downturn made angel investors scarce. In a last-ditch effort, the founders put all their expectations on partnerships with large companies in the hope of creating a lasting relationship to provide YouCastr much needed support and longevity to survive. Unlike startups, the large independent companies moved too slowly to approve and fund YouCastr, resulting in its death.

I'm sure by now you're seeing the constant thread here. Perhaps you even hear an elder relative's voice whispering in your mind, "Don't put all your eggs in one basket." Either way, co-dependency and SOPF issues will sink a company faster than the iceberg that took down the *Titanic*.

For a slight variation on the SOPF failure, I offer you Barings Bank. This particular case study shows how a SOPF doesn't only apply to new companies.

In 1762, Barings Bank began at the hands of a wool merchant from Exeter and his father, John Francis Baring, who started the John and Francis Baring Company. Within a few years, they had offices in Cheapside, London, and the Mining Lane district, and helped finance the United States government during the War of 1812.

After more than two hundred years as a powerful entity, the company was brought to its knees in 1995 by a massive trading loss committed via fraud by twenty-eight-year-old Nick Leeson, a former chief executive and current employee. Without any oversight of his trading activities, he could hide his bets in Singapore by reporting it to the London branch as profit. The loss escalated at an unprecedented pace due to internal and external factors unrelated to the fraud. To cover his behind, he changed a branch error account in the office and blamed one of his colleagues for purchasing twenty contracts on a buy-and-sell basis costing the company £20,000 each. By December of 1994, Leeson had cost over £200 million on top of the additional £102 million reported to Britain's tax authorities. Allowing one person so much power without oversight was the SOPF that sent Barings Bank to its grave.

The Fix: Diversify

I'm not saying that one couldn't make millions creating content for Play-Station alone. What I am saying is that one shouldn't count on making millions creating content solely for PlayStation. If you're this hypothetical game-maker, you'll want to consider branching out and creating games for Xbox and a few other platforms as well. You could do this using the superb gaming platform Unity, which we'll return to later under organizational failures as an example fix. You'll probably also want to distribute your product directly to your end-clients—cut out the middleman. Once you've covered those bases, you can think about building diversification and expansion into your business's five- and ten-year plans. Remember to always be on the lookout for a single point of failure or co-dependency concern. If you determine you're already in one of those situations, you need to take action now. Here are some steps to avoid allowing one big customer to dictate the future of your entire business.

- **Size doesn't matter** (that much). Even if a customer is large, they aren't entitled to all your attention. You are in control of which customer segments you choose to work with. Make sure you can quickly adapt your strategy to the size of the customer and the acquisition costs. It's completely fine to start with smaller customers but keep in mind point number two.

- **Customization kills.** Offering each customer ultimate customization is a timely venture that rarely nets the returns you want. Ensure you have a reliable product and a command of the market before offering any customizations. If you plan to find a solid foothold in your industry, you will need a solution that applies more generically with only minimal customizations available, if any.

- **You can't serve one person all the time.** Limiting yourself to only one customer who monopolizes all your time and resources will send your doors closing faster than you can imagine. You'd be better off having many smaller customers rather than one large one. Remember, good news travels, so the more small, happy customers you have, the more potential new customers you'll have knocking on your door.

- **Save your capital for creation.** The temptation to upgrade your office suites, create fancy new video ads by a young creative director, and so on can kick you in the backside. As you grow, save your capital to create improvements for your products or services. These can be pricey if they require hiring new people, finding new suppliers, or making capital improvements!

- **Don't micromanage.** No matter what your product needs, you've hired the best of the best to make it happen. Let them do what they do best. Back up and let them do their jobs. Don't fall into the micromanagement trap because it stifles creativity, productivity, and innovation.

A final note on diversification: if it's unavoidable that your company will cater to a single industry, then make sure your business plan spells out exactly how you'll defend your company if your primary marketplace crashes.

Business Model F*ckup #5:

Terrible Timing

Who knows the cliché "timing is everything"? Like most clichés, this one is true. Understanding your industry gives you great timing insight.

It sounds obvious, but I'll remind you anyway: please be mindful of your timing.

A quick check-in with our data paints a grim but obvious picture of the packed startup cemetery following the burst of the dot-com bubble, from roughly 2000–2003, and another dip at the Great Recession, around 2007–2009, with fewer investments, less job creation by startups, and so on. And then we're just getting warmed up with today's interesting business climate.

Factor in how long it's going to take you to bring your fantastic idea to the marketplace. If you're making a physical product, how long will it take to create the designs, produce your samples, refine them, turn all of that work into a salable commodity, and distribute it? Is your industry regulated? And if so, how long will it take you to get your final product approved?

Timing is everything. It's a cliché for a reason. Take the e-retailer Boo.com that launched in late 1999. Ready to go with an online outlet offering specialty and branded sportswear, Boo.com had direct agreements with the production teams for the products, owned offices and distribution centers in four countries, serviced six different countries, and had over two hundred employees at launch. Lest we forget to mention the high-tech website, it offered 3D images, Flash, and a virtual assistant who acted as a personal stylist. This well-thought-out venture, technologically advanced for the time, couldn't get off the ground for a few important timing reasons. First, their advanced features for their online sportswear shop required web users to have broadband internet. While the site serviced customers in huge markets like the US and Europe, less than 2 percent of the households in these countries had broadband service. In preparation for their launch, the founders sank a ton of money into advertising and marketing before their product was market ready. This led to release delays and, ultimately, a loss of potential customers who attempted to utilize the service prior to the "actual" go-live date.

This sad start for clothing retailers online ended a scant few months later for Boo.com. Only seven years later, the clothing, shoes, and accessories market won the first-place slot for all articles being sold on the internet. Boo.com is a prime example of a business ahead of its time and not ready for its marketplace.

A lesser-known example of terrible timing is Haburi.com. A Danish company launched almost simultaneously as Boo.com, in early 2000, they offered an online outlet shopping experience. I helped develop various campaigns for Haburi.com, via my company at the time, Shockwaved, and judging by the solid campaign budgets back then you could tell they were in a hurry. Like Boo.com, they had contracts with the manufacturers, but they stood out by offering low prices to consumers looking to get the outlet pricing with an online shopping experience. After posting a large deficit in their first year and the dot-com crash, Haburi.com hoped to pull it together during their second year. Unfortunately, problems with investors as well as departing founders kept them from becoming profitable. In 2003, it was handed over to an established German textile company at a loss of $1 million USD per month during its time alive.

Remember The Poultry Exchange from only a few pages back? Beyond the Idiot Industry Failure, they also had the misfortune of bad timing. As luck would have it, they also won the double whammy lottery by entering the market around the same time a major antitrust lawsuit wreaked havoc on poultry pricing.

I'm pretty sure if I mention the online coupon site Groupon, over 90 percent of you reading right now could tell me what the company does. However, if I mention LetsBuyIt.com, I would assume the response would be completely different. LetsBuyIt.com was a pan-European service offering group-buying discounts to customers. Sound familiar? It should. And it entered the marketplace in 1999, a whopping nine years before Groupon.com. Can you venture a guess as to why this online startup failed? You guessed it—bad timing.

When LetsBuyIt.com launched, not only were there not many small businesses online, there also weren't many consumers. The "build-it-and-they-will-come" approach totally backfired for Lars Johan Magnus Staël von Holstein, the founder. I can only imagine how he felt when, years later, Groupon arrived in the marketplace and became a huge success.

One last classic example of the Terrible Timing Failure is brought to us by Hummer. This company launched a street version of the military gas-guzzler in 1992, just before the climate crisis became a topic of international concern. Initially designed by AM General, the Hummer was used by troops during the Persian Gulf War and in Panama. During conflict news coverage, the vehicles were often featured and quickly gained popularity with celebrities such as Arnold Schwarzenegger, who bought a fleet. These hunkering vehicles were a novelty to be seen, but weighing in at over ten thousand pounds, they were an expensive vehicle to drive. Getting less than ten miles per gallon with the original H1, the customer base was small. While the truck included some creature comforts separate from the military counterparts, like comfortable passenger seating and air-conditioning, they didn't take the market by storm as planned. Sold to GM in 1999, a smaller version, the H2, was released on the market boasting all the power with a lighter frame. A mere two years later, the world found itself amid an oil crisis. With the fuel cost skyrocketing, the "cool factor" Hummers offered was lost to other SUVs' practicality. But did GM pivot? No. They doubled down and designed the H3. It was smaller and lighter than the H2 but still got less than fifteen miles per gallon on the road. By 2009, GM filed chapter 11 bankruptcy, and the Hummer line was discontinued. Arriving late in the game, the first electric Hummer hit the market some fifteen years later in an effort to resurrect the brand. Only time will tell how far their battery-powered re-envision of the former military vehicle will fare. Oh, and Arnold Schwarzenegger? He has also changed gears—now building awareness of the climate crisis and having founded the Schwarzenegger Climate Initiative.

The Fix: Be Nimble

I know, without the advent of a crystal ball (or Magic 8-Ball as we will talk a bit about in chapter 9), how does one truly overcome bad timing? The reality is, sometimes you get lucky. Other times it's all about planning and researching your market. If you do everything right and timing works against you, there's not much you can do other than be ready to pivot.

Creating a layer of flexibility in your business plan can go a long way toward heading off any potential timing situations. If you know anything about technology, you've heard of If-Then statements. Heck, you might even know them from spreadsheet programs, or math classes some of us prefer to forget. Regardless, an If-Then statement addresses the potential of a hypothesis or question with a solution. For example, if it rains and I don't have my umbrella, then I will get wet. Building these basic statements into your business plan can go a long way toward planning for the unforeseeable future.

Mind you, some of those statements should address aspects related to timing. Say if your product launches and the internet dies, how will you get it in front of consumers? Is there a point when you have exhausted your planning and need to cut bait? Companies who build these components into their business planning stage tend to be more prepared in the event life hands them a ton of lemons. Those are the companies that don't try to get by making lemonade like everyone else. No. They make margaritas, lemon squares, lemon-crusted fish dishes; you name it. They have a plan and are willing to be flexible.

Business Model F*ckup #6:

Mini-Mindset

Entrepreneurs have a tendency to think "too big" in early stages of a startup, but many startups fail because the founders think too small too soon.

Please plan on your business going places! Sorry, flower-shop founders; I'm going to use you as an example again. It is not okay to tell yourself, "All I need is to have a cozy little flower shop on the corner that makes just enough money to pay my bills until I die." You need to aim much higher—not only because it would be nice to strike gold, but also because you actually do need to make more than enough to pay the bills until you die. You need to build a buffer into your business plan to account for all the things that will go wrong once you open your doors.

If you're a business school student or graduate, you already know that I'm not being pessimistic. There are two problems here.

1. Thinking a small profit is okay (it's not; something will go wrong, and then the small gain becomes a slight loss).
2. Thinking too small in terms of what is possible. Why make a local kid's company walking dogs if you could almost equally make a nationwide dog-walking company hiring kids? It's nearly the same work, but 100x the result if it works.

Unforeseen obstacles are inevitable—not because you didn't do your homework, but because stuff happens. Change is constant. There will be days when you don't get the twenty customers a day through the store you need to make a modest profit. There will be days when you get three customers. There will be unforeseen weather events that drive the wholesale price of tulips through the roof. There will be broken refrigerators for which you didn't allot repair costs. As they said once upon a time in the Old West: There will be blood. And if you think small from the get-go, when challenges arise, you'll be dead, end of story.

Bottom line, if you start your business thinking of it only as a "small business," you've already sealed your fate in 99.8 percent of the cases. Granted, that statistic may be skewed,[3] but the reality is if you decide

---

3. Of course it is. As you perhaps already know, 83.7 percent of all statistics are made up on the spot. My point is to illustrate that if you think small, you're missing out on so many possibilities. I always recommend putting your "small" idea to a "big" test.

your business will be small because the idea of thinking big is too scary or overwhelming or far-fetched, you'll be setting yourself up for possibly a quick flash-in-the-pan success if you hit the market right, followed by a sudden exit, leaving the customers you gained with a bad taste in their mouths over your lack of concern for their long-term dependence on your product or service. Or, more realistically, you'll be too buried under the fear of "thinking too big is bad" to grow and improve your business, products, and customer promise. It's the business equivalent to "cutting off your nose to spite your face." Don't make the mistake of pigeonholing yourself into being a "small business" out of fear.

This particular failure was one I witnessed. My parents owned a small laundromat next door to my childhood home as well as others locally. As long as they brought in enough funds to pay for family vacations and "extras," my parents were happy. Despite my parents having an entrepreneurial spirit, they always looked at those pursuits as additional income or a way to fill gaps and find some small growth, rather than a true lifestyle or career choice. Interestingly enough, their laundromats were my first glimpse into the potential of a subscription model. The idea of having a business that could run on autopilot intrigued me. Had they chosen to devote more time to their business ventures along with applying growth formulas, they could have both given up their "day jobs" and perhaps enjoyed a different level of success and accomplishment.

The Fix: Apply the 10x Rule and Skip Small

The 10x Rule, which we could also nickname the Antifragile Rule (inspired by Wall Streeter and scholar Nassim Nicholas Taleb), for reasons I'll soon explain, starts with a simple calculation. The core idea is to stop shooting for average, and instead multiply your goals by ten. It's

---

If you can see the vision working big without an excess need for cash flow initially, or see ways to scale with time, "go big or go home," as they say. Although, who "they" are is still up for grabs.

the most straightforward math you'll do when creating your business plan. Just 10x everything. Once you've determined how much you'll need to make in sales to pay your bills, multiply that amount by ten. Now, develop improvements that will increase your revenue by tenfold. And there you have it: your new business model. Perhaps 10x reminds you of the BHAG—"Big Hairy Audacious Goal"—as coined by Jim Collins. And yes, it sounds simple but the idea is good because it forces you to look at your goals in a different way, and actually includes both the effort (consider it 10x harder, and account for that) and the desired result.

Like a runner's bones, which get stronger when subjected to stress, your business will thrive on chaos if you've properly braced and buffered for it. That's what the Antifragile Rule does—ups your ambitions, in tandem with your prospects for success.

Flower-shop founder, I can already hear your argument: "I just wanted to net $100,000 a year! That's all I need—and besides, there's no such thing as a boutique florist making $1 million. Get real!" To that, I say two things:

1. If you can't find a way to multiply revenue by ten, you shouldn't start this business. It will be too fragile, and it will fail. Likewise, if you dream of a comfortable life that doesn't fit with what it will take to make that 10x leap from a fragile business to an anti-fragile company, it's possible the startup life might not be for you. That said . . .

2. I want you to try it anyway: think outside the box to find your ideal way to get to 10x growth. Yes, it will seem unrealistic at first because everything seems unrealistic before achieving it for the first time. Look at 1-800-Flowers. They bring in over $80 million USD yearly. It can be done.

Skip Thinking Too Small in Different Categories

Targeting niche markets is a successful approach that startups agree works. Most people misinterpret the word *niche* to mean "small." However, it actually refers to a specialized segment of the market. Your nest. Just because your target market segment is specialized doesn't mean it's small and limiting for your growth. In fact, if you position yourself properly, you can create a brand that scales beautifully from a niche market into larger markets. Keep in mind, your product or service needs to be scalable to succeed beyond a niche market starting point. If you find that your product or service isn't scalable at any point in your launch process, you should understand you're only selling a product and not a business concept. A strong business concept is scalable, answers a problem with mass-market appeal, and can potentially gain global influence.

Flexibility is key. No thought is too small. You should always have an avenue for growth and development within your company. Open your eyes to look beyond today, tomorrow, and next week, and plan big. Create the road map to gaining widespread inclusion in your market. Seek out new partners, opportunities, marketing ventures, customers, products, and inspiration. In doing so, you'll change a small-thinking mindset into one of possibility. In that, you may even happen upon something you never expected, a new and improved you. Think big. Don't limit your potential.

Remember Roger Bannister, the first person in history to run a mile in under four minutes? Remember how long it took someone to beat Bannister's record time of 3.59.4? That's right, forty-six days.

Everything is impossible. Until it's not.

A Final Word on Business Models

So now that you know how to ensure you have a viable business model for a product in an attractive industry that solves real problems customers have, which alone could save you from startup failure, we're going to show you how to avoid the pitfalls that cause 90 percent of startups to fail. And we'll poke a little fun at Google and illustrate how three products of theirs all fall into market research failures.

Remember, this book is about avoiding the most common startup failures before they happen.

So I remind you of my opening quote from Robert Heinlein about teaching pigs. Or perhaps you'd prefer J. R. R. Tolkien's version: "It does not do to leave a live dragon out of your calculations if you live near one." No matter which speaks to you, do us both a favor and make a plan for success. Don't bother giving a pig a singing lesson or ignoring a dragon when one works next door. Write a darn business plan and address the questions: "Is my industry an idiot or attractive?" "Am I offering a solution to a valid and widespread problem?" "Am I making assumptions, or do I have concrete data to support my venture?" "Am I co-dependent, or can I stand on my own two feet?" "Is my crystal ball back from the shop?" Wait. I'm pretty sure I told you they aren't available yet for entrepreneurial use. So make a bunch of If-Then statements and create a plan for being flexible. Don't pigeonhole yourself into thinking too small.

I know you can do it. Better yet, I know it won't even take you as long as you think to accomplish these exercises either. Sit down with your co-founders and hash these things out. Your business will be the better for it, and your bottom line (and bank account) will thank you for putting in the effort.

Chapter 3

Market Research F*ckups

As we've established, it's a cornerstone of entrepreneurship that the majority of businesses fail. With that risk in mind, you should bolster your venture from the start with solid market research.

Before embarking on any new venture, I first identify the top competitors in my industry and download their annual reports. These are available for publicly traded companies and often for privately held companies as well. I don't spend hours analyzing each report, but I do make sure to look closely at employee numbers and turnover, profit margin, and capitalization. Even these basic metrics offer a treasure trove of knowledge to work with. One hour spent with the annual reports of three top TV production companies, for example, told me that none of them were making money. That was all I needed to decide not to invest in a compelling TV startup that had tempted me.

On the other hand, early market research for my CRM company, Simply, revealed that our main competitor was seven years old and doing very well, despite having a subpar product. That was incentive enough for me to dive into the customer relationship management (CRM) space in Denmark. But should I plan to expand internationally? To find out, I used a simple tool, Google AdWords, to estimate the volume of ad clicks available for purchase in Germany, Sweden, and Norway. Though hardly an exact science, my rudimentary advertising-channel research gave me insight into market demand in those countries, telling me that Simply would be well positioned to expand beyond the Danish market.

What if you start researching and find that your would-be venture has no comparables in the marketplace? Sorry, that's no excuse to forge ahead blindly. It's a cue to try twinning or looking for data on companies in a neighboring market or country.

Once armed with a fundamental understanding of who, where, and how successful your competitors are, you're ready to dive deeper into your market research and analysis. Beware: there are more ways to mess up this homework than you probably think.

Market Research F*ckup #1:

Doppelganger Danger

Cloning usually fails. Copy all you want, and you'll always be one step behind. Stay original with your startup and let the world copy you.

Time and time again, I've heard pitches from aspiring entrepreneurs who think they've got a winning idea but can't tell me definitively if it already exists. Remarkably, they haven't even Googled their fabulous idea to see if a doppelganger business pops up. It's almost as if they would rather bury their head in the sand than look at what they're really up against in the marketplace.

What is the danger of a doppelganger? Essentially, a doppelganger is a clone or copycat business. A delicious example of a frequently copied company is Pinterest. And it makes sense from a business perspective since a study compiled by Shareaholic showed the platform drives more traffic to websites than Google+, YouTube, and LinkedIn combined. The doppelganger sites popping up are further proof that Pinterest is doing something right. Interestingly enough, the founders of these copycat platforms all say the same thing, "It's Pinterest for _____ [insert whatever portion of the market they want to capture]." Feel free to make up your own "Airbnb for _____" or "Uber for _____," "Amazon for _____," and so on.

I find the staggering number of failed Pinterest clones already washing on the shores of copycat island amusing. A few honorable mentions are:

- Pinspire: a Pinterest for Pinterest users
- Stylepin: Pinterest for style
- Wanderfly: Pinterest for travel
- Gtrot: Pinterest for globetrotters
- Kulish: Pinterest for social commentary
- Manteresting: Pinterest for men
- Snatchly: Pinterest for porn
- Hunuku: Pinterest for families
- Urbantag: Pinterest for places you've been
- Singtrest: Pinterest for Singapore
- The complete.me: Pinterest for dating
- Discover: Pinterest for designers

- Pingram.me: Pinterest for Instagram
- Reclipit: Pinterest for deal lovers
- Sworly: Pinterest for music
- Tailored: Pinterest for weddings
- Chill: Pinterest for video
- SparkRebel: Pinterest for fashionistas
- Stylepin: Pinterest for fashion
- Pin style: Pinterest for fashionable fashionistas
- I Wanna Nom: Pinterest for recipes
- Pin Cat: Pinterest for pinning cats to Pinterest

Okay, I went a bit overboard with the failed Pinterest clones, but the answer should be clear: doppelganger danger is real. Keep in mind that all of these copycat businesses launched and closed. This fact proves the threat is real and should be taken seriously when creating your startup.

Ideally, your startup won't have copycat-itis, but hold it to the doppelganger standard and see what shakes out. Now, some doppelgangers may have the capacity to hold water and stand against the competition, but that's because they already have other solid benefits, such as a stronghold on the market and enough faithful users to compete. What if you're Facebook? Hobbi, launched in 2020 and owned and backed by Facebook, was a photo-sharing app where users could capture and organize their creative processes. For those unfamiliar with Facebook's other attempts at competitive apps, you only need to look at Whale, Bump, and Aux, none of which have been a unique product for Facebook's New Product Experimentation team. At this point, you can probably guess what happened to Hobbi with Pinterest ranking so high in the market. Yup, it closed its doors a few months after launch.

Another fun doppelganger is Wimdu, a German take on Airbnb, created by the Rocket Internet startup factory, which is notorious for creating international clones of other successful American businesses. Wimdu sent out requests to Airbnb members, attempting to poach them from the program or persuade them Wimdu was a partner program. Launched in 2011, the company was able to corner some of the market in Austria and Germany, but they never made enough impact to get bought out by Airbnb like some other, more successful clones. In 2016, Wimdu merged with another doppelganger, 9Flats. Still unable to compete, they were acquired by another European entity owned by Wyndham Worldwide. Later, it was again sold off. In 2018, the website was shut down, and all employees were let go.

The Fix: Differentiate to the Better

Doppelganger danger is not to be taken lightly, but don't let it scare you off your idea completely. If you find out—even on the late side—that an identical concept to yours already exists in the market, you don't necessarily need to burn your business plan and go running for the hills. I strongly suggest that you go back to the drawing board to figure out how your company can bring something new and different to the table. Can you deliver this desirable service more efficiently than your competitors? Can you build a more straightforward path to profitability? How is your product better? Perhaps you can tweak your selling point to gear your product to a slightly different market than your competitors'.

Interestingly enough, in a multitude of marketplaces, you can hear reassuring mumblings of doppelganger danger.

But perhaps the great American entrepreneur Mary Kay Ash, founder of Mary Kay Cosmetics, put it best: "Ideas are a dime a dozen. People who implement them are priceless." Point being, there is no limit to ideas. Most of them are not going anywhere unless someone with a plan and passion uses their intelligence to bring an idea to fruition.

If you plan to essentially copy an already existing company, let it go. Especially if it's an exact doppelganger. If you need the reminder again, read back through the Pinterest list. However, if you believe your idea is a new take on an existing idea and you can differentiate from the current company in at least one (but preferably more than one) aspect that can outperform the competition, go for it.

I highly recommend the aspect that beats the competition isn't only the price. Going back to Michael Porter from the previous chapter for a moment, another of his strategies states that you want to avoid being stuck in the middle as a business, especially if you're competing one-on-one with an existing player. If you find yourself in this position, you can adopt one of his generic strategies: cost leadership, differentiation, or focus.

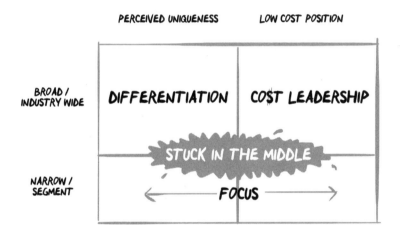

Cost leadership is relatively straightforward: you aim to be the preferred choice because of your pricing. You have the lowest prices in the target market segment—or are at least perceived as the lowest price-to-value ratio, i.e., price compared to the value the customer receives from you. *Perceived* here can be a key word as there are several markets where pricing is not fully transparent.

The problem with cost leadership? In theory, there is only one player in the market that is the cheapest, so everyone else loses this game. And as a startup, you will rarely have the economy of scale to support the pricing. There are, however, exceptional cases if you can find old monopolies, where their cost-to-serve is too high, and they have legacy/structural barriers preventing them from competing on a lower price.

Differentiation is my personal favorite (fortified after many years running communications agencies), which basically means that you need to differentiate from the pack. There are many possible angles—you can differentiate on design, features, usability, time-to-market, support, and so on. Volvo and BMW both make (good) cars, but they are both differentiated. Volvo is differentiating from a "safety" positioning and BMW from a "driving experience" positioning.

Focus means narrowing your focus to a particular market (perhaps geography if language/location is a parameter or other segments/niches), and servicing that market better than others in this industry. Here you can also apply differentiation or cost focus in the selected segment.

Unnecessarily Original

The difference between unique and unnecessarily original is the difference between success and failure.

While you want your idea to have that unique selling point, if your research finds that the market you're trying to enter seems somewhat empty, use caution. Chances are, there's no other ice cream delivery service or edible shoe company out there for a reason. After all, with thousands of entrepreneurs working on startups 24-7, how could it be possible that no one has previously investigated your concept?

More than likely they have, and discovered that it's just not profitable.

Now genius, one-of-a-kind ideas certainly do exist. But they're incredibly rare, and to assume that your idea, lacking any evidence of a market foothold, is just that special would be akin to hearing hoofbeats and assuming zebras are on their way.

One of my favorite examples comes to you in the form of Washboard, a startup designated as the "Worst Startup Ever" by the *Washington Post*. They lasted a solid week and boasted having "more than ten customers." To be fair, they tried to create a problem that didn't exist for the laundry market: people needing quarters for the machines, delivered to their door.

I'll wait while you take a second to reread that last line. Yeah. They offered to deliver quarters to your home for use when you went to the laundromat. For $20 worth of quarters, they charged $27.

Remember the laundromats I mentioned my parents owning? My mother had two, along with her daytime job doing pensions at SAS (Scandinavian Airlines System), and my father had several laundromats. He had earlier built houses and invented printing machines for Aller, where I would later go to work as CCO in one of life's full circles.

Their laundromats were how I learned about subscription-type income and the idea of putting a business on autopilot. Having a laundromat meant paying rent, adding soap and detergent, cleaning up the place, and, of course, collecting money from the machines (as well as chasing away petty criminals and drug addicts in the middle of the night).

This was all small-scale, trial-and-error type business, but it was inspiring just to try things out and see what happened. It clearly gave me the idea to become an entrepreneur.

For this reason alone, I can also come up with many other easy ways to do Washboard's coin idea. You could probably add even more. While I can't speak for your experiences, the last time I went to a laundromat, there were machines filled with those little coins. You feed a bill into the machine and receive the matching number of coins, no surcharge needed. I'm honestly surprised they lasted a week. Washboard makes for an example of an overly original idea. Yes, it could belong to many categories, but it fits best here with ideas created alongside the problem they solve.

Ah, and lest we not forget Agister, a service where you could upload your picture and then have people judge your age. Essentially allowing others to guess your age based on your appearance wasn't a problem anyone needed fixing. While the idea was original, it lacked the major hallmarks of a potentially profitable business venture in that it: a) didn't answer an existing problem in the market, and b) lacked a repeated revenue stream. I'd argue this service may have created more problems than it ever addressed, especially with the body positivity movement taking off. Needless to say, the service died rather quickly.

The Fix: Formulate from Familiarity

Even if you're passionate about a marketplace and, with extensive research, discover no one has done anything like your idea, consider those similar ventures as opportunities. Is there something in those similar ventures you can reinvent, streamline, or market in a new way? If so, consider that new idea and apply the same standards. If not, add it to your not-to-do list and move on to another idea.

If you still feel your idea needs to see the light of day in some shape or form, look back at Porter's differentiation. Within his wisdom, you may find what you need to pursue the venture. But perhaps, put your idea on the back burner for just a bit while we learn about other market research failures. There's likely to be more problems coming that can direct your idea toward either the trash bin or the business plan.

Competing with the Network Effect

A Network Effect is very hard to build—and extremely hard to break. Giants before you have tried and failed. Going for a network requires Herculean effort.

It's (almost) impossible to compete with the Network Effect. Take Facebook, for example. Due to its wide acceptance in the social media market, it has grown, adapted, and continued to find new ways to keep its portion of the market share while still bringing in new users daily. The value people gain from interacting with the platform only keeps their feet more planted in the network Facebook created. To my point, the greater the network of users who use a product, the more valuable it becomes. Imagine the complexity—and serious probability of failure, almost despite whatever funding you could get your hands on—of launching a competitor to Facebook or LinkedIn today, having to outrun those existing networks' hordes of users.

There are four types of network effects:

1. Direct Network Effects: Occur when the value of your product increases exponentially with the increased number of users using your product

2. Indirect Network Effects: Occur when your product value increases due to other complementary products in the market that add value to your business

3. Two-Sided Network Effects: Occur when there are "supply" users and "demand" users both coming to the same network for different reasons, but both add value

4. Local Network Effects: Occur when there are smaller subgroups within the network offering a secondary benefit to users, which encourages more users to join

Avoid confusing network effects with a viral product. Whereas the Network Effect increases its value with the number of users, a product is viral when the rate of adoption increases with adoption.

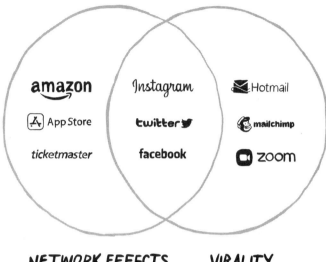

NETWORK EFFECTS   VIRALITY

As you can imagine, there have been many attempts to rival the network Facebook created in the last five to ten years, but so far, none have succeeded in any way greater than a quick flash in the pan before drifting back off into obscurity.

The allure of becoming the "new and improved" network will keep companies chomping at the bit to rake in those sweet, sweet dollar bills. Case in point, Google's attempts to claim some of Facebook's market share with Google Wave and Buzz.

Starting in 2009, Google made multiple moves to try and steal market share away from Facebook in the creation of their own social media platform. Google Wave launched in 2009 when it seemed Google couldn't lose and yet it failed epically. Google Buzz took its place in 2010 and also epically failed. Neither endeavor was exactly a wave or a buzz.

Both platforms allowed users to share posts with friends privately or publicly with an extensive list of integration partners that included Twitter, YouTube, Flickr, Blogger, FriendFeed (a new Google feature), and others.

Both projects ended up causing massive issues surrounding their privacy policies and user complaints. Yeah, you guessed it, Google axed the projects.

Not to be defeated, Google laid low for a bit as they developed yet another product designed to capture a piece of that Facebook fandom. In 2011, they launched Google Plus. While Google Plus was a revolutionary platform in providing new product integrations that helped improve our experience when conducting online searches, even today, it merely shows itself at the end to be Google's aborted effort at trying and failing to take on Facebook.

If we take a ride in the looking-back machine, it is easy to see what Google was trying to do—dissect popular services like Twitter, Facebook, YouTube, LinkedIn, and Gmail and Frankenstein their parts into a shambling new machine. Combining many beloved parts will make a monster that is universally loved, right?

Wrong. The story's antagonist was of course Victor Frankenstein, not the monster.

The *New York Times* broke the news in 2014 that Google Plus was an underhanded attempt by Google to connect user accounts in one place, similar to a hub. Their own project management VP, Bradley Horowitz, was quoted explaining the previously undisclosed goal of the product: "It gives Google that common understanding of who you are."

October 8, 2018, is forever doomed to remain in infamy as the day the Google Plus machine came crumbling down. That fall Monday morning, the *Wall Street Journal* reported that Google Plus had exposed hundreds of thousands of users' private data—a major security breach in every meaning of the term, opening up the company to expensive probes and lawsuits. A flaw in the API was responsible for the information breach and had been discovered in the spring but went unreported as Google feared stricter regulations.

Google announced the same year that the service would be shutting down. The cause? "Low usage and engagement." They stuck to some version of the reported API breach as being unfounded. Sure, they agreed there was a potential for a breach in the API, and of course, they were working on a patch for it, but there was no proof of an actual breach they would admit to.

More user data was leaked or exposed to muddy the soup further after the software was patched through in November. Google then began taking action by deleting profiles from there while maintaining that there was no evidence that developers had taken advantage of the platform's weaknesses.

Part of Google Plus's problem was that it wasn't even a social network—it was more akin to LinkedIn than Facebook. In fact, underneath the hood, Google Plus was a design for an "identity service" used by the United States federal government.

It offered not much in the way of desired features to its users and, in fact, usually frustrated them. Users who were used to using Facebook's streamlined systems slammed the social site for having too many seemingly unrelated menus and options. It died a death on the vine, never really having taken off. Studies conducted on usage and implementation of the products showed that the average user only used the platform for less than five seconds.

Social media is a prime example of a complicated industry due to the network effect, plain and simple. There are many people blinded by the valuation of Facebook, thinking that some are the new black. Fact is, they aren't.

A discussion on the network effect wouldn't be complete without MySpace. Yes, it launched before Facebook. Yes, it's still online, people work there, and there's an office. Try going to www.myspace.com—it still works! However, MySpace has fallen *far* from being the giant that it was as one of the first true social networks. Falling from the most visited website in 2006 worldwide to the loss of millions of users through the 2010s was definitely an iteration of the network effect.

It seems MySpace went through an identity crisis, now rebranding as a music site. During a poorly performed server change in 2015, all content from that year was deleted. Gone. In April 2019, the Internet Archive was able to reclaim a large amount of the data, known as the "MySpace Dragon Hoard."

Nervous yet?

Don't be. You know we have a solution.

The Fix: Convert Your Liability to an Asset

It would be easy to assume you shouldn't get into a market where the Network Effect could be your downfall, but that's not the case. It is important to consider if the network you are entering is already at critical mass. If so, then there is no need to launch a competing product or service. Perhaps you'd be better off focusing on a complementary one instead. However, if it appears your product or service is in the same market as a huge "Facebook-esque" player, there are a few key things you should do.

1. **Ensure that your product fits the market.**

   Remember, you don't want your juicer to have to connect to Wi-Fi and be so highly priced that only millionaires can afford it. Do the features, product details, cost point, service level, and marketing of your product match your target market? You're not going to stay in business for very long without making sales.

2. **Focus your efforts.**

   Remember, even Amazon focuses on one area—providing services to customers through online retail (replacing the brick-and-mortar store for items from video rentals to groceries)! As you craft your startup, sit down and hammer down your niche. Airbnb offers rentals to outdo hotel sites. Etsy offers handmade goods compared to eBay, which is more akin to a mass-marketplace for secondhand items, not so much homemade. What is your niche? How does it compare to your closest competitor?

3. **Use the correct business model for your business type and niche.** A subscription model won't work for a onetime product, just as a onetime-purchase meal kit won't survive for very long either.

4. **Use actionable metrics and throw out the ones that only make you feel good.** Unless you're in the social media or video sales business, the number of watches-without-action on your video ads won't mean squat. Customers through the door who don't purchase anything don't count toward your sales goals. Some metrics, like the ones mentioned above, are comfortable, like views on videos or the number of people moving in and out the doors. However, if these metrics do not suggest actionable strategies, they are not worth your time and effort to understand.

5. **Fight to retain your customers.** You'll need to develop programs such as coupons and discounts, customer loyalty, create games, or set up referral programs.

6. **Customize your platform to fit your needs.** Businesses are a lot like life itself—you must adapt to survive. If customer demand begins shifting toward a specific segment, it is important to step forward and embrace that change. For example, when Netflix launched, it offered DVD rentals only. As the market changed and streaming became increasingly viable, Netflix slowly shifted into the digital market, eliminating its DVD use over time.

If after addressing each of these key considerations, your product stands to successfully compete with the network, go for it! To increase your chances of a win, consider these additional three points:

1. **First to the market wins.** People will say you can be second if you're faster with upgrades and additional rollouts because there's a proven market, but that's baloney.

2. **Viral marketing makes movements happen.** Mobile and web products and services that succeed with network effects can gain even more traction with viral social media promotion and exposure.

3. **Compatibility with the market leader will allow users to add to their already good experiences.** Offering something that integrates or enhances what currently exists will go a long way toward helping you win.

Customers— What Customers?

Founders & CEOs, meet your true boss: your customer. Your customer is in charge and can fire everybody in your company. Pay adequate attention to them.

In Eric Ries's book *The Lean Startup,* you can read all about the saga of the massively funded online grocery delivery service Webvan, which failed in 2001 because the founders forgot to consult their customers. Webvan's founders thought they had a no-brainer offering: groceries delivered to your doorstep. So they skipped the focus groups and surveys and took their service straight to market. As a result of their haste, they deprived themselves of some invaluable insights about the average American's grocery-shopping habits. Two of Webvan's many oversights were that they neglected to offer shoppers coupons and they required orders to be placed twenty-four hours in advance—a concession that shoppers weren't yet willing to make.

If someone suggested or illustrated the idea of projected client market share by estimating 1 percent of the market, they would have done you a disservice. There's no room for wishful thinking in your business model. To be viable, your numbers must add up in reality! This means if you're starting a flower shop, you don't get to assume that thirty customers a day will come into your shop and buy an average of five tulips each. Even if that's the number it will take to show you can make a profit, it's not a safe assumption. By rigging the numbers in your favor in your business plan, you're only cheating yourself in the long run.

Over and over again, I've seen founders write business plans that assume capturing 1 percent market share to succeed. Starting with this false notion, they retrofit their numbers to show how this tiny, supposedly easy-to-capture market share will be a no-brainer to win. But let's get real: 1 percent of any robust market isn't small at all.

Assumptions will also come back to bite you. Suppose you build your business model around the belief that your market is heading in any given direction, versus building your product for the market as it exists today. In that case, you're in for disappointment. The truth is that none of us has a crystal ball. A smart investor usually won't sink their money into a product that will take ten years to build. You shouldn't drop your own money and time into building such a product—no matter how sure you are that the world will need it in a decade.

The Fix: Survey Away!

I highly recommend getting one-on-one feedback on your idea from as many experts in your market as possible. But an even better way to find out if your startup is truly needed is to get feedback from the customers themselves. Surveys conducted through social media can provide invaluable feedback about the validity of your idea. And I don't mean that you should email your seven best friends a questionnaire about your precious business idea. Sure, you can start with them, but if you want to hear it straight, you'll need to move to a broader group representing your target market.

Facebook is an excellent survey platform.

Before we launched our renewable energy company, Nature Energy, my partners and I used a company to call one thousand people and ask if they would be interested in switching to a clean energy provider. Not only did this help us gauge consumer interest, it allowed us to find out exactly how much the respondents would be willing to pay for our service.

Another great way to gather consumer feedback is through split testing, otherwise known as A/B testing. You present two different versions of a concept to your target audience to determine which performs better. You might do a split test by putting out two ads for your product using different calls to action, offering different price points, or featuring models from different age groups. By presenting only one difference between the ads and then measuring click-throughs, you can easily gauge why one ad performs better than the other and customize your consumer marketing plan accordingly. I split tested titles for this book, as a simple example.

It's a fantastic idea to include some data-based predictions in your business plan. If you have research-backed insights into where your industry is heading and can outline the ways in which your company will adapt and evolve over time, your business model will be all the stronger for it. Just make sure that your model also makes sense now if your predictions don't come to light.

Once you've consulted your customers, it's time to get even more specific with your market research by building a viable prototype. Let's talk about that, shall we?

Messed-Up MVP

Not having a Minimal Viable Product makes your startup as likely to succeed as a team without a single Most Valuable Player.

Another way to increase the risk of failure is to either do your MVP (Minimal Viable Product) wrong or downright skip it altogether. The term *MVP* was coined by Frank Robinson in 2001 and later popularized by Steve Blank, Eric Ries, and hordes of others. It's a product with just enough features that it's usable, which is then sold or tested with its customer base to get feedback and verify if the idea is good enough—kind of a sellable prototype.

Google Glass qualifies as a problem-less solution, which it is, but they could have known all of this had they only done an MVP, which they did not. Ah, Google, you should know better, right? But as we move through this particular portion of the book, you'll see Google has a history of market research debacles. They have a tendency to do "moon shots" and hope for the best. Because of their size, they get away with it more than most.

All that aside, Google Glass was announced with a fancy video and a full-fledged prototype. The spectacles were supposed to be the latest and greatest way to send and receive messages, take photos and videos, and find one's way through a new cityscape. With the release of these techno hipster glasses, fear began to mount. Privacy concerns surfaced along with people's safety concerns trying to multitask while driving, walking, or pretty much doing anything. Added to the pitchfork-led revolt was the concern for having private user information vulnerable to hacking.

Had they created and tested an MVP rather than roll out what they expected to be the newest, biggest, most exciting new tech gadget and interface, they would have saved a lot of time, money, and credibility.

While creating the MVP does take (some) time and (some) money, the investment is well worth it. It is a step in your startup's right direction toward developing your product or service. And, more importantly, testing a version of your product in the market will result in a massive amount of feedback, improvements, and even concerns, which allow you the time and data you need to ensure every *i* is dotted and *t* is crossed before you release your product to the mass market. Side note: be prepared to get loads of negative feedback at this stage. It's not fun having your business idea ripped to shreds, which is probably why so many entrepreneurs want to skip this step. But trust me, it's better to suffer the haters now rather than later. No matter what, don't get defensive. It's crucial to listen closely and take this feedback seriously.

The Fix: Prioritizing Your MVP: Apply the MoSCoW Method

As I've said, you've got to take your MVP seriously: it will help you prioritize your product road map by gathering validated customer feedback. To give the MVP the best conditions, you will need to prioritize the functionality of the MVP, and this is where the MoSCoW method comes into play. The prioritization method was originally developed by Dai Clegg in 1994 during his tenure at Oracle for Rapid Application Development, but can in practice be applied much more broadly. It can be used with timeboxing, where you fix the deadline and adjust the functionalities of the product—making it an obvious choice for developing your MVP.

The term is an acronym for the four categories of prioritization:

- M: Must have
- S: Should have
- C: Could have
- W: Won't have

And someone threw in some lowercase Os just to make it sound cool. Prioritization should (must) be central to your idea development when deciding on the potential features for your (minimum viable) product.

I cannot stress how important it is to create an MVP, even if it isn't perfect, and test, test, test it. Oh, and maybe test it once more. Because as you move your MVP through the market, you'll truly see if your product or service can compete and win the market share it needs to be a success.

INCORRECT

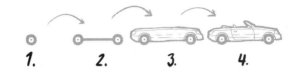

1. 2. 3. 4.

CORRECT

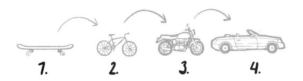

1. 2. 3. 4.

My son, Wilbert, loves skateboarding. To encourage his entrepreneurial streak, I helped him set up a small online skate shop when he was nine—both to test consumer interest and Wilbert's interest in selling these products. The shop is functioning as our test market, so of course, we don't keep an inventory of goods to sell and ship. Instead, we advertise Wilbert's favorite products for sale. If someone orders something, we buy it from our competitor and ship it to our customer. While there's no profit to be made from our little venture, it's a great way of gauging which boards and gear our customers want most. Looking back at the MoSCoW Rules, Wilbert is primed and ready to strike as he's learning his market, customers, and products without attracting attention from his competition. If he decides to take the business fully to market, he will have a ton of great data to guide his MVP creation.

Analysis Paralysis

Bogged down by statistics, research, and more? Stop and take a breather. Research is essential to making sound business decisions, but don't let it stop you from making a decision at all.

There are two ways to consider analysis paralysis. In terms of market research, the quote by Yogi Berra, "When you come to a fork in the road, take it" best exemplifies the sentiment. All too often, founders get stuck in the trap of testing and analyzing forever. If you're asking yourself if forever is an exaggeration, the simple answer is: If you never make a decision, then you are, indeed, taking forever in my mind. So MVPs and timeboxed MoSCoW are great allies.

The secondary application of analysis paralysis is seen in Big Bang Releases. We'll go into that in more detail in chapter 5 when we delve into product development f*ckups. You'll see the similarities, but the marketing and product development aspects are close cousins with completely different purposes.

These days, there's an assumption that investors want every startup idea to be backed by big data. It follows that entrepreneurs have become very test-centric about their market research. Remember how we talked about split tests in the Market Research chapter? We do split tests of everything. We test colors. We test pictures. We test a period versus an exclamation point. And that ad we're testing? We spent five minutes writing it and an hour doing the test setup. The result is rarely a success.

In fact, while it *is* a great tool, all of this data analysis can also keep us from ever launching our business in the first place. At the very least, it will cost us precious time. And if we do launch our data-driven enterprise, our idea's original spark has inevitably been snuffed out, replaced by something gimmicky and artificially complicated.

Many car companies have been taking too long to innovate. Volvo has even admitted that they're lagging behind green-powered car companies like Tesla.

Then take Google's self-driving car project, Waymo, which launched in 2009, and still hasn't (really) delivered their product to the world. "We're building the world's most experienced driver," they tout on their website. I think that copy should be revised to read: "We're *still* building the world's most experienced driver."

By attempting to finalize every last detail before releasing their car, Waymo is doing the opposite of market research.

I'm a firm believer that you shouldn't wait for 100 percent. Your goal should be to get your product in front of real customers, real people, as soon as possible.

The Fix: Test it Like Tesla

Back to the fork in the road wisdom, all decisions have more real value than not deciding a thing. Whether you choose to go one way or another, choosing a path is better than standing still. This way, at least you are moving forward to success. And if you happen to realize you made a bad choice, you always have the opportunity to learn from it, correct it, and move forward again. I'm sure you are seeing my pattern here by now. But, to be blunt, any movement, any decision, is better than no decision at all.

Don't get me wrong: I'm all for testing. The details do count, and testing helps us to refine those details. But rather than attempting to make a product 100 percent perfect before releasing it to real customers, companies should make those customers integral to their testing process. Take Tesla, my favorite car company.

While Waymo and Volvo continue to "perfect" their self-driving cars, Tesla's self-driving cars are already on the roads. Since 2014, they've been releasing their autopilot features step-by-step. The first Tesla Model S would steer itself as long as I was in a specific lane on the highway. That was the starting point. Later, a simple software update allowed the car to self-drive on roads other than the highway. A year after that, the car updated to self-parking services. Now it can drive its way out of the garage. Step by step, Tesla continues to launch more features. And each one works better than the last, thanks to constant real-driver feedback. Probably reminds you of our earlier discussed MVP.

Now, I'm well aware that not everyone is as gung ho to test like Tesla as I am. And I'll acknowledge that the car isn't perfect. That said, you can't get a car with a higher safety rating than a Tesla.

So how do you test like Tesla if you're launching a virtual flower shop or a tutoring service or a frozen croissant company? Just follow these three rules:

1. If it's not something that would enhance your value proposition, i.e., make it easier for you to make a profit, don't test it.
2. Do only as much research as you need to do to understand what your product should be and how your offering should be constructed.
3. Bring your MVP to market as soon as it's viable—that means sellable, not perfect.

Cheating and Ripping People Off

It sounds like a no-brainer, but the temptation to cheat your way to possible success is a real problem in the startup world. Spoiler alert: it never ends well.

At first glance, the title of this failure might seem a bit judgmental or like a lesson in morals, but it isn't. Really. There are so many startups that sound like a good idea on paper until you look under the hood and realize the core value comes from stealing from others or ripping customers (or investors) off. These tend to go down in epic flames at the end and can result in jail time. So before investing a ton of time and energy into a "get-rich-quick" business, I recommend finding a legitimate venture to spend your time and energy on.

One of the most notorious examples in this category is founder Billy McFarland of both Magnises and Fyre Media. Magnises was meant to be a club card for millennials that offered black club card perks to non-black-card carriers; the idea was to fake wealth and importance or at least pay for the appearance of it. McFarland used this company's doctored success portfolio and valuation to secure investor funding for his second company, Fyre Media. This company also had a series of fake books along with a mainly fake music festival, which they sold tickets to. We'll discuss Fyre Festival a bit later because it is one of the most epic examples of a sales failure recorded, but to say he defrauded both his investors and customers is an understatement. McFarland was sentenced to jail time for fraud. While out on bail during the trial, he started another fake venture to sell fake tickets to high-end events by using the list of buyers from his last scam. In late 2018, he was found guilty and sentenced to serve six years in federal prison.

While running Shockwaved, I received a call from the Danish Scientology office, where they had a substantial budget to do online marketing. As Scientology is rotten to its core, I obviously had to reject the offer, but being a small startup with crap liquidity, it actually did hurt saying no. L. Ron Hubbard writes the antithesis of actual science in the science fiction genre as a writer, but he was also pretty anti-business in his business ventures as well. To be more specific, after writing his first publication, *Dianetics: The Evolution of a Science,* he saw an influx of exposure and used his earnings to start the Dianetics Foundation. While Hubbard outwardly banked on his snake-oil science, making people believe his teachers could fix something intrinsically broken within them, he himself lacked a desire to grow the business into anything other than a cash resource. He stripped the company for money and looked for as many loopholes as possible to capitalize on people's misfortune. After two years of fraud, Hubbard's greed and personal misuse of the money kicked off the swift decline of the foundation. The movement, and his foundation, died. Of course, a taste of the limitless income from suffering people led him to his next venture, one with greater shielding from business limitations—a religious organization. Also on his batty to-do list was trying to take over the town of Clearwater in the late seventies, spying against the US, as well as continue his work after his death—from another plane of existence, of course. Enough with the drugs already.

Another prime example includes World Patent Marketing, an invention promotion firm. Founded in 2014 by Scott Cooper, the company used false success stories to lure in new clients and followed with intimidation tactics and threats to keep victims from filing complaints. Their board consisted of a wonderful who's who of famous doctors, scientists, former presidential advisory council members, military generals, and the like. As it turned out, most of the company's clients were sold a bad bill of sale on products that didn't pass the patent process and never received a patent, nor were sold. The Federal Trade Commission shut the company down in 2017 for defrauding the investors seeking to market the proposed inventions.

Similar statements can be made for the tobacco industry, which has taken several hits over the years for previously not disclosing the health risks associated with smoking. While getting its customers addicted to their product, but not disclosing the risk of addiction or death, companies opened themselves to a host of lawsuits and regulations. The industry keeps trying to pivot, but their products, no matter the delivery system, are still unhealthy and causing health concerns.

Funnily enough, this translates to the drug trade. I bet you never considered drug lords to be business owners, but indeed they are. Of course, by systematically poisoning and killing off their customers, they are at the mercy of other customers to persuade new customers in the door. And due to the illegal nature of the industry, someone like Pablo Escobar, Colombian drug overlord, lived most of his life on the run and died from a gunshot to the head. Competition in the industry is literally deadly.

The Fix: Go Legit

Startups take a lot of time and effort. You will ultimately spend as much time and energy on an illegal or shady enterprise as you will on a legitimate one, so save yourself the scruples and jail time and go legit. Don't fudge the numbers to get investor buy-in. If the numbers don't support the business venture, it's likely because you don't (yet) have the solid foundation needed to find success. Take a step back and review the business from all aspects to see where the failure to have the numbers is coming from. We discuss a lot of options throughout the book, and more than likely one of them will be the problem you face.

Building an empire takes time, patience, practice, and fortitude. Spend all of those on something that can be your legacy if it's successful rather than something that gets you fitted for prison orange or a nice oak coffin.

Final Thoughts on Market Research Failures

Market research is, unfortunately, an undervalued component of startups. If there's only one thing you take away from this book, please let it be "do your market research." If you must, imagine me wagging my finger at you in disapproval until you get it done.

Boiling down market research into easy-to-manage steps might include a list something like this:

- Complete your business model canvas from chapter 2.
- Check for doppelgangers in the market.
- Look at potential networks already in place in your market. Can you realistically compete?
- Write out your assumptions about the market, your product, your clients, everything.
- Test the assumptions with your client base. Make sure you target the people who will buy your product or service.
- Create your MVP and test it. Often.
- Take the data gained from your MVP testing and make decisions. Don't sit around picking apart the numbers for eons.

I understand that it may seem overwhelming or complicated to do the market research, especially if you already aren't sure the data will support your vision for the product. But there's no room for excuses here. Do the work. Believe it or not, if you can make it through this portion of the process, you're well on your way to a successful launch.

The next chapter is the topic I probably get asked the most questions about: So how do you plan to pay for that?

Chapter 4

Funding F*ckups

There is one overarching, repeated explanation why most startups fail. It's the (very) short story founders spill the most, and which their understanding audiences apparently seem to accept. It's a five-word reasoning, called "we ran out of *money.*"

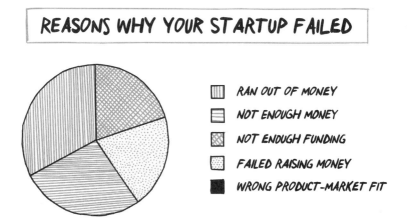

REASONS WHY YOUR STARTUP FAILED

- RAN OUT OF MONEY
- NOT ENOUGH MONEY
- NOT ENOUGH FUNDING
- FAILED RAISING MONEY
- WRONG PRODUCT-MARKET FIT

A stubborn myth, ranking up there with favorites such as how bulls get angry when they see the color red (like other cattle, they're actually red-green colorblind), that goldfish have a few seconds of memory (make that months), and how we only use 10 percent of our brains (yes, I also found the 2014 Scarlett Johansson–starring movie *Lucy* entertaining, but of course we use virtually all parts of our brains).

Do you believe that the key to turning your great business idea into a reality is to secure outside funding? That an investor's monetary "blessing" will all but ensure your company's success? If so, you're not alone. When I talk to founders in the early phases of building their businesses about how it's all going, their focus, nine times out of ten, references their pitch deck. Sometimes they include which big-name venture capitalist they're wooing and the pie-in-the-sky valuation they're seeking. I'm sympathetic. That's what people seem to do these days, and a crappy cash flow can crush even the strongest ventures. Still, I don't hesitate to warn founders about the many funding failures that can and will derail their startups if they're not careful.

Funding F*ckup #1:

Getting Funded

If you aren't independently wealthy with money to burn, funding is something that cannot be ignored when creating a startup.

The first problem you can run into when funding a startup is getting funded at all. The stats on this are actually surprising for most who have entrepreneurial spirits. As we'll see later in this chapter, those investments are a challenge. Read that to mean not impossible, but tiresome. When the time comes, a significant proportion of your time will be devoted to pitching, making acquaintances, making investment deals, and so on.

The early days of your startup can sometimes get so hectic, and in all that chaos, it's easy to lose track of primary objectives—getting the best product possible and landing those early sales. Now, this is easy to say, but we all know that stupid feeling after a hard day's work, when you finally hop into your bed expecting to get some sleep, and thousands of insignificant, exaggerated worries immediately come to your mind. "How will I do this? How will I do that?" And then you "realize" that you need to step up your game and get more funding.

The reality of things is this: The early focus on funding is often less rational than we want to believe. I'm not saying funding isn't significant because we all know that funding is essential for a startup to survive. What I'm saying is that early on in your startup, the focus needs to be on the product, the business, and the market you're entering. Chasing funding rather than focusing on a product your market wants is just as dangerous as running out of money.

Hmmm, sound familiar? It should. I designed this book to take you through all the areas of a startup. It showcases where you might find the pitfalls, but it is also structured to prioritize each aspect. The fact that funding is buried in the middle of the book in chapter 4 means it's something to think about, but not the most crucial factor early on.

No matter how brilliant a founder is or how groundbreaking their product is, those that focus on funding before all else find an imbalance in their business. This imbalance can take them from a startup success story to a cautionary tale in less time than anyone would expect.

Take, for example, Pearl Automation. This automotive startup was founded by former Apple engineers Bryson Gardner, Joseph Fisher, and

Brian Sander, who hired more ex-Apple employees, hoping it would help them gain that slick Apple feeling.

And it did. Pearl Automation made an elegant rearview camera, which acted as a frame for license plates. You could connect this camera to your smartphone. Though the company was founded in 2014, it didn't launch its first product until 2016. By 2017, their doors were closed permanently.

What went wrong? A combination of high-reputation founders (who can easily convince investors) and too much focus on early funding.

Pearl Automation received $50 million from venture capital companies based on the founders' reputations, and nobody thought about early sales. Fifty million is quite a lot; I would argue more than they needed, considering I honestly don't see where that $50 million went. The product was simply too expensive, and if you were ready to pay $500 for a rear camera, you probably already had a car with this option. Nobody wanted to buy it. Everything looked good on paper, but once they started selling it, everyone knew Pearl Automation wouldn't see the end of 2017. Their burn rate was way too high, sales too low, and what was a good idea— making rear cameras available to everyone, not just those who had enough money for fancy cars—got dissolved by the early focus on funding.

Some of the VC firms that funded Pearl Automation were Accell, Venrock, and Wellcome Trust. You can imagine the amount of time that went into talking with these large reputable firms, convincing them that your previous Apple experience is enough for success. They could have spent this time much more wisely.

While Moore's Law (which roughly translates into the doubling of processing power every two years) might be declining, it's still important to point out that dealing with hardware is pretty complicated. It's a field in constant development, but it's not as simple to make adjustments as it is with software. From needing replacement batteries and reconfiguring layouts, to constant innovation and update requirements that could change the product's entire design, hardware is a pain. You will find yourself running to and from the factory (which will probably be quite far away), getting that prototype done. Then you'll fret about its reception because each adjustment in serial production can be quite expensive. Combine that with the constant innovation and advancement coming from every corner. It is easy to get a high burn rate on a hardware startup.

Hardware startups primarily fail due to lack of product-market fit, which we will discuss in a later chapter. Overspending funding dollars comes in at a close second place. Pearl Automation hit both those mines.

The Fix: Know When & Why

Get funded to prove your case, or prove your case to get funded? Obviously, this is an existential question, much like whether the chicken or egg came first.

I digress not only for the entertainment value it can bring to the topic but also because there are a ton of different solutions that all come at this failure from differing angles.

Back in 2006, a team composed of a geneticist, philosopher, and chicken farmer worked together to answer the all-consuming question finally. No, this isn't the beginning of a "three men walk into a bar" joke.

Drum roll, please. The egg came first.

Professor John Brookfield, specialist in evolutionary genetics from Nottingham University, settled the discussion in an interview with the BBC, explaining that the DNA in the egg would have to be the same as that of the chickens, noting, "The first living thing which we could say unequivocally was a member of the species would be this first egg, so I would conclude that the egg came first." No more sleepless nights over that one.

As I mentioned earlier, there are multiple ways to approach the problem of proving your case for funding or funding to prove your case. But like the three experts who determined the egg came first, I'll side with many other VCs on the sentiment that, first, you must prove your case for funding.

Why? It's simple. Having funding at the outset of your startup can inadvertently hide the fact that your product is utter crap. Having the cash on hand allows you to ignore that your product is too costly for consumers, has too low of a price point to be profitable in the long run, or is facing any of the other myriad issues. When you have extra cash lying around, you don't have to immediately deal with the financial stress of an MVP or a product itself not performing well.

Face it: money doesn't solve your failures.

Getting funded too early is going to be too costly.

If you come to me or any VC asking for funding and it appears to be a huge risk at the stage you're in, the investor will want more equity to cover the investment. While the initial influx of cash may seem incredible, think six months down the road when your equity isn't what it could have been. How about twelve months? Eighteen? How's that pit in your stomach feeling right now? The longer your startup exists, the greater the chance for change, and the constant pressure from VCs may be more hassle than helpful in the long run.

"So, smartypants," you ask, "how can I finance a company without funding?"

"Elementary, my dear Watson,"[1] or whatever your name is. How do you bring in money to any company?

Get a customer. Or a few customers. Heck, get a bunch of them.

Consider Glossier, which started as a beauty blog. Glossier began with Emily Weiss, a former fashion editor at *Vogue*. She's a champion of putting customers precisely at the center of her business. Unlike Pearl Automation, who focused on creating a product to amaze their VC firms and pay their investors back, Glossier started very, very slowly. After a few

---

1. Our favorite and famous Sherlock Holmes quote that did not actually appear in any of the Arthur Conan Doyle books but was instead synthesized by its readers and assigned to him. It wasn't until some forty years later that the line was used in the 1929 film *The Return of Sherlock Holmes* as its final high note.

years of blogging and interviewing various potential customers, Weiss had enough information to start her brand. The customer feedback directly fueled the Glossier brand—most notably, even though it was evident that Emily Weiss succeeded in creating a stable business, because she didn't want to rush funding. Glossier didn't sell to stores, necessitating a completely different infrastructure and thus more investments.

With Glossier, we see that getting investments can be a good thing once the timing is right, and the market research proved her case. Emily Weiss pitched a lot of VCs, and some decided to fund her. Keep in mind that Emily worked on her product for years and only decided to seek capital when it became apparent she needed a way to keep customers interested over a long period.

Pearl Automation, on the other hand, had a great product on paper, but listening to its users, it became obvious that the company focused more on pleasing the VCs than customers.

Worse yet was the realization that in the US, since 2018, by law, car manufacturers have had to put rear cameras in all cars. This could have been easily predicted if a random commenter saw this coming in 2016. Instead, the founders were much busier running around, convincing VC officials that their Apple experience was enough.

One more thing, and then we'll leave Pearl Automation to rest in peace. It was obvious that with minimal adaptation, they could have made their way into a potentially significant market—rear cameras for classic and significantly older cars. Enormous markets outside the US exist where people drive slightly older cars.

Funding F*ckup #2:

Convoluting Capital

There is such a thing as "too much money" just as there is "not enough money." Keeping capital simple is essential. A good startup can get funded. A bad startup can burn through capital.

I learned the hard way that bootstrapping is best. I spent my first ten years as an entrepreneur convoluting capital—thinking it was more challenging than it was to secure outside funding for my businesses. If I'd not succumbed to this failure, I do not doubt that several of my early ideas would be businesses today. Instead, I tied myself into knots, trying to figure out where the money would come from, exhausting myself to the point that I let many promising ideas die on the vine.

Even with the first (real) business I bootstrapped, Shockwaved, I ended up overcomplicating capital. About two years in, a marketing platform we were creating for a customer ended up being much more time consuming than we'd thought. Two months turned into five months, and we were in dire need of our final "due upon completion" payment. At this point in the game, it would have been entirely justifiable to seek funding. An easy solution would have been to book meetings with one or two of the angel investors I'd gotten to know through networking channels and propose a simple deal that boiled down to: "My company is growing, year over year, and we need an immediate infusion of $100,000. Here are the numbers that show you'll likely make five times that in five years. What do you say?"

Don't let articles with titles like "Why 99.95% of Entrepreneurs Won't Get Venture Capital" get to you. Even if it's true that most businesses won't even get the chance to see the inside of VC offices, there are many other sources of funding, including angel investors, private placements, even rewards crowdfunding or equity crowdfunding.

That being said, there are many ways you can screw up by either overcomplicating funding or completely ignoring it, which are facets of the same failure. This happened to the Walnut mentoring platform, founded by Arpit Kothari. You've never heard about it because this guy, of course, didn't get the VC support, but neither did he try to fill the gap through other sources. Arpit wanted Walnut to be a sort of side thing, something that would bring him money without him doing anything. All he had to do, so he believed, was to start it, and the money would come all by itself.

"From my traditional Gujju-Marwadi upbringing, I was never in favor of raising funds," he stated. This was the first and most crucial mistake he made. While the company was profitable at the very start because Arpit Kothari focused on short-term gains, ignoring long-term goals led to the ultimate decline. In a way, Arpit overcomplicated capital by ignoring it because he simply thought it was too much hassle. He didn't want his life to revolve around business so he chose to run it as if bringing in capital were something scary. Although, as any entrepreneur can attest, it happened inevitably, but not because he got motivated and enthusiastic. He had to work more because things started crumbling in front of his eyes, and he always had to fill the gaps. Watching his business start to collapse ultimately forced him to confront capital needs.

This begs me to make an additional point here: If you're looking to make a passive income, don't start a new business. Drop-shipping isn't a passive income business model, no matter what some online articles will try to say to the contrary. If your goal in life is to make a passive income without working at something, I hope you're already independently wealthy and have a solid understanding of investment principles. Of course, that would be a topic for a completely different book.

But consider this: the unheard-of Okami Pack. Okami Pack was a field survival pack developed by Tim Chad, a thirty-two-year-old American living and working in Japan in 2014. One day, while at the office, an earthquake hit. He reached under his desk to find a pitiful, outdated emergency kit. With Japan being one of the most earthquake-prone countries globally, he felt he could design something people could use with an appeal to millennials. He partnered with a colleague and, together, they went to work. Quitting his day job, he spent the next ten months putting together a Kickstarter page, researching products for the kit, having a prototype designed and produced, and finding industry experts to review the kit. Want to hazard a guess what he didn't do? Launch the Kickstarter campaign. By June 2015, he had less than $1,000 in the bank and no prospective investors. In meeting after meeting, he realized if he clicked "launch" on his Kickstarter campaign, he wasn't just launching a product but an actual business. With much introspection, one more point became painfully clear: he had no real attachment to his business. The next day, he deleted the ten-months-in-the-making Kickstarter page he never launched.

Back to funding. Don't sweat the small stuff here. It's important to spend some time and attention on the topic, but if you find yourself getting overwhelmed and ready to walk away and completely ignore it, you're only doing your business a huge disservice. This is a great area to reach out for assistance if it's not in your wheelhouse. We've discussed mentors and business partners already. These key people may hold the answers you need to address your biggest funding worries. People experienced in applying for and attaining funding can offer a lot of insight into the process and what is required from a business to achieve their funding goals in a variety of ways. Not every startup needs a venture capitalist firm backing them. As we discussed, the opposite is more likely. However, there are other funding avenues that can get you the funding you need to launch your business.

Having originally never sat on the investors' side of the table, as I often do now, I simply couldn't believe funding could be easy. And it really is. Unless you're operating during a recession, getting funding isn't that complicated.

The Fix: Know How to Pitch

To give yourself maximum leverage in the negotiation process, you'll, of course, need to have a comprehensive knowledge of your business model and all its numbers (which any founder should have). Then, just show up to your meeting armed with a pitch deck that clearly states your value proposition, your modeling numbers, and an angle that maximizes your market validation and attraction. You'll need to show your potential investors all the key metrics, including what it costs to get a customer, your churn rate, any forecasted expenses, and predicted revenue.

A good elevator pitch is a representation of you as a personality. Your business ideas, as well as current and past projects, are, of course, something to be mentioned, but not in a way you would present a business plan (which I'll explain below). You want to present *yourself.* In other words, an elevator pitch is a great thing when you're attending a social gathering with a lot of potential investors, clients, and business partners. Quite often, nobody expects to strike great deals during these events, only to make acquaintances that might turn out to be good business opportunities in the future.

If you're presenting your business plan to VCs, you'll need a pitch deck.

You'll want to highlight anything and everything attractive about your business. If you have a team with a strong track record, that will go a long way—much further, in fact, than having the perfect business model.

Finally, you should pitch like a king, not a beggar. It's not: "Can I please have some money?" It's: "Here's how I'm going to make you lots of money." And it's also about asking what they can offer you in addition to money, such as contacts or joining your board in an advisor role.

You may have to talk to twenty to fifty different investors, but if you approach the process in a fairly structured way, you should be able to get this over with reasonably fast. And it's okay to bundle them up a bit. It does not hurt an investor to know that you have a meeting with a competitor later the same day. It's actually more of a requirement that you let them know that you have other options (politely and subtly, obviously). From there, it's really just a game of statistics in the same way as with any other sale: the more you have lined up, the more good meetings, the more proposals, and so on. If you've presented them with all the proper building blocks, there's no reason why several of the investors you meet with shouldn't be competing to fund you. As they do, make sure to have more than one negotiation going on at a time. This will give you a) options and b) ammunition. The more interest there is in what you have to offer, the more confident you'll feel—and appear—in your negotiations, and the more the investors will want what you have to offer.

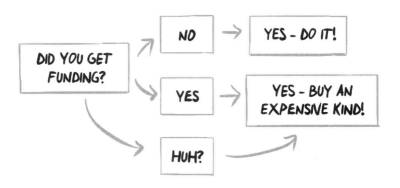

Again, I didn't know any of this when I was twenty-two. So what did I do? I took out an unsecured loan at a horrible rate to cover cash flow at Shockwaved. It was a stupid move that ended up costing us dearly and could have been avoided altogether if I'd practiced better budgeting.

This brings me to our next funding failure.

Bad Budgeting

Balancing your startup budget is like going to heaven. Everybody wants to do it, but nobody wants to do what it takes to get there.[2]

---

2. Phil Gramm

It's all too easy to miscalculate the cost of running the different functions in your company. Rush through your budgeting process, and chances are you'll fail to assess your burn rate accurately. This is what sends the vast majority of companies down the drain. Don't make the same mistake.

For many companies, one of the most significant expenses is the staff. It's a common budgeting mistake to hire too many employees too quickly, like Jim Picariello, founder of Wise Acre Frozen Treats. Founded in 2006, Wise Acre Treats made organic oxidants. Wise Acre didn't grow that much in its first eighteen months—Picariello was the only employee. He made these organic popsicles out of his kitchen. After a year and a half of hard work, he hired one employee, and then thirteen more after six months. Picariello moved his production to a three-thousand-square-foot facility, and everything seemed to be going well. Seemed. Wise Acre went bankrupt by the end of that same year in which it "grew exponentially." Along with other budgeting mistakes—like taking on too large a lease for their headquarters—Picariello cited overstaffing as a critical reason why the company went bankrupt less than three years after being founded.

On a much larger scale, take Zynga, a massive game development company that created wildly popular games like *Words with Friends* and *Mafia Wars*. In 2011, the company was doing so well that they invested heavily in staffing and building their own data centers, the latter to reduce costs—at the expense of $100 million. Building. Their. Own. Data centers. What the heck were they thinking? By 2015, Zynga had closed down several of those centers and laid off 364 employees. The company is still around today, but it's far less successful than it was a decade ago—a depressing fate that could have been avoided if they'd avoided the Bad Budgeting Failure.

Finally, let's look at Skully, a company that fabricated AI-equipped bike helmets to allow motorcyclists the ability to "have eyes in the back of their head." The helmets were promised to crowdfunding investors to provide a new level of safety and security while on the open road. Not only did Scully's founders, Marcus and Mitchell Weller, underestimate their cash requirement, but they also underestimated the savvy of the Securities and Exchange Commission, which investigated them for wildly misspending their investors' money. After three years of living the high life, blowing their company's cash on lavish vacations, strippers, and expensive sports tickets, the brothers were brought down in 2016.

The Fix: Meet the Devil in the Details

You can't be too detailed when it comes to your budget. The metrics you need to isolate and keep in your head at all times are your fixed versus your variable costs for the next twelve months. Your fixed costs are your rent, insurance premiums, loan payments, and any business costs that remain constant no matter your output. Your variable expenses are salaries, advertising expenditures, direct materials, commissions, and anything that fluctuates with your production. For example, if you're selling furniture, you'll calculate the expected costs of everything from your phone bills to your deliverables to your vendors to your transportation. If you're a tech company selling subscriptions, you'll need to assess your CAC, or customer acquisition cost—what you'll spend to move each customer from the point of their first visit to the point of their first purchase and beyond. Also, what's your churn—how many customers will you lose over time?

Once you've plugged these key metrics into Excel, Numbers, or Google Sheets (or whatever program you like) to create a static budget, you can play around with different parameters and their budgetary consequences dynamically. Work out, for example: "What would happen if I fired this person after two weeks? Six months? What if I hired three salespeople in the first year? What if I reduced my advertising budget by 10 percent? Or if my conversion base was improved by 5 percent?" By manipulating these parameters, you'll start to get familiar with the many different scenarios you might encounter from year one through three—and budget for the most feasible scenario.

Funding F*ckup #4:

The Cap-Table Capsize

There are only a few mistakes that cannot be undone. Messing with your cap table is one of those. Be the captain of your cap table.

Your cap table, or capitalization table, shows who owns what in your startup—how much each of your company stakeholders owns, who invested in each financing round, and how their equity has been diluted over subsequent rounds. Sounds simple enough, but you can still f*ck up massively by forgetting to keep a close eye on your cap table. Take your eye off this vital record, and the precious vessel of your company risks capsizing into dangerous waters. In other words, you may allow your share in your company to become overly diluted, which means you lose control. This failure is practically unfixable. Once you've sold, say, 50 percent of your company, you're obviously not in a position where you can just buy that stock back. If your investors even allow it, chances are you'll pay far more than you should, and certain percentages can mean that you lose votes, influence tax, etc.

We can find an early example of the Cap-Table Capsize in Christopher Columbus's story, whose voyage could be considered one of the first significant venture capital deals. While Columbus's ship made it to its destination intact, Columbus, all the same, suffered from the Cap-Table Capsize. In a nutshell, the Spanish crown had promised the explorer 10 percent of all revenue from any lands he discovered, in perpetuity. Ten percent of all of North and South America, forever? That's a pretty good starting point.

It's interesting to think about Columbus's voyage as one big investment. Most people focus on how he discovered America (probably discovered by my fellow Vikings some five hundred years before he was born, but history is forgiving since it had already been "discovered" by its original inhabitants living there when he landed), forgetting that the whole expedition was just barely realized, thanks to Columbus's incredible enthusiasm and zeal. In a way, it's like he had this great idea and knew how to make it happen but just needed the funds.

One thing Columbus didn't overcomplicate was capital—he knew very well how to pitch his idea to the big players. He was an Italian but knew that Italians wouldn't give him the money, having tried his luck with Genoa and Venice, the wealthiest city-states. So Columbus asked the king of Portugal, who rejected him on two separate occasions. He then focused on the king of Spain, and these negotiations lasted from 1486 to 1492. While this was happening, Columbus didn't want to rely solely on Spain's king, so he sent his brother to England to request finances and ships from English royalty. Pirates captured his brother (the perks of living in the fifteenth century), and by the time he was released, Columbus already had a basic agreement with the Spanish crown. Besides the 10 percent of all lands, Columbus also negotiated another great deal—he had the right to buy at least one-eighth of commercial ventures tied to the land he would discover. While they did do a quite elaborate contract (Capitulations of Santa Fe), the Spanish crown ultimately rejected his demand for payments. Bummer.

Roughly five hundred years later, the entrepreneur Steve Jobs would find himself in a similar position to the one Columbus faced. He embarked on a journey, and he wasn't quite sure how it would all end. Neither did his business partners, Steve Wozniak and Ronald Wayne. The latter made arguably one of the worst moves in the history of the business. He sold his 10 percent share in Apple just twelve days after the company was founded. In total, he received $2,300 for his 10 percent of Apple. A major Cap-Table Capsize, in my humble opinion, despite Ronald claiming to have no regrets.

Wozniak and Jobs were shrewder. After the first fundraising round, Jobs had 26 percent ownership, which was reduced to 11 percent in 1985, before being removed from Apple. Perhaps, when the Apple executives expressed their intention to replace him in a moment of anger, he sold almost all of his shares and left Apple. Wozniak did the same thing and also sold his share to about 7 percent. Sure, they didn't commit the same mistake as Ronald Wayne, especially Jobs, who invested in Pixar, made some serious money, and then repurchased some Apple shares. Jobs wouldn't repeat the same mistake. He held on to his Disney share—a comfortable 7 percent—to the very end.

The worst thing is, most entrepreneurs are forced to give up on their original cap table. This happens way more often than you would expect because entrepreneurs who had their companies taken away from them are silenced in every way—typically legally but also illegally.

The ways you can be forced to give up control and shares come in so many different shapes—and are mutating so fast—that they are impossible to list here. Just be aware that majority control of your company can be reached by malignant investors in a number of different ways. They make a very complex legal case that includes reverse stock splits, stock dilution, and down rounds. In other words, everything an entrepreneur doesn't have time to get into, or at least is not an expert in. These guys can make a 99 percent ownership turn into a measly 1 percent in a single day. Make sure that you have qualified legal help before entering into any agreement.

The Fix: Talk Specifics and Get Legal Support Before Making a "Great Deal" with the "Big Buys"

This problem has a two-part solution, due mainly to the multiple components of the problem: know whom you're working with and accept dilution.

In addressing the basics, every startup needs to create a capitalization, or cap, table to designate company ownership. If you're founding the company with a co-founder or two, you'll want to make sure you vet them thoroughly, as their stake in the company will be outlined in this document as well. (Don't panic. Co-founders and how to vet them will be covered in chapter 6. There are plenty of mistakes to make here also.)

Any investors you consider getting into business with need a thorough vetting as well. Keep in mind, you should never only have one candidate. Considering multiple people as potential investors will give you the time to make a proper choice. The same is true when selling a company. You'll want to aim to get "smart money," which is money that also comes with a network, knowledge in the startup world, and easier access to more capital later. On top of that, make sure any potential investors are people you can work with since they will own a stake in your company. If you find them to be a real a-hole, reconsider. The advantage of having multiple parties to consider for these roles means you have the ability to help let the market dictate a reasonable sales price. This advantage will give you a better chance to know you made a good decision in hindsight.

That covers part one. Know whom you're working with, whom you're borrowing from, and have specific conversations about who owns what percentage of what.

The second part of the solution is: accept dilution. Yep, it sounds scary (and to a certain extent it *is*), but if you need the cash, then it makes sense. If you, as an example, get funding plus a great mentor for your business, *even though* it might cost you 51 percent of the company, then it's not the worst situation. Many founders worry about dilution, but the reality is, eventually, it will happen. Stop worrying about what can't be controlled because the harsh truth is you won't have control over your business's valuation entirely.

This brings us sliding into the second part of the solution for any cap table failures.

Before signing hefty contracts, you should hire a contract attorney, usually on a freelance basis. If you don't have that many yearly contracts, you don't need to hire a contract attorney full-time as they don't come cheap.

What to do when you don't have a contract attorney? Get one anyway. But in addition to this, good old reading will help and reduce the cost. You should do what you never do and read the terms and services very, very attentively. Each page is important, and sometimes the crucial information is strategically put in places where it's hard to notice. Every word in a contract is important. And even while doing this, always hire an attorney.

Next, even when everything's okay and there are no signs of foul play, you should still have your paper version of the contract. Nowadays, there are so many online document signing services, and we sometimes forget how it was back in the day when a paper form was the standard. Having a printed, paper copy gives both parties the added security of a "hard" or "wet" copy. Sign all pages. Some contracts are required by law to be maintained in the paper form, especially when doing business outside your country of origin and for certain holdings like real estate or some international employment agreements.

Before you make any deals with big investors or VCs, consult your legal counsel. Do your due diligence researching the people you'll be working with, and make sure you understand how to protect your ass(ets) best.

Funding F*ckup #5:

Amateur Accounting

When it comes to running a business, if you don't have a background in business accounting, save yourself a lot of time and hassle by finding an expert who can help.

A friend of mine has borrowed several books now and has never returned a single one. He should consider becoming a professional bookkeeper. All startups need one.

It's a common mistake: a founder with zero professional training in accounting will decide, inexplicably, to handle their own finances. Not only will they make numerous errors, which can sometimes turn out to be serious issues, but when they realize that they cannot do it on their own, they'll try to outsource it to some faraway accounting company for cheap.

One example is LeSports, an online live sports streaming service, launched in 2014 by founder Jia Yueting. In his zeal to expand the business, he began racking up some serious debt. In 2019, however, amid scandals over his excess debt and his questionable accounting practices, Yueting filed for bankruptcy. This left his creditors about $3.6 billion in the hole.

The big guys also have failures with accounting, especially relating to taxes. In 2018, Toys "R" Us, one of the biggest US retailers of toys, faced administration, which is the British way of saying "bankruptcy," after accounting irregularities resulted in $15 million in tax debt. Soon after, the UK branch of Toys "R" Us was closed, followed by the Australian and finally US branches. Although the company reemerged as Tru Kids in 2019, it still only has two stores in the US.

Lindsey Reinders is the co-founder of the Beardbrand startup. They sell everything connected to beards, man, and machoism.[3] Note that Lindsey already had an accountant, but she figured that she could save some money and try to "reinvent the wheel." This is not necessarily related to the exact topic we're debating, but Lindsey's story is also an example of how many people try to make some small improvements and tweaks in things that are working perfectly fine and end up making a complete mess out of it. And as we all know (let's say it in unison):

If it ain't broke, don't fix it.

---

3. No, read it again. I wrote machoism.

Regardless, she immediately purchased a $23,000 yearly subscription with accounting and finance software company ScaleFactor.

Mind you, ScaleFactor appeared as this very ambitious startup with aggressive marketing that emphasized how the company was using AI to revolutionize accounting. Their slogan went something like: "Evenings are for family, not for finances." Pretty good, right? When you're working all day, doing the essentials, you want to go home and spend time with your family before your kids go to bed. Or you want to relax a little, whatever. So ScaleFactor got a lot of clients who believed in what they said.

The main point here is that owners of other startups and businesses thought: "Wow, this is an easy and cheap way to do my accounting! I won't have to think about it again in my life." Realistically speaking, that's absurd. And guess what? Other people will probably try to make some easy money from this, like ScaleFactor.

ScaleFactor came and advertised this fancy AI they had for doing finances. There were no accountants, just the computer doing the work. There was nothing better for a small startup owner because they all want to avoid the expense of getting a pro accountant to work with them.

Lindsey, excited to be getting into this fantastic service early, figured all her accounting worries were gone. And for the low, low price of $23,000 (read: I'm not that impressed), she believed she could ignore her accounting to a degree. Sadly, ScaleFactor's AI was so glitchy that they had to hire real accountants to do the work. But the scale of the work was so vast that the company decided to outsource a portion of the work to a Philippine-based company. So the outsourcer hired an outsourcer—great! This just shows how important it is to have someone who knows you and your company. Each company has some very specific nuances, and a second-level outsourced Philippine company cannot really get to know these nuances.

Even with outsourced help working on ScaleFactor's accounts, things got pretty glitchy, pretty fast. Lindsey had some bills paid twice, while others not at all. Reports were full of errors and ScaleFactor customers, like Lindsey, had to work a lot to sort this out.

Lindsey Reinders learned this the hard way—a ScaleFactor error made her lose $17,000 (on top of the $23K yearly subscription). The $17K was credited to a customer. By mistake. Can you imagine? Because Scale-Factor was so chaotic, the error went unnoticed for six months, and by then, it was too late.

These accounting mistakes didn't necessarily ruin Lindsey's business, but it sure lost some money and, more importantly, it took a ton of time for her to get her accounting and finances back to normal. Oh, but don't worry—ScaleFactor closed shop back in 2020.

The Fix: Call in a Pro

Now, I'm not saying you need to hire an expensive CFO from the get-go. But just as you wouldn't attempt to handle all of your marketing, sales, and website design, you shouldn't try to DIY your finances. At the very least, dear founder, hire an accountant to help you create a solid financial framework for your business early on. In time, you can transition to hiring a part-time CFO or whatever makes sense as your company grows.

Before you go out and hire an accountant, figure out what types of services you need by considering the following:

- **Management accountants** do the budgeting, financial forecasts, risk management assessments, and are basically involved in the company.
- **Financial advisors/consultants** are well versed in taxation things, especially the consultants.
- **Project accountants**, usually independent contractors, work on short-term projects. You might utilize a project accountant if you need someone to sort out your invoices, plan the budget for a specific project, and approve billable hours.

- **Cost accountants** prove to be valuable in businesses that have elaborate supply chains. They seek to minimize the inefficiencies in the supply chain that ultimately increase the cost.
- Although mainly working in the financial industry, **investment accountants** might also be willing to work as independent contractors on a short-term basis. However, their hourly rates may be somewhat Western. Pricey.
- There are also **staff accountants**, who are all-around players doing various things, such as analyzing financial data, creating financial reports, arranging the bank accounts, budgeting, and financial regulation.

This is where the good-old person-to-person communication kicks in. A real-life accountant, not a flimsy software like ScaleFactor, will get to know you and your company. When you eventually find a good accountant, you'll have someone who has probably worked with many companies and has valuable experience, so they'll be able to offer advice here or there when things start to get a bit dodgy.

Startup founders are notorious for their enthusiasm and utter disregard for tedious jobs such as accounting. Most startups don't hire accountants on time or wait to do so until things start to get bad on the financial side.

This didn't happen to David Ross, now a billionaire entrepreneur and the first CFO of Carphone Warehouse. He was an accountant and a damn good one. But he initially wasn't an entrepreneur-type guy. He worked at a well-off holding company, one of the best in the world.

But a guy with an idea, Dunstone, wanted Ross as a CFO of Carphone Warehouse. The two knew each other well, and Ross was probably already involved in Carphone Warehouse's making. Anyway, CFO is perhaps a too-strong expression since the company was pretty small at the time when Ross arrived. Four years later, they had twenty stores, quickly becoming Europe's biggest independent mobile phone retailer. Ross decided to step down recently and do his own thing.

Note that the company progressed at a steady pace. They didn't try to over-expand and repeat the same old mistake that closed down so many startups.

You can say that Carphone's success has nothing to do with Ross and his accounting skills. This maybe was a pure coincidence. There are a lot of successful companies that don't have accountants as co-founders. Yes, that's right, but let's see what Dunstone, the founder, has to say about Ross's contribution: "He's my secret weapon."

I'm not saying that your accountant should always be your business partner. That's not the point. The point is, a good accountant will know when to warn you about certain things, the wider economics game, and can always offer you more efficient tax solutions. Don't be afraid to ask for help!

Inadequate Early Profitability

Startups live and breathe under the ticking clock of cash. There is a breaking point for profitability, and it's often sooner than expected.

Surprise! You do not have all the time in the world to hit profitability. And if it takes you too long, your plan should merely be to fall back on (yet) another round of funding. It needs to offer more longevity than that. How long it takes to reach profitability depends on your industry, business model, and many other factors. But looking into my Magic 8-Ball (okay, admittedly, it's actually just a large database), the answer would be between two and four years as a (reasonably loose) rule of thumb, depending on various factors such as industry, business model, and so on. Getting there in a timely manner is crucial for long-term survival.

Take Oryx Vision. Founded in 2009 by Rani Wellingstein, the company had developed a light detection and ranging camera system (LiDAR) for self-driving cars. The device was supposed to convert light into an electronic signal that translated to autonomous vehicles' AI, accurately detecting oncoming hazards. Despite having some of the best and brightest at the helm production-wise, there was little room for early profitability. Unfortunately, the lack of profitability continued as autonomous cars' invention and adaptation kept changing and shifting, therefore not becoming mainstream as initially projected. The market slowed down and Oryx Vision closed in 2019.

Ever heard of the company called Fieldbook? Conceived in 2013 by Jason Crawford and Ben Bernard, Fieldbook was a pretty cool spreadsheet-type product designed to track projects and workflows. Crawford, the CEO, had been thinking about the idea for years before taking his startup leap. "I was inspired to give data superpowers to non-technical end-users," he explained to me. After securing a small seed round in 2014, Crawford, Bernard, and their single employee created their MVP. By 2015, they had their first paying customers. A larger seed round followed in 2016, putting two years' worth of cash in the bank, so the founders could focus on growing their team. Alas, staffing up proved difficult, and a long search for a designer took Crawford's attention away from what he should have been doing: product management. From the beginning, Crawford has admitted, his product was too complex, requiring its customers to "learn a new paradigm in order to fulfill the promise that had hooked them in." Despite their valiant attempts to simplify Fieldbook, the product limped along, struggling to find its focus. In 2018, with Annual Recurring Revenue (ARR) under $60,000, they gave up the fight.

Jason Crawford explained everything that went wrong, focusing mainly on the growth model, which was, in his words, "the reason behind Fieldbook's failure." The company focused all its strengths on the idea. As we've seen, the idea was good (as it often is), but the materialization wasn't there. And because Fieldbook was somewhat complex and not that easy to use, the company didn't focus on appealing to a broader public, which hampered growth, especially in the first quarter.

On the other hand, you might say the company could have moved upmarket. I discussed this with him, and to this, Jason replied, "To make this work, I think we would have had to relaunch as almost a different company."

The enterprise level was utterly different, something neither Jason nor his associates had experience with. Remember, Fieldbook started as this tool that combines spreadsheets and databases and makes it available to an individual user. So Fieldbook was somewhere in no-man's-land. Instead of making a quick decision about the company's direction, Jason admitted he hung around and waited for a long time—years—believing that they would eventually make something revolutionary. And after a few years of waiting, investing millions of dollars, much time spent recruiting various experts, the whole project amounted to nothing.

And suppose you remember back to our discussion of Pearl Automation. In that case, you can see that their focus on funding and not developing a strong product that would work in the market fell victim to not bringing in enough revenue to keep their vast VCs happy. Their early profitability was abysmal, but not abysmal enough for the guys to stop believing in their Fata Morgana.

The Fix: Don't Be Afraid to Make Concessions

The idea of making concessions, especially early on, can be daunting. However, it's important to realize that every idea you tie into your business or product may not live through the first initial stages of your business. If you choose to be very concrete about each component of your product and business, you are limiting yourself. If you are still working on developing your MVP two years into your company's life without having anything in the marketplace or an avenue to bring in some level of profit, your company is living on borrowed time. By opening the door to potential concessions, you give yourself more time, flexibility, and profitability.

Airtable is a cloud collaboration company founded by Howie Liu, Andrew Ofstad, and Emmett Nicholas. This company was Fieldbook's closest competitor, and it will help us show what went wrong and how you can avoid it.

As opposed to Fieldbook, Airtable got much more traction early on. Instead of trying to make something revolutionary in just a few years, Airtable, from the very start, closely observed their ARR and made changes accordingly. Even though Airtable has roughly the same functions as Fieldbook, the former still had some essential differences that ultimately made it much more profitable.

First of all, Airtable had much more emphasis on the mobile experience. Back in the day, this wasn't as important as today, but still, it was undeniable how the platform trends were changing and where they were going. Fieldbook simply didn't take much note of this, and their complex product would probably be impossible to use on the phone anyway.

Moreover, Airtable focused more on formulas for data analysis, which was just at the sweet spot between complexity and usefulness. The same goes for data modeling options in Airtable—they were much more appealing to customers than what Fieldbook offered, which resulted in quicker growth and ultimately made the difference between staying afloat and sinking miserably.

As a result, marketing and onboarding were much easier for Fieldbook's closest competitor, resulting in steeper growth. The app now has a lot, really tons of downloads, and quite an active community. It's everything that Fieldbook lacked, and only because they chose a different growth model. Back in 2018, Airtable was valued at $1.1 billion; in 2021 it was valued at $5.77 billion, and it keeps on rising.

What it boils down to is, rather than listening to the "experts" drone on and on about growth versus profitability, take a step back and realize the two can coexist. No hard and fast rule says there must be a trade-off. As an investor, I always look at a business through its funnel and determine its health from its customer base viewpoint. We'll talk more about how to do this in chapter 7 when we discuss sales failures.

Funding F*ckup #7:

Death by Overfunding

Too much of a good thing can be bad for you. This is even true for money. The startup cemetery is filled with deaths from overfunding.

When it comes prematurely, massive funding can put undue pressure on a young company to grow rapidly, which isn't necessarily a healthy objective. "Never eat more than you can lift," as Miss Piggy says.

WHAT REALLY GETS YOU

WON NEW CUSTOMER
PROVING YOUR BUSINESS CASE

AN INVESTOR OFFERING YOU (ANY AMOUNT OF) FUNDING
FOR (ANY AMOUNT OF) SHARES IN YOUR STARTUP

Death by overfunding, as coined by the highly successful entrepreneur and investor Sramana Mitra, happens in more cases than most founders would expect. An infamous case is the meteoric rise and fall of Nasty Gal, which started as an online vintage clothing reseller on eBay in 2006. For the first three years, the company's twenty-two-year-old founder, Sophia Amoruso, operated alone from her bedroom in San Francisco.

When Amoruso's little shop became an overwhelming success on eBay, she took it off the platform and started her website. From there, Nasty Gal grew organically, in leaps and bounds, earning $30 million in revenue in 2011 and (unsurprisingly) attracting the rabid attention of venture capitalists. Long story short, Amoruso couldn't resist accepting $50 million from venture capitalists who essentially said, "Wow, you're doing a great job on your own. Let's see what happens if we give you a ton of money."

At first, some exciting things did happen. In 2015, Nasty Gal earned $300 million. But the company's core identity as a vintage reseller had been lost, and Amoruso, caught up in the hyper-growth mentality promoted by her VCs, mismanaged the company into bankruptcy. In 2016, the once ever-so-promising Nasty Gal was sold to a British online retailer,

Boohoo, for $20 million, a fraction of its value just one year prior. Everyone involved lost their shirts.

Another case of death by overfunding belongs to Silicon Valley startup Jawbone. Founded in 1999, this consumer electronics company created wearable technology that had the potential to rival Fitbit and other wearable Bluetooth device-making companies.

As VC money came flooding into the company, the valuation soared to $3.2 billion in 2014. Still, unfortunately, the wearable fitness tracker aimed to compete with Fitbit wasn't making the splash they hoped for. So, even after raising more than $900 million in capital, Jawbone couldn't meet investor demands and began liquidating its assets in 2017. This is one of the most extensive failures of a highly funded company. Experts agree, had Jawbone entertained smaller angel investors and sovereign wealth funds, which wouldn't have raised the valuation so quickly, they might've stood a chance.

Too much of anything is bad. Except for champagne, of course. Too much champagne is just right.

The Fix: Bootstrap It

I'm often asked for a silver-bullet tactic for landing millions in funding. Sorry, but I prefer to suggest something very different: consider bootstrapping. Let me be more precise: my best advice to founders is to fund their business through the early stages if at all possible and only seek outside capital, if necessary, down the road. While this approach may not make for great news coverage like Nasty Gal's mega-infusion, it's a surefire way to avoid death by overfunding. And it's healthy. The truth is that the biggest success stories out there—from Facebook to Apple to Microsoft to Github to Dell to Cisco to eBay—are companies that bootstrapped it initially.

As a novice, I can't say I bootstrapped intentionally; I went at it alone because I thought raising capital was much more complicated than it really was (see Funding F*ckup #2), but all the same, I've benefited from this tactic. While I've yet to build my own Cisco, I credit the millions I have made to the fact that I've never sought early-stage funding for my companies.

So what does it take to bootstrap and self-fund your company early on? It takes whatever it takes:

- Get a side hustle.
- Sell some stock.
- Deplete your savings.
- Get a cheaper apartment.
- Quit drinking or eating out or smoking or taking flying lessons.

If these extreme measures simply aren't feasible for you, I'd suggest looking into a grant or loan program—especially if you're in the nonprofit sector. Otherwise, consider a crowdfunding platform, a startup accelerator, or even an angel investor. I strongly prefer angels (individuals using their funds) to venture capitalists (companies that buy, grow, and sell other companies).

Even for the founder with some resources, bootstrapping is definitely scary. I can just hear the chorus now. "Spend my savings? Move out of my loft? Are you crazy?" I prefer to call it risk-averse. Bootstrapping means going all-in with your own money, which is far from foolhardy; it's a sign that you've conquered your attitude failures and are wholly committed to your startup. American investors call this putting your skin in the game, originating from derby races. Danish investors have a different saying, which translates, awkwardly, to "Put your hand on the stove." The idea is that by placing your hand on the stove before things get cooking, when it's still cool, you're proving that you're willing to take the heat when it comes—you're risking something yourself. This will pay off in the future when you're ready to seek outside capital.

And when should you seek that capital? A good rule of thumb is to wait until your equity in the company will be greater post-infusion than it was before taking the investment. If you can show this by whatever metric you're using, go ahead and take that money to develop your software, get the real estate you need, or do whatever you need to do to grow.

Final Word on Funding

In this chapter, we've covered everything from Getting Funded all the way to Death By Overfunding, and plenty in between. There are a ton of options when it comes to funding, and with each one, there's a potential pitfall waiting for you if you aren't careful.

Bootstrapping is, by my reckoning, the best initial approach. I mention it often because I believe in it. Plain and simple. But if you don't have the capital to bootstrap, look at angel investors rather than large VC firms early on. When the time comes that growth and expansion fit your business model and your company's scope, then go after the investors you need to continue being profitable and a competitor.

As long as you know your profit thresholds and often reevaluate so you don't miss opportunities to pivot, change product scope, or determine if a component is deadweight, then you're bound to work out okay. And worst case, if you need to go out, go out on top!

In the next chapter, we will examine product development failures. When you consider the number of products brought to market each year compared to the number that succeed, you'll see there's room for potential failures.

We'll take a look at the downfall of WeWork and Fashism (the company, not the political philosophy) and see how to avoid the most common product development failures startups encounter.

Chapter 5

Product Develop-ment F*ckups

Every year, about thirty thousand new products launch into the market. Some are pretty awesome, while others are complete head scratchers. To illustrate the point, Coke released a ton of new products that were epic failures despite holding the preferred spot in the cola market over Pepsi. I still remember being puzzled by Coca-Cola Water Salad on a trip to Japan, but perhaps you remember a few of these fantastic failures Coke offered:

- OK Soda (designer soda for the supposedly cynical and disillusioned Gen X audience)
- Vault (to compete with Pepsi's Mountain Dew)
- Green Tea Coke (which was supposed to have antioxidants)
- Sprite Remix (fruity Sprite)
- Coke C2 (a half-sugar and carbs version of Coke later replaced by Coke Zero)
- Tab Clear (to complete with Crystal Pepsi)
- Diet Coke Plus (added vitamins and minerals to the original Diet Coke but still obviously far from healthy)
- Vio (a carbonate milk product with fruit flavor)
- Coca Cola Blak (to compete with coffee)
- New Coke (Coke made to taste more like Pepsi)

The most interesting problem I see founders face is their limited thinking when it comes to their product. They get so stuck in their vision of their product that they forget it should be a direction instead of a destination. I love drawing and painting, but admittedly only one in ten of my drawings turn out good. Look at paintings by some of the world's greatest artists. Before they ever put paint on canvas, they make sketch after sketch to perfect and evolve their idea into something that eventually works beautifully. Then, and only then, do they begin painting. A startup product should be viewed the same way—as a general sketch to guide the path to its evolved final product. Many products these days never actually arrive anywhere, but are rather constantly evolving.

While it may seem silly, products like the Evian water bra, the wine bra, the potato parcel, or Neuticles (testicular implants for pets, anyone?) all hit the market at different points in time. Not sure about you but sending an engraved potato to a friend or family member never occurred to me.

Better yet, consider these services that have been introduced over the years into the marketplace: restaurant for dogs, potty training coaches, snake massages, dead flower deliveries (for those times you want someone to know you really dislike them), ice cream delivery, and cuddle parties. Yeah, there are some interesting ideas in the bunch, but the point is, someone launched them as a business venture.

Now, getting back to the thirty thousand new products and services released yearly, it's safe to say over 95 percent of them fail. However, failure, as my son can attest, is all about perception. How you measure is one of the universal loopholes.

My ten-year-old son considers my height of 178 cm (5 feet 10 inches) to be of low standards, giving him a lousy genetic start in life. My take on the matter is to qualify the number via anthropometry (*anthropo* meaning "human," and *metry* meaning "measure"—a clever topic I know very little about, but throwing in a bit of Greek and Latin usually shakes my opponent). This concept states that I'm of above-average height in most regions, excluding only a few countries. Denmark, where I was born, is one of these exclusions, but he does not know this (and his English reading skills are poor for now), so I believe my secret is safe. I'll stick with the ability to measure without the exceptions since it provides me with the advantage.

You can see how the perception of how we term a failure can affect the numbers, but it's safe to say that product failures come in many shapes and sizes. That is mainly because product development isn't only about creating a product but tackling the many challenges that come with it. The more exposure you can get to potential failures with your product, the better. If you can't win, then you can learn.

No project is ever perfect at first. Failures are inevitable and can appear at any time during the product development process. If you can find the failures before they find you, however, then you can get pretty close to perfect.

So let's take a look at the most significant product development offenders out there and the solutions for them.

Product Development F*ckup #1:

The FNAC

Feature, Not A Company: clever as they might be, a set of product features does not make a company. And you will have to make money someday. Soon.

In startup jargon, FNAC stands for Feature, Not A Company. It's VC shorthand for a service component that doesn't add up to a stand-alone business—despite an eager founder's desire to see it as one.

When a potential investor uses this term, it's often a direct challenge to an entrepreneur: dig deep and consider the real value of what you're offering.

There are many hurdles in getting your company out there in the big bad business world, but none more significant than dealing with venture capitalists. Remember that these people have seen it all and, thanks to powerhouses like Apple, Microsoft, and Google, who have built successful cash cows giving features away, VCs are less likely to invest in something they might deem as FNAC. So, before you hit that hurdle, ask yourself the following: Can your company make enough money to sustain itself?

If you'd prefer to avoid that uncomfortable reckoning, remember the following three rules:

1. **Your Company Isn't Your Product**

   PepsiCo is known for Pepsi (you know, that drink you get when there is no Coca-Cola available), but they also are Lay's potato chips (and Quaker oatmeal, Tropicana juice, and other names you'd likely recognize) because Pepsi is only a product and not the company. It's a tad specific, I know, but you must separate the two in understanding FNAC.

2. **Your Customer Experience Isn't Your Product**

   Sure, Apple fanboys and girls love to film reaction videos unboxing their new iPhones with their recently old iPhones or MacBook Pros (until they realize that Apple changed the ports again so that you can toss all your old wires). Apple does a great job creating buzz around their customer experience, but that experience isn't everything. Experience is subjective too; not everyone is going to feel the same way about your product. It's like the great debate on Macs versus PCs or gaming versus having a social life.

3. Your Marketing Plan Isn't Your Product

Getting someone excited about your product isn't the same as having a product. Take Kuri, the much-anticipated and -funded home companion robot that danced and could take a video of you and your family (somewhat creepy). Debuting in 2017 and touted in *Popular Science*, electronic trade shows, and crowdfunded, Kuri was abandoned before it could ever get to market. Sure, the marketing plan had people excited enough to throw money in the game, but that wasn't enough to create a viable product.

Let's dive into WeWork, and their massive fall from a $47 billion valuation in 2018 to a mere $2.7 billion valuation in 2020. How could I write a book on failures and ignore WeWork?

Since its inception, WeWork, a real estate company masquerading as a tech company, has been all over the place. Known for their "work hard, party hard" ethos, they offered free beer on tap in their co-working spaces and enjoyed a freewheeling atmosphere in their corporate offices.

Ultimately, their initial product was co-working or shared office spaces, which to an outsider with an eye for any level of detail appeared to be a real estate market product. The initial concept had been for individual contributors to each procure a space in a communal business office with the added benefits of being able to network with other small businesses to create a physical social networking workplace. By offering things like monthly VC meetings and social events, WeWork believed that if they built the office space, the individuals renting space would become a more intertwined, cohesive business venture.

All the while, WeWork has been having an identity crisis of sorts. One of their most reckless practices was WeWork's serial purchasing of companies not at all relevant to their core business. Between 2015 and 2019, WeWork purchased the digital marketing startup Conductor; the events platform Meetup; a software engineering program called Flatiron School; a mobile app for construction workers called Fieldlens; and the tech companies Case, Welkio, Unomy, and Spacious, which was shut down just four months later.

Beyond the insanity of market hopping to change its product's core value, WeWork has been losing money at an alarming rate ($3.2 billion in 2020). Not to mention the exit package the former CEO got for stepping down. The failed executive was given a $445 million package while over four thousand employees got let go to try to save the business.

But ultimately, the most significant point of failure came from their insistence on being a tech company rather than what they really were, a real estate company. Mind you, their co-working spaces were designed and marketed to people in the tech industry, but marketing isn't your product. The product-market discrepancy was their undoing. Investors viewing the company as a contender in the tech space expected a much higher profit margin than the commercial real estate market offered.

The Fix: Understand What Your Product Is and Keep It Simple, Simple, Simple

The cure for FNAC is simple: be crystal clear about what your product is, and how it offers value to its target market. If you're not there yet, circle back to some of the tactics we discussed in the market research section.

A relatively unknown app called Burbn hit the market full of features that made users feel overwhelmed (a bit like our old friend MySpace). Burbn didn't know what it was doing until CEO Kevin Systrom stepped in and focused on only one thing: mobile photo sharing. Burbn was reborn, offering users the ability only to upload photos, and then filters, and then hashtags. They also renamed it, by the way, as Instagram, and the rest is history.

You want your product to be simple. Does it offer an excellent solution to a current problem? Is there a gap in the market for something that your product could provide? What makes your product so unique to any of your competitors?

Often, you have to take a step back and ask yourself probing questions to get the right answers. Once you know exactly what your product is, stick to it. When you know your product inside and out, you develop the gift of anticipation.

Anticipation is one of the many superpowers of a VC. If you can present your product in its most simple form, then a VC can evaluate future opportunities. Venture capitalists and investors pay great attention to current trends and the potential surrounding them. When you have your product boiled down to its simplest form, chances are you can handle the bombardment of questions from VCs. You might get asked things such as, "What competitors do what you do differently?" or, "What is your target audience and how do you satisfy their needs?"

The real emphasis here is one thing: defining your product and making it simple. Once you can do that, things will start falling into place.

Product Development F*ckup #2:

The Big Bang Release

Releasing products with a bang might sound sexy, but in practice it is dangerous and might end up burning your business.

Whatever the cost, Rand Fishkin, the founder of Moz, an SEO software company, wanted a Big Bang Release, a showy drop of multiple new features at once. His latest offering, Moz Analytics, would offer a bevy of bells and whistles. The year was 2013, and Fishkin's team had already pulled off three other big bang Moz releases in recent years. The latest was especially important to Fishkin because he wanted it to coincide with his rebranding from SEOMoz to Moz. When colleagues raised concerns that the project was too ambitious given their resources and timetable, Fishkin pushed for his big bang anyway. "I thought this would be another release like [our others]," he would later write. "A little late, but worth the wait." So the team rushed forward, delivering a mammoth new product that was disappointing on multiple levels. The product ended up hurting the company's bottom line. As Fishkin would later reflect in a postmortem: "Had we been listening to our customers, iterating on the projects and products that mattered to them, and not consuming all of our development time and energy on a long-delayed, poorly launched mega suite that did lots of things they didn't need, we'd have been in a much different place at the end of 2013." Ironically, after all that cost and effort, the rebrand and the release ended up happening separately.

The lesson? Though it may be tempting to "shock and awe" your marketplace with a Big Bang Release, the headache and deadline issues will probably not be worth it. Ultimately, you'll put yourself in a situation where you're under-delivering on what you've promised to your target audience. There is also the matter of cost. Working toward one big launch will cost a lot of money and time, which, for some companies, could make or break them.

The Fix: F*ck It, Ship It

Instead of trying for a big bang, parse your offerings into smaller, more frequent releases. That way, you'll be a company that's known for being on the move. Your customers will come to expect regular innovations, and they'll be happy to wait for the next great feature.

The concept of the "big bang" is pretty much over. Sure, it worked well before the internet, when you could focus on most of your intended target audience through TV or radio. Still, nowadays, people consume content like candy on Halloween. Even the average attention span has dwindled in the past two decades from twelve seconds in 2000 to eight seconds today. So how do you get your audience's attention now?

Instead of one big bang, consider breaking it into smaller, more frequent releases through strategic growth planning (aka "growth hacking"), a highly focused methodology based on fast-paced marketing experiments.

Growth hacking emerged from the startup scene in Silicon Valley as an innovative way for new entrepreneurs to quickly grow their businesses on a tight budget. The term is terribly overused, to the point of giving me nausea, but the idea behind it is great.

The main goal is to test and optimize continuously, and to learn from your mistakes each time you do a launch or release so you don't make the same mistakes again—thus unlocking your growth potential. Through experimentation across many marketing channels, you will find out your target customer's habits and behaviors and utilize that data to develop solutions for the next release. While failure in a big bang scenario could have a disastrous outcome, failure is here seen as progress.

Dropbox famously managed to utilize growth hacking by gathering lots of feedback, improving their product, and continually meeting with VCs. From 2008 to 2010, Dropbox managed to double its user base every three months, resulting in an impressive 3,900 percent growth within fifteen months.

Growth hacking is not about finding that one silver bullet, but really about developing systems and processes, discovering weaknesses and overcoming them, prioritizing and analyzing. And if you have a product that fails because nobody wants it, it is best to move on and save time, money, and energy. It's preferable finding out through a small, manageable release than a costly big one.

Product Development F*ckup #3:

The Mashup

Mixing two good things does not necessarily make something great. In the world of startups it's actually quite often the opposite.

We see it all the time—new movies pitched to audiences as mashups of previous box-office hits: X new thriller is billed as "*Shutter Island* meets *The Shining*." Or Y's new comedy is sold as "*Bridesmaids* meets *Back to the Future*." You get the picture. And movie marketers aren't the only ones guilty of falling back on the old "X meets Y" trope. Entrepreneurs are also overly fond of what I call the Mashup Failure. It's understandable, I suppose: By appealing to consumers of two massively popular products, founders believe they can double their market share, multiply their magic.

As we discussed in chapter 4, adding Wi-Fi or AI or any other technology to an existing product won't guarantee market acceptance or success. Companies like Teaforia, Skully, and Juicero were huge flops because adding a tech component to something that already worked and charging a bundle for it insulted the consumer's intelligence. Remember, if you aren't actively solving an immediate problem for the consumer with your technology-improved version of a product, you are creating a mashup f*ckup.

These days, another common Mashup Failure is when an old, established company tries to infuse its existing product with a little startup-culture hipness. I call these startup-wannabes intrapreneurs. In 1990, Maxwell House jumped on the intrapreneurial bandwagon by creating what they billed as "a convenient new way to enjoy the rich taste of Maxwell House Coffee." Maxwell House Ready-to-Drink Coffee came in a foil-lined carton with a convenient screw-on cap. It was a mashup of coffee and convenience, you might say. A potential "disruption" of the established coffee culture!

The only trouble: the product couldn't be microwaved in its original container. The key incentive to buy ready-to-drink coffee—convenience—was taken away. While I don't qualify, as I'm a tea drinker, I do also think it sounds slightly unappetizing. The product failed.

The Fix: Mashups Work Better for Pitches Than Products

It should be said that adding Wi-Fi or Bluetooth to an existing product can be a game changer, but take a moment to stop and think about it. If a company has a super successful product that can benefit by adding a mashup component, don't you think they will?

Most mashups fall victim to not actually solving a problem, a failure all its own as we discussed in chapter 2. With that in mind, keep your mashups for those elevator pitches and create something groundbreaking and problem-solving. Do yourself a favor and avoid forcing a square peg into a round hole and calling it revolutionary.

Product Development F*ckup #4:

Identity Crisis

Founders fuss about identity. The fact is that most identities do not contribute or impair much. Spend your energy accordingly.

You've already read about a few of the many mistakes I made with my first company, Shockwaved. Here's one more.

I admit with some embarrassment that I spent the entire lifetime of Shockwaved, all seven years, debating with my employees about what it should be called. I'd named the company quickly and had never particularly liked my choice. The main problem was that it resembled Shockwave, a *much* bigger and more successful company. I felt the similarity was confusing for the consumer, and most of my employees agreed. This was back when paper business cards were still a thing, and my team begged me relentlessly to provide them with their cards so they could have some semblance of professionalism at meetings with new clients. I desperately wanted to finalize our identity and held regular naming contests, offering incentives to whoever could come up with the perfect name. The topic consumed the majority of our time at weekly meetings. But month after month, we failed to land on our identity. I was an idiot. Those cards never did get made.

I hate to think of what we could have accomplished in the many wasted hours we spent worrying about our company name. But even worse than that, lost productivity was the psychological toll the dilemma took on my team. When a founder isn't comfortable with their company's identity, that ambivalence becomes contagious, seeping into every aspect of the business. Employees feel uneasy about the present and the future. They ultimately begin to worry that their jobs might not be secure.

Another example here could be Fashism. The flippant name was definitely not ready for cancel culture nor was the idea on track to bring the professed body positivity movement forward.

Developed to be an online and web platform where people could upload their pictures and get real-time feedback on their outfit choices, Fashism landed in the fashion sector with many similar startups in the same space. Just what the internet needed in 2009, a platform that allowed people to be critiqued online. All for their appearance. In late 2010, Fashism raised $1 million in funding from multiple high-profile famous types, including image-conscious Ashton Kutcher and Nina Garcia, a *Project Runway* judge. Two years later, Fashism attempted to pivot into e-commerce to save their failing darling but could not find more funding. Essentially, for three years, they hosted a "hot or not" web app with no real business goal for profit.

When it comes to identity, a name says it all, right? Well, sometimes the name says more than we bargained for. Thanks to various algorithms intending to block names that may be censor-worthy,[1] we see plenty of issues with names being flagged and rejected. Take Plymouth Hoe. A seafaring landmark in Devon was labeled by Facebook as misogynistic rather than the beautiful panoramic ridge offering views across the Plymouth Sound. But this doesn't just apply to place names like Scunthrope, Penistone, and Clitheroe (to name a few), but also individuals with last names like Weiner, Cummings, or Dickman (again, only to name a few) have had social media accounts rejected, emails blocked, and so on. So, if you're blessed in that direction, skip the last name as a part of the company name.

The Fix: 80 Percent Sure = 100 Percent Sure

Who really cares about your logo? No one but you cares whether you go with a sunburst or a shooting star, or whatever you're debating between. I'm not saying that your logo isn't important, or that your name isn't important, or that your website or your business card or the paper on which you print your business card isn't important. It is. The identity of

---

1. Ah, the Scunthrope Problem. By building filters into internet searches, spam filters, forum moderation, and more, these algorithms inadvertently blocked towns, people, and events from a natural life cycle online. People from the town of Scunthrope, Lincolnshire, England, couldn't create accounts with AOL because of their town name containing the word *cunt*. Even the popular Super Bowl naming convention had problems with Super Bowl XXX on search engines.

your company matters. And yes, I get it: the identity around your company is closely tied to your identity as the founder. You have every right to take this decision personally. But you have to balance that importance with the importance of developing the product that your logo represents. The product should be your foremost priority. I think most founders understand this intellectually, yet, in the early days, at least, they spend disproportionate amounts of time and energy trying to get their websites to look perfect. Why? Because doing real work is harder.

How to break out of the identity crisis? Stop waiting to be 100 percent in love with your brand identity. You'll never get there, trust me. All you need is to be 80 percent satisfied with what you've got. In other words, 80 percent sure is as good as 100 percent sure.

This is what I call the 80 percent = 100 percent rule. It's one I've been using again and again in many situations. Use it in any decision-making process, and you'll save an incredible amount of time. Any decision is better than no decision.

Product Development F*ckup #5:

Overcorrecting Success and Failure

Once founders find success with their first startup, it's easy to believe that the next will be an equal or greater success. Interestingly enough, the opposite is normally true.

In one study conducted at Copenhagen Business School (the largest business school in northern Europe), Rasmus Toft-Kehler and his team analyzed 65,390 startups over eighteen years. Speaking with Rasmus, he described how they found that most first-time entrepreneurs believed that once they were successful, things would be easier. Yet, for most, a second startup would significantly underperform the first. And a third startup would fare, on average, no better than the first. But wait, there's hope: entrepreneurs who dared to found a fourth startup would finally find their early success not only matched but exceeded! On average, an entrepreneur's fourth startup will ultimately outperform their successful debut.

You can see this pattern with the founding team of FeedBurner. The same team that led the web feed management provider collaborated on four startups in a row. The first three ventures, Burning Door, Digital Knowledge Assets, and Spyonit, followed the same pattern discovered by Toft-Kehler and his team. It wasn't until their fourth venture, Feed-Burner, launched that founder and CEO Dick Costolo and his partners found success.

Similarly, you can see this in action with creators in all industries. Look at The Strokes (yes, the band). Their first album hit it so big that the second album's pressure was crushing to the band. No matter how much press and hype, when *Room on Fire* dropped, the world held its collective breath, listened, and then walked away. You get it. The sophomore slump was in full effect.

One last worthy example is brought to us care of Janus Friis, the co-founder of Skype. Prior to creating Skype, Friis founded KaZaA, the infamous peer-to-peer file sharing platform often used for (and often illegally) sharing music files. Thanks to the acceptance of peer-to-peer sharing, he co-founded Skype, which they sold in 2005 for a ton of money (and yes, that's the exact number). After the sale of Skype, Janus founded Joost. Built on the same peer-to-peer networking idea as Skype, Joost was supposed to be a way to distribute online television programming. I really liked the concept when it launched, but found it more a platform than a hub for content. Unfortunately, Joost underperformed and was closed. Next, he launched Rdio, which met a similar fate in 2015. But, true to the pattern, his fourth venture, Starship Technologies, seems to be gaining ground. Only time will tell its future.

The Fix: Failure Breeds Success

The fix here is to practice, and allow yourself to practice. Many people fight with themselves about starting a company. When (if) they do start one, and it then fails (with the other 90 percent that do), they are so disappointed that they never repeat the experience. This is a great fault, as the second, third, and fourth time will most likely be much better.

And, at the same time, you should be aware that just because you did well with your previous venture does not mean that you can walk on water. You still need to use the magic ingredients of arduous work and staying on target.

The whole point of my Rule Zero of Startups, which as you may recall is "Don't die," is to ensure that you are able to try again.

Product Development F*ckup #6:

Overzealous Outsourcing

Do what you do best, outsource the rest. Just always know the what, why, and for how much—and ensure outsourcing doesn't cause costly complications.

In 2013, a hip eyeglasses company called Rivet & Sway secured $2 million in funding. Just sixteen months later, they folded. What went wrong? It came down to overzealous outsourcing. With competitive companies nipping at their heels, founders Sarah Bryar and John Lusk felt immense pressure to scale quickly—more quickly than they could afford to do with their $2 million cash infusion. Their solution was to outsource production. In a postmortem on the business, Bryar notes that she would've waited to scale and outsource if she could go back and redo it. Outsourcing increased the cost required to acquire new clients—something not maintainable so early in their business.

PatientDox, a medical records software service, made the same mistake. Because none of the founders had a background in software engineering, their tech startup needed outsourced help. Unfortunately, 90 percent of the initial costs associated with a tech startup come from product development. Without a technical founder, any required changes or feedback-driven adjustments took more time and money than budgeted.

Another outsourcing example is seen with Nextt. Founder Mark McGuire had two previously successful startups that both were acquired by Microsoft and CSC, respectively, so when he launched Nextt, he did as usual. Like his previous ventures, he collaborated with an outsourced development firm. Unlike his previous ventures, this didn't go smoothly. After wasting precious time and money, he decided to hire an in-house iOS developer. He reminds other entrepreneurs of the importance of having an in-house development team: "If you are building a software company, get your dev team in house from day one or you will take one step forward and two steps back."

If you're in the early phases of building your startup and lack the funds to hire a dedicated team, it can be tempting to hire outside contractors. But this is not the time for outsourcing. It's simply too risky.

Finally, outsourcing is demanding. When your team isn't working alongside you, it's challenging to stay on the same page. This is especially true if you're outsourcing to workers in another country. Shortly after

Simply was established enough to outsource safely, we contracted with developers in India and Ukraine. Luckily, my background in technology anchors me in ways McGuire wasn't. These outsourced relationships taught me a lot about managing employees from other cultures. For example, my team in India appreciates precise directions more than my sense of humor. In contrast, the team in Albania appreciates having more creative leeway. They also get my jokes (they don't actually laugh, as I'm not funny in Ukraine either—the cultural similarities just make my jokes more understandable). I've learned how to adjust my management style accordingly, but I wouldn't advise a new founder to add this complex layer to their day-to-day operations.

The Fix: Outsource Non-core Functions Only

Save outsourcing for when your business is on solid footing, and you're ready to start optimizing your non-core functions. I repeat, non-core functions. This means anything that supports your business. Depending on the scope of your business, non-core functions may include website design, content creation, logo design, physical office cleaning and maintenance, IT support for employees, and so on. If a need arises that affects the business at its core, it is not non-core and should not be outsourced. Oh, and coffee beans—those I would normally also just buy somewhere and not produce myself.

For example, if your core product needs enhancement, sorry, no outsourcing for you. If your product is an app, you can't outsource the app's optimization itself, period. That said, you can outsource parts of your sales and marketing functions if necessary. And if you're really in a pinch, it's probably safe to hire some outside support for your in-house developers—as long as you and your leading developers maintain absolute control of the process.

Speaking of control: it's tough to have it if you don't understand the function that you're outsourcing. I've relied heavily on outsourcing for several of my tech companies, and it's worked out fine as I'm fairly technical myself. I'm a terrible programmer, but my firsthand programming knowledge allowed me to keep a firm grasp of what my contract workers were doing. But all the same, I still waited until my businesses were on solid footing before I employed offshore contractors to help my team scale up. Because the remote teams weren't responsible for the core product, if they didn't work out for any reason, I would just delay my schedule and reassign the tasks to my in-house team. And, of course, I made sure not to give away any company secrets to outsiders.

Now, there may be rare instances in which outsourcing early in the game is simply unavoidable. Say you need to build a complicated prototype, requiring a team of ten experienced programmers, and your budget is exceptionally tight. In this case, you may have no choice but to hire more affordable offshore contractors. This is the situation Joe Fernandez, the founder of Klout, a social media influence resource launched in 2008, found himself in. He believed in a hands-on approach to getting things done. So much so that he moved to Singapore to get the initial website built and he met in person with the former owner of the domain Klout.com to make his purchase offer with cash in hand. As someone who didn't have the know-how on how to build the algorithm for the app, he needed a team that could. To make it happen, Fernandez went to India to work in person with his development team and slept on one of his developers' couches for three months until the prototype was finished. Unfortunately, after ten years and several investments, acquisitions, and a company sale later, Klout closed its doors. It was not, however, because they miscalculated Justin Bieber to be more influential than then-President Barack Obama. Their initial decisions to keep things in house gave them the control they needed to steer the business successfully through the marketplace. But controversy surrounding the product itself, which both lost relevance and was challenged by the introduction of GDPR, ultimately led to their demise four years after their acquisition by Lithium.

Product Development F*ckup #7:

Not Stealing from Giants

Learn from those who've paved the way before you. Their example can be your best source of navigation in the world of startups.

"If I have seen further, it's by standing
on the shoulders of giants."
—Sir Isaac Newton

Sir Isaac Newton, a notably humble genius, generously used and credited his predecessors in the scientific field for the knowledge they passed up to him. This is the spirit I wish every founder would adopt. Vigorously using existing knowledge, tools, and ideas, that is. But all too often, I see founders who—operating from the misguided mentality that they're at war with all competitors and "all is fair in love and war"—don't just build on the giants' ideas in their fields; they attempt to reinvent and re-create them.

Let's unpack that difference. Whatever field you're in, whether technology or product development or kitchen design, you will obviously want to learn about and avail yourself of the latest innovations in your space. It's perfectly acceptable, for example, for a software developer to use and build upon open-source software, and for the kitchen designer to use Blum's kitchen accessory components. Why reinvent the wheel?

But then there's the opposite extreme.

As mentioned under the failure of Competing with the Network Effect, Google Buzz launched (after the failed Google Wave) in 2010. The platform was Google's take on Twitter. Integrating seamlessly into Gmail, it offered users the capability to post photos, statuses, links, and videos. As is customary when Google isn't first to the marketplace with an idea, they failed. In only twenty-two months. It was destined for failure with privacy concerns and nothing worthy of enticing people from the more successful Twitter.

Choosing to go it alone rather than partner with someone in a similar or complementary industry can be as bad as not finding a sufficient mentor. Wesabe's founder, Marc Hedlund, says of his personal finance software that their mistake was not partnering with a company to utilize an aggregation solution already created. Instead, they insisted on building the solution in house, wasting costly time and resources. Mint, their main competitor, worked with Yodlee to use their aggregation software to build their platform until they were purchased by Intuit. Hedlund says they had considered a partnership with Yodlee, but decided against it to their own demise.

Another company that missed the mark by not partnering with the giants in a similar market includes Mac & Mia, a children's clothing delivery subscription service. Despite launching before Stitch Fix offered a service for children, they didn't have enough to stand alone. Had they partnered with one of the adult services, or other big-box retailers, they may have stood a chance. Instead, major retailers and already established companies saw the market acceptance of the idea and swept in, pulling already loyal customers back into their fold and away from Mac & Mia.

In 2019, Daqri, a company focused in the cloud space and AR technology, closed after ten years in operation. Their AR glasses gained a lot of investor attention initially, but as the marketplace cooled on the technology, capital dried up and left them broke and unable to compete with Magic Leap and Microsoft, who already had institutional partnerships they could leverage. Their AR glasses were aimed at enterprise customers rather than a more general audience and therefore had difficulty getting buy-in from the employees using them.

Neglecting to learn from others in your (or an otherwise related) market is as shortsighted as it comes. Those founders who refuse to see their counterparts in the market as mere competition tend to find themselves on the losing side.

The Fix: Mentor Up

There is no such thing as an original idea, really. I've had conversations with other founders I know who have all had similar ideas for the same market space. If it's possible for two or more in my personal circle to share the same idea, there are even more also with the same idea outside my circle. What makes each of our ideas special, and therefore unique, is the execution.

Entrepreneurs are known for being creative "idea" people. This is how innovation and progress occurs. And if many people have a similar or the same general idea, at least one of them will have an execution strategy well enough designed to bring it to market.

Along the same train of thought, it's important to know whether you are the right person for the idea. I've had countless ideas over my career (remember my not-to-do list?). Many of them weren't a good fit for me in one way or another. So, before sinking a ton of time, energy, and money into a new venture, make sure you're really the best person to bring this idea to life.

The key takeaway for this situation is to find a mentor. We discussed mentors before and it's worth mentioning again in this context. If you can find someone in your marketplace doing well, ask them questions. Ask for advice. If you look to a mirror market outside of your geographical radius, you're likely to get some great returns on the time investment.

A great example of this is the Walmart Superstore. Sam Walton consulted with Raymond Bartolacci Sr., the founder of a small grocery store chain in eastern Pennsylvania and northern New Jersey called Laneco. This chain was founded in 1946 in rural farming communities where there wasn't a lot of retail available. Even back in the early days of the store, Bartolacci Sr. saw value in offering a one-stop shopping experience to his customers. Known for offering all the staples of a grocery store, the company also offered textiles for the home, clothing, shoes, auto parts, toys, basic furnishings, and a pharmacy. Even though, at most, they operated sixteen stores in the region, they gained the attention of the Walmart founder, Sam Walton. With the geographical distance great enough to initially not make Walmart a competitor to Laneco, Walton reached out for advice. He used the Laneco model to develop the Walmart Supercenter. Interestingly enough, when Laneco closed, a bunch of the properties were bought by Walmart and converted to Walmart Supercenters.

In chapter 3, I told you about the Doppelganger Danger Failure and how putting a small twist on an existing idea can help you avoid looking like a copycat. This fix is similar. To develop and grow at a reasonable and cost-conscious tempo, by all means, ask yourself: "What's out there already that I can adapt for my purposes?" Just make sure that you alter whatever you're building upon by at least 5 percent.

Final Thoughts on Product Development

I'm sure you're starting to see the pattern of product development: Don't be a copycat; seek advice, not ideas; and understand the cost of getting into product creation. Don't waste money by cutting corners and producing something that's ultimately better suited for the garbage can than someone's office or home.

Make sure you know your actual product and haven't confused its identity with that of your company. When you're intimately involved with the product, it can be easy to confuse the two. Make sure your product is ready in time for your release date. Don't rush ahead with marketing a colossal release when your product is still in development and testing. Missing a release deadline will flatline your customers' enthusiasm faster than you can blink.

When it comes to making decisions that don't affect your business's outcome, like font colors, logo images, and so on, being 80 percent in love with it is the new 100 percent in love. Cut those minimally significant issues a break and focus on what's really important: your product, your finances, your marketing strategy, your sales strategy, your business plan, your organizational structure, and pretty much anything that will forward your business's success from day one.

The "giants" are meant to be teachers as are failures, so don't lose perspective.

Outsource with caution. Understand the unique challenges and benefits before handing your baby business over to people time zones away who may have a language barrier.

And leave mashups to the movie screens and bookshelves of the world. Unless you can answer a need by mashing two industries together, don't. Remember that thirty thousand new products are created each year. If you can avoid the failures listed, or at least overcome them, you stand a greater chance than the majority of founders who started with you.

With the knowledge that product failures are both avoidable and fixable, I think we're ready to move on to bigger things, like your organization.

As we all know, your business is really only as good as the people running it. In the next chapter, I'll tell you why (and how) I like to fire everyone in my company every six to twelve months.

Chapter 6

Organiza-tional F*ckups

We all know the mantra: your team matters most. Your team members are the building blocks of any startup, the LEGO you build your dream with.

I'm not only a fan of great teams, but also of LEGO. As a kid, Christmas was, for me, the yearly chance for a new fantastic LEGO set. Today, my kids have almost outgrown the plastic blocks, but even after they do, we will still have some of the original (now vintage) toys they made, from when LEGO started as a wooden toy manufacturer.

I've also had the pleasure of having LEGO as a client over many years, which has always been exciting on many different levels. I'd go so far as to say that their only failure remains mine when a loose piece finds its way into the bottom of my foot in the dark.

Although it should be stressed that this was not a direct failure of their own making, LEGO has also been associated with less impressive situations.

Let's take a look at Mindscape, the developer of the 1997 LEGO video game *LEGO Island*. The fantastic team developing the game worked on it for two years before release and had even begun working on the underwater sequel when Mindscape fired the whole team and sold off the business. It's believed the company didn't want to pay out the huge bonuses and royalties that were contracted for a successful game to the team that had created it. Ditching the team seemed like the best way to save cash.

Once they continued operations under the new management group after selling itself, Mindscape didn't win the contract for *LEGO Island 2* or any other project. Without the original team on board, their most valuable assets were gone.

So does the team matter most? Is this philosophy exaggerated? Overrated? A meaningless cliché? No. Your business is *really* only as good as the team of people behind it.

Let's take a closer look at the delightfully many ways you can go entirely wrong with your startup's organization—ending up in jail being one of the most extreme outcomes.

The Flawed Founding Team

Surround yourself with people who are smart, hardworking, and fill in your deficits. The best teams are complementary in nature rather than carbon copied.

Two types of successful teams are traditionally found at startups. The first comprises skilled young workers who can survive on a minimum of cash and dedicate fifteen hours a day to develop the business for however long it takes. These kids are content to live on Ramen noodles and Coke Zero to stay alive until you're up and running. The second type of startup team is just the opposite: they're mostly older, more experienced, and have probably left well-paying jobs to join your venture. You're likely able to raise more funding if you've assembled this type of team. And thanks to their combined experience, your startup's chances of survival are probably greater than they would be with a younger, less experienced, less expensive team.

Of course, there are pros and cons to each of these team-building approaches. Which is right for you? It comes down to your funding and the particular needs of your company.

One startup that picked a too-experienced-and-expensive team was Vitoto. Founded in 2002, Vitoto was a collaborative video app for mobile phones. After raising some seed capital, they built their MVP, relocated to San Francisco, and launched their product. So far, so good. Except for the fact that their team was outsized for their needs and budget. Most of its members were at the stage in life where they had kids, nice cars, and hefty mortgages. No all-nighters and Ramen dinners for them. They probably didn't even drink Coke Zero. This was a massive shame because Vitoto didn't need such heavy hitters. For them, a tenacious and scrappy team of crackerjack coders and managers would've fit the bill perfectly. They were making a fun video app, not a lifesaving heart medication, after all. As it was, their senior team worked too methodically and drained the company of its resources before it even got a chance to compete in the marketplace—long story short, Vitoto bit the dust.

Whether you go with a green team or a seasoned one, it's essential to assemble a group of people with shared values and complementary strengths and weaknesses. This is especially critical with your founding team, who will most likely be allotted a significant amount of company stock. If that stock is owned by people who don't contribute significantly for the long haul, you're in for a rocky road ahead.

Remember my plate-spinning debacle in chapter 1? Well, here's the ugly truth of what trying to keep too many things going at once, mixed with the wrong co-founding team, can do to a person. And if you guessed it might land you in a padded cell, you're half right. This failure landed one of the founders in the clink. If you thought that founder was me, give yourself a high five and feel free to laugh at my expense.

To accurately set the stage for this not-quite-made-for-television story, let me take you back to 1997. Back when gas was $1.22 a gallon in the US and scientists were busy cloning Dolly the sheep. Perhaps less notably, on a worldwide stage, I partnered up with a guy to start my very first business. We sold digital products to e-commerce (yes, just two years after a startup called Amazon started, so most of our customers took credit card numbers by phone) and webshops. Nothing super fancy, but exciting to us, nonetheless.

Fast-forward approximately five years. Picture the night before my girlfriend's thirtieth birthday party. I was twenty-five years old, the founder of two businesses, and starting up a third. At around 1:00 a.m., just as we were going to bed, there was a knock on our apartment door. I opened it to find two police officers, who politely informed me that I was under arrest.

I remained calm, probably because my girlfriend, who was racing around the house, tearing apart every drawer in a frantic search for my lawyer's phone number, was doing enough freaking out for the two of us.

The police declined to tell me why I was being arrested, flashed a warrant, and said that the charges against me would be clarified once we got to the jail. However, they allowed me to pack my laptop and change into a suit (I thought it might help me get out of whatever mess I'd gotten myself into if I looked more presentable than my pajamas). I also brought my wallet with around $100 in it.

Arriving at the jail, I turned over my laptop, wallet, and everything else to the clerk. After a restless night in my rubberized jail cell—which wasn't all that bad, it being a Danish jail—I was led to a courtroom to hear the charges against me. Lo and behold, I owed thousands of Danish kroner, about the equivalent of $10,000, in unpaid business taxes. Without my knowledge, they had already gathered most of this amount by withholding tax refunds. But there was still a small balance—and a fine—left to pay. All of this was news to me, as I'd left the finances of the company that owed the money in the hands of my business partner, and actually thought we had closed the company years ago. He was (and still is) a great guy! But apparently, his administrative skills were even worse than mine at the time.

In a small plot twist, my then current CFO had actually taken care of the matter (great hiring on my part). As it turned out, the Danish tax authorities had actually made a mistake. I was then able to prove my innocence within fifteen minutes. The tables had turned. Instead, they canceled the fine, and owed me all the money they had taken (well over $9,000).

While I never got an apology or the $100 that had been in my wallet (which had mysteriously disappeared since I handed it over to the clerk at the police station), this brief stint in jail taught me one of the most valuable lessons I've learned in startups to date: your founding team makes all the difference in the world if you plan to succeed.

Long story short, I understood how critical each founder's focus on their portion of the business was. No matter how great the team looks on paper, if each member can't contribute to a deficit another founder has, the team is destined to wind up in hot water (or on a cold prison bench).

I'm not the first, nor will I be the last, founder to make the mistake of having a flawed founding team. Take Steve Blank, the CEO at Rocket Science Games. His founding team lost $35 million due to a business model that could not match the founding members' skills. The gaming company's executive staff included no gamers, nor did anyone have any gaming industry experience. Heck, not even one of the board members was an actual gamer.

Mike Tuchen is the current CEO of Talend, the open-source leader of integration software. Before his current leadership role, he was one of the founders of failed startup ParaMark, a nascent technology space company. Tuchen cites the failure of ParaMark as an experience that taught him valuable lessons that have put his career on a successful trajectory. Through the failure, Tuchen clearly identified strengths, weaknesses, and best practices that served him as he went on to the next startup.

The first significant mistake Tuchen pointed out was choosing the wrong co-founders. They didn't behave as a cohesive team, facing a massive amount of conflict, which led to sluggish decision-making. Next, Tuchen didn't take the time to identify the gaps in the leadership team. For example, Tuchen had never worked as a salesperson, so he wasn't adept at identifying the necessary talent and skills needed to make a successful sales team. His lesson was to admit knowledge gaps and weaknesses and ask for and find credible help. Tuchen ended up hiring an advisor to help hire the right salespeople.

Perhaps you've heard of Zirtual, an online company offering virtual assistants (Zirtual Assistants) to entrepreneurs and small business leaders, so they wouldn't have to hire a full-time employee. Within five years, Zirtual had grown to more than five hundred ZAs on staff and operated in thirty-nine of the fifty US states. Within months of their fifth anniversary, they raised approximately $3.3 million in funding and brought in about $1 million each month. Sounds good, right? A month later, Zirtual laid off four hundred employees overnight. By email. Charming and effective. A case clearly under what author, consultant, and speaker Christian Ørsted describes as Lethal Leadership in his bestselling book by the same name. I wish that Zirtual management had read it.

CEO and co-founder Maren Kate cited "burn," lack of checks and balances on the board, and a lack of financial knowledge in leadership as their reasoning for the major chop job. The leadership team had been dedicated to both the brand and the mission but didn't understand how to scale the company properly. They grew too fast and had no one acting as the Chief Financial Officer or the Chief Operating Officer.

The Fix: Take Stock Early and Often

If you have the vision of building a successful and sustainable company, selecting the right team is crucial.

Make sure that everyone on your team is moving in the same direction. Having a team with different goals and objectives for the company means differing priorities and no solid order. Some companies exist where people act as if they were stranded alone on an island, therefore thinking solely of their personal goals, motivations, and expectations, rather than thinking of the people around them or their ideas.

People in a team may play different roles and have different strengths, but if everyone does their job and makes sure they're available to support one another, the entire team will have a better chance of finding success. That applies to both individual teams and companies. No matter the role a person plays in the organization, if they are aligned with their peers on goals, the team will land a win.

There are many mistakes to be made if you do not have clearly outlined responsibilities, direction, and key performance indicators that are measurable and tracked routinely. Without that road map in place, it's easy to waste time and money as everyone flounders around trying to "wing it." Sadly, this lack of clear direction (also known as leadership) can cause a catastrophic failure. To help avoid failing not only yourself, but also your company, surround yourself with smart, talented people—and give them ownership of their tasks and allow them to make mistakes.

You can't succeed with your startup without hard work. Like, seriously hard work. And then some. Hard work in turn requires commitment, vision, and passion—but doesn't mean that you can't have fun.

When you work hard, and your team wins and achieves great things, it's the team that wins. Managers and coaches set the direction and rely on the team to implement it, but the best team relies on a collaborative approach. Teammates collaborate and exchange ideas. Successful teams look to their leadership in a supportive capacity to help circumvent major organizational obstacles. No matter what, a good team keeps their eyes on the final destination as they work together to identify, develop, and implement the best road map to arrive successfully.

Work on flexibility. Your role is to set the overall objective and trust your team to execute. This does not mean not giving people autonomy to exercise themselves, but they must first fulfill their primary role. Once people understand their roles, their ability to cooperate and act improves significantly. Keep roles loose and flexible to encourage individual creative thought.

Go to trade fairs and universities, find people smarter than you, and then hire the talent that fits. You need to define the role that suits you and your team and the needs of the company.

A big part of leadership is articulating your vision and communicating the result so that people can see, feel, and taste it (victory requires cake, obviously). Imagine the bigger picture to spark passion and set and communicate clearly defined goals and milestones so that everyone in the company can feel like a winner when the company wins. If you are passionate about your idea and can articulate how things work, you will attract the best and brightest.

A problem in many companies is that people feel disconnected from what is happening around them. Try to focus on meeting your team where they are, walking around and explaining to people how what they're doing is related to the bigger picture. The more you believe in yourself and have passion, and the more you buy into it, the more you are willing to do what it takes to win.

There is a lot of uncertainty and ambiguity in every company, especially in a startup. Sometimes the plan needs to be adapted to the current real-time circumstances, sometimes not. Big companies start with a good team—good coaches and managers know how to do it, and good players win the vision. Make sure you aim high and understand how your contributions fit into the overall picture. Let the best players work together toward a common goal, which is to win, and let them win together.

Don't forget to celebrate milestones with your team along the way, work hard, and adapt when needed.

The Missing Co-Founder

A team gains its strength from the people in it. If an integral part of the team goes missing, the entire organization suffers.

Having a co-founder is essential. This partnership creates accountability, which helps you to avoid some of the pitfalls of being a single charismatic leader. Plus, a co-founder will have skills that you don't have.

I say this as someone who's launched multiple companies on my own before learning this lesson. I launched my first *real* companies, Shock-waved (digital entertainment/marketing) and Octane (hosting), without a co-founder because I wanted total control, honestly. I wanted to ensure that these companies, my brainchildren, stayed true to my vision. I worried about partnering with someone who would care less than I did and whose expectations might be lower.

The fact is, most every company established by a single founder will suffer from the same fundamental handicap: the lack of accountability a single founder encounters in operating their startup. As the CEO and sole owner of Shockwaved, I had some ridiculously fantastic colleagues but I didn't have a co-founder by my side, day in and day out, to challenge and support me. It was all too easy to let myself off the hook if I missed a deadline or failed to achieve one of my ambitious benchmarks. Once I'd fallen behind, getting myself up to speed again was almost impossible. Even when working around the clock, it was difficult to sustain the non-stop output a startup requires.

Ready to meet another victim of the No Co-Founder Failure? Let me introduce you to Melissa Tsang, the founder of Cusoy, a restaurant-finding site for diners seeking gluten- and allergy-free meals.

I actually believe that Cusoy could have been a success. The business plan was solid: Tsang had identified a real pain point and tapped into an avid and receptive user demographic. And, despite being self-admittedly "non-technical," she successfully designed the site herself, using Word-Press templates.

But Cusoy also had some handicaps, like problems with funding and no clear revenue model. Most of all, Tsang was working solo without a co-founder. Tsang did actually try to find one by searching for a potential partner through Meetup groups and several Hacker and Founder lunches. But she could not find a candidate who shared her values and vision and would also be willing to leave an established company to come to Cusoy. Tsang spent six months working solo on Cusoy, only to decide not to launch, after all.

Ultimately, Tsang recounted in a postmortem on her blog: "I needed strong user growth numbers and concrete evidence before I would have leverage to use when talking to restaurants to advertise and partner with Cusoy. I couldn't get those numbers yet working by myself (especially with no team or funding)."

The once-promising venture had proven "overwhelming both physically, mentally, and emotionally," according to Tsang. As she explained: "Without anyone else to keep me accountable or really caring about Cusoy as much as I did, it was hard to deal with all my self-doubt and still persevere."

The Fix: Board-Up, Partner-Up, or Both

As Cusoy's Melissa Tsang discovered, if you're a solo founder with a great idea, it can be challenging to find a partner who believes in your vision as much as you do—and is willing to take on the risk of starting a new venture from scratch. Here are the top three tips I've assembled for finding a partner:

1. Write and commit to heart a "job description" for your ideal partner.
2. Network to find co-founders.
3. Look for a partner who complements your shortcomings. Be open to working with someone halfway around the world, from a different geography and business culture.

The point is that having a partner will increase your chance of success. So make it a priority.

Friends and Family On Board

The temptation to hire who you know may be strong when it comes to selecting your founding team, but there's something to be said about looking outside your circle of influence.

The temptation to start your business with a friend, significant other, or family member can be enticing, but I promise you, it's not all sunshine and rainbows. It's not to say it can't be done successfully, but there are enough cases where things ended badly to warn you off from it. I can say from personal experience that working with a significant other can cause additional stress. When my startup Shockwaved was bought, my girlfriend and I both wound up working for the same company. She had been there for a while in another division and had spent countless months turning her area around when I was acquired with my company. We had to work very hard to keep work at work. Unfortunately, we had many more work conversations at home than important conversations about our kids, groceries, bills, or anything other than work. It wasn't until she moved on from the company that things at home shifted back to normal. I've even hired friends from school to some of my startups, and co-founded companies with others. We're still friends, but it's not the surest way to maintain those relationships.

Domino's Pizza offers another example. Founded in 1960 by brothers Tom and James Monaghan, they started the first store and bought a used '59 Volkswagen Beetle for making pizza deliveries. Eight months after taking over the initial pizzeria called DomiNick's Pizza, James traded his 50 percent of the business to Tom for the delivery vehicle. Now, I truly believe that a Volkswagen Beetle has a charming design, but had James instead stuck around, his 50 percent share would today be worth half of the over $10 billion yearly the company brings in.

Another fantastic family business failure comes by way of one of the most famous cereal companies. Dr. John Harvey Kellogg was a renowned anti-masturbation advocate in the US. He believed both sex and masturbation were bad for one's hygiene, mood, stiff joints, acne, epilepsy, and a whole host of other maladies. While working at the Michigan Battle Creek Sanatorium, he focused on healthy eating ideas to combat the desire to masturbate. His first invention, granola, led him to the discovery of a flaked bran cereal meant to be a healthy anti-masturbation tool. This was the invention of Corn Flakes. His brother Will also worked at the sanatorium as a bookkeeper. Will disagreed with his brother's mission, but did see potential for a ready-to-eat breakfast item. Together they founded the Kellogg Company. On all accounts, the brothers coexisted in a constant state of feuding for decades.

Back to couples who start business relationships. If the staggering divorce statistics are something that might scare you away from marriage, add to it the failure rate of new businesses. With a 90 percent potential failure rate, the stress and angst of running a startup tends to bleed into other areas of one's life, including personal relationships. When your partner at work is the same as your partner at home, the line between work and home disappears and the stress increases tenfold. Studies show married business partners have a greater likelihood of experiencing divorce and a failed company.

The Fix: Don't Mix Business with Pleasure

Sure, it's a twist on the cliché we've all heard a thousand and three times, but it's true. Mixing business with pleasure can be detrimental. The social conventions of relationships in business vs. personal relationships sit at opposite sides of the scale.

The best thing you can do when looking to find co-founders for your business is to ask friends for recommendations and not ask them to join you. Think of it this way—if out at dinner, would you ask your friend to recommend a bottle of wine or to make one with you?

Friends who understand the startup life and all it brings are great commodities and should be valued. I have several friends who are founders (most of them, it seems, these days), and we can discuss a ton of things, like which direction to go, product design, how the new sales guy is performing, and so on, with no strain on our relationship. We will never have any goal dissension, power struggle, or conflicting financial interest. They can be great resources for information, support, feedback, and commiseration. And no matter how much you like hanging out with them, the bleed of personal relationships will usually overshadow the business's needs at some point in ways that hurt and hinder the company and likely the relationship you had at the beginning.

Rush to the Altar

Selecting the wrong co-founder(s) is worse than having none, and it's one of the most costly decisions in any business. Get it wrong and spend forever trying to correct it.

Suppose every business is only as good as the team of people behind it, and that team starts with the company founders. In that case, it follows that the single most important relationship in your business will be the one between you and your co-founder.

This partnership will ultimately be like a marriage, and it shouldn't be entered into lightly. How are you supposed to choose the person with whom you'll be spending so many hours of your precious life? You need to do some dating.

Just as you would in your romantic life, you need to carefully vet your prospects, get to know them well, and refuse to rush into anything.

Tell your potential business partner how you deal with conflict, and ask them how they deal with it. Do they yell when they get angry? Retreat into themselves and give the cold shoulder? Whatever their way of coping with stress and conflict, it can be all right as long as you can build a structure that compensates for it. Focus on providing an outlet for you and your partner (or partners, if you're in a multiple-co-founders situation) to keep the lines of communication open at all times—through thick and thin, the good times and the bad.

When dating your prospective partner, you'll want to learn as much as possible about their work ethic: How do they work? How hard do they work? Are they insightful? Are they skilled? All of those things are important in terms of ensuring that you get the right founding-partner match.

It's also important to explore your common interests outside of work. Think of co-founder matching like a dating profile. You want to be different enough to complement one another with your working styles, but you need some common interests to discuss over dinner. These relationships are long term, so make sure you know who you are sharing your company with. Make sure you can stand the way they chew their food and what team they cheer for (okay, so one of those is more important with dating than co-founding, but I'll leave it to you to decide).

Once you've gotten to know your co-founder personally, it's time to start negotiating and documenting your roles, including who's the CEO. No matter how equal you feel, there can be only one decision-maker. Asking the difficult questions is essential before agreeing on roles and responsibilities.

You'll also want to sit down and iron out the major milestones and the Key Performance Indicators (KPIs) you'll diligently monitor for the business. This should determine whether you have a shared business vision or not. If not, cut your losses and find another co-founder. If you can't agree on the company's principal goals, it will only get harder to agree on decisions as you go.

The Fix: Go Slow

Admittedly, this advice works for both business and relationships, but I digress. Any business partnership is as precious as a marriage and has to have elements of compromise, good communication, and open-mindedness to be more successful and lasting. Without really knowing the person you're getting into business with, you're liable to learn they aren't the person you thought they were.

Taking the time to really get to know potential partners and vet their business (and, in some cases, personal) history can give you a more well-rounded view of who they are, how they work, and what to expect concerning their leadership style, work ethic, strengths, weaknesses, and so much more.

In keeping with our marriage analogy, I'm sure you have heard divorce horror stories from friends, family, or unfortunate personal experience. Everything is a fight. Anyone caught in the middle is affected by the tension and infighting, and any semblance of trust and harmony disappears. Imagine that in your company—that kind of strife causes multiple failure points and often leads to epic dumpster fire BBQs. Getting married is far too important to rush the process (besides, getting divorced takes at least ten times longer), so take your time with it. There is no rush to find the perfect partner for your business venture. Take it slow, give it the time it deserves to respect the importance of the decision, and trust your gut. This partnership should be ready to stand the test of time and the stress of a startup.

Hiring Freeze

Not hiring can backfire. Startups often struggle with knowing when and who to hire, and are reluctant to take the next step. Avoiding hiring has dire consequences.

Hiring too quickly is fatal from a financial perspective, as we learned in chapter 4 where we discussed funding failures. But not hiring is also a huge problem. I don't subscribe to that cliché advice to "hire slow, fire fast" (the first part of it, but I'll talk about firing later in this chapter). At least not any more than I listen to entrepreneurs and wantrepreneurs who extoll the virtues of big data, growth hacking (oops), synergy, and [insert buzzy startup-world trend here].

Sure, it is possible to start a successful small company with zero employees. But that success will likely come sooner if you propel the business forward by bringing at least one employee on board as quickly as possible. Up your stakes and bring someone on as soon as you can afford to do so.

With someone else on board, you'll be forced to set a firm start time for every workday. In giving them structure, you give yourself much-needed structure.

Also, employees can bring a completely different angle to your company than founders can. Of course, founders have skin in the game, and that's important. But you get different perspectives from employees.

With my company Nature Energy, my partners and I would initially debate the smallest decisions endlessly. The three of us theorized and agonized for months over our pricing structure, positioning, and product-market fit. We researched, ran endless numbers, and called up potential customers to ask them about price bonds. Much of this preparation was (very) useful, but it wasn't until we went out and hired two people that we really got the ball rolling at Nature Energy. Now, if we weren't efficient with our time, we were wasting their time too—and as we paid for their salary, that was nasty. The idea of paying employees to sit around and twiddle their thumbs while we got our acts together and gave them work to do was too painful for my partners and me to withstand. So we made sure there were prospects for them to call, process and software development tasks to manage, and customer interactions for them to handle.

The Fix: Hire When Ready

As soon as you have the basic framework for your company in place, hire someone to do a component you can't do yourself. Having an employee you are accountable to will keep you moving forward and stop you from making excuses, letting deadlines slip, and so on. It focuses you, and also adds more energy and new thoughts.

At the very beginning, it's okay if you hire someone who won't be with you for the rest of the startup's life. This really isn't the worst thing that can happen.

That said, don't rush the interviewing and hiring process itself. When done right, this process takes time.

And it goes two ways. Research shows that carefully considered hires are more sticky than rushed hires. An employee who's been thoroughly vetted feels that they've earned a significant and competitive position. As a result, they invest more of their time and energy than employees who were hired quickly.

On the other hand, employees hired quickly are likely to have a "that was too easy" mindset. They tend to quit more easily, with average tenures lasting shorter compared with employees who undergo lengthy interview processes. Back in the eighties, Ellen Jackofsky (who used to be Associate Professor Emerita at Southern Methodist University's Cox School of Business) and others actually concluded that up to 60 percent of undesirable turnover came down to poor hiring decisions.

This is why even if I know I've found the person I want for an open position, I still conduct a minimum of three interviews for the role. While doing so, I let my top choice know that they are one of the leading candidates. This way I force myself to spend more time on the process, while ensuring that the candidate knows they're being cherry-picked, and not risk losing them in the process.

Horrible Hiring

Not all hires are good hires. Plain and simple. Hiring the wrong team can be detrimental to any startup.

I did just say that your first hires do not necessarily have to be permanent, but still remember that with every hire you make, you're building the culture of your startup. This is why I tend to agree with the expression "Hire for attitude, not aptitude." An employee with a bad attitude can quickly dampen company morale in a small startup. That single wrong hire can mess up everything. They might be the customer service agent who calls all of your customers idiots as soon as they hang up the phone. They might be the employee who makes all the women in your office feel uncomfortable.

I didn't always know my way around the problems with Poor Hiring. In my early days, I tended to err on the side of taking too much time for interviews and being overly friendly and encouraging when I liked a candidate. Hiring always takes much effort, and doing it like this makes it downright exhausting. This is a common problem with young founders.

One entrepreneur I know was considering two nearly equal candidates for a sales position at her communications agency. Wanting to keep the process moving along, she gave each of them a copy of the company's standard employment contract to review, while negotiating the salary with both candidates. Unfortunately, this tactic sent the wrong message to one of the candidates, who believed she'd actually been hired and immediately quit her current job. It was, however, not her that was ultimately hired. Ouch. It was a regrettable situation that reflected poorly on my friend and her company. (Although it did reassure her that she'd made the right choice in not choosing the more naive candidate who'd leapt before she looked.)

If you haven't already heard of Zenefits, you'll be in for a treat. This startup had all the makings of a success on paper, but once implementation began, so did the nightmare. In 2013, Parker Conrad founded Zenefits, a human resources service for small businesses and startups. The concept was a hit and gained more than a billion dollars from initial investors. By 2015, Zenefits was serving 14,000 businesses and bringing in $20 million in recurring revenue.

Unfortunately, Conrad mishandled his human resources within the company. He never hired an office manager, IT workers, or receptionists. With these oversights, the company became disorganized, dropping the ball on key tasks and deadlines. On top of that, they sold insurance without a license because there wasn't anyone to tell them not to. By early 2016, Parker Conrad was forced to resign due to (obviously) serious failures of regulatory compliance.

Fix: Hiring Hot Sheet

Hiring can be a stressful process. How do you find good people? How do you know who the best candidates are, and what happens if you hire the wrong candidate?

You can, of course, interview yourself to death, but two shortcuts I always use are a very compressed interview format and personality assessments like the Carl Jung–inspired Myers-Briggs Type Indicator (MBTI) to see if a potential hire would be a good fit.

I usually know in the first ten to fifteen minutes if the candidate is someone I could work with or not. This is impossible to tell just from an application, and because of this, I need to interview as many of the candidates as possible, in the shortest possible time. My compressed interview format means that I invite the candidates to a fifteen-to-twenty-minutes-only interview. I ensure that they know about the company in advance (so I don't have to waste time talking about it), and that they complete the MBTI before the interview, so I also have an idea of their personality type. Armed with this, fifteen to twenty minutes will do fine, and then I'll add ten minutes between each interview for notes. Bam! Ten candidates in five hours flat, and only a slight brain-fry on my part.

Hiring (white, heterosexual) Men

Lacking diversity in startups is bad for business—and everyone around it. Diverse teams perform better. Often, the right man for the job is a woman.

Getting the disclaimer out of the way: First, I identify as male and I'm fairly white—to the degree where my skin only has two settings: albino and tomato. I also have avoided discussing my demographics in a book on startups mainly because it's not meant to be political and I expect there is no need to preach to you that everyone, regardless of their gender, race, age, ethnicity, sexual orientation, and so on, is equal.

However, from a business perspective, I'd be remiss if I didn't discuss the shortsighted issue of only hiring (white, heterosexual) men. You'll notice this area may sound familiar. It should. Hiring a team of similarly gendered individuals as yourself is closely linked to the gender data gap, skillfully covered in Caroline Criado Perez's book *Invisible Women*, and in practice a variation of survivorship bias, which excludes other genders.

A recent failure of this magnitude can be seen in the company that designed Pinky Gloves. The company, spearheaded by two men and their (male, of course) investor, designed pink disposable gloves with a strip of adhesive designed to be used by women during their periods to remove and dispose of their tampons and pads. The glove-turned-disposal-bag received a lot of backlash, rightfully so, considering their product was aimed at fixing a nonissue while shaming an entire gender for the way their body was designed to work.

The entire concept was a bloody shame. Really. Had they consulted even one female about their product idea, they could have saved themselves a ton of embarrassment and negative press. But no worries, the market will easily correct their blunder.

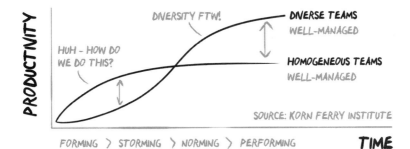

Similarly, the auto safety industry did not invent the wheel. For decades, they conducted their safety research with crash test dummies mimicking average males behind the wheel. When they finally added female test dummies into the mix, they continued to work under the same gender survivorship bias that Pinky Gloves did. They only looked at what was important from their perspective and put the female crash test dummies in the passenger seat. While in some families it may be true that a man drives while a woman rides shotgun, what about when the woman drives to work alone? Shouldn't the potential consequences of a major impact / crash be studied with an average woman behind the wheel? The short answer is "yes." The longer answer comes from a long-lasting ignorance to other perspectives.

So how is the situation for women founders? This, I was discussing with Louise Lachmann, a highly successful tech-entrepreneur, investor, and modern-day superwoman, who told me about the stats from Europe (which inspired this section): 90 percent of capital raised by tech startups went to teams without any female founders. Not a single female.

These are not imaginary numbers—Agnieszka Skonieczna and Letizia Castellano from the European Commission confirm this in their discussion paper on *Gender Smart Financing.*

So if the companies that get venture are almost exclusively led by men, who will then be our future investors when exiting their startups? Men, of course. A downward spiral in the making.

The Fix: Diversification Develops Dividends

We discuss diversification in other areas of the book, but it should be applied to not only your team of colleagues but also your founding team.

Ignoring the idea of political correctness, there is solid reasoning to have a diverse founding team. One comes from Lone Christiansen and her team from the IMF's Research Department. They have researched on the topic of gender diversity in businesses vis-à-vis their performance, and it seems safe to conclude that diverse teams outperform market benchmarks and provide stronger returns.

Lone Christiansen and her team found that companies with a larger share of women in senior positions have a significantly higher return. Greater diversity equals more money. That in itself should be all the argument you need.

In addition, they found that gender equality is even more beneficial for companies in industries that already have more women in the labor force. The same is true for industries that are knowledge intensive and high-tech.

While this section primarily focused on gender, when founding a startup, you should of course work from a wider perspective.

Getting facts straight: LGBT identification is on the rise, with roughly 6 percent of US adults identifying as LGBT according to Gallup. And there are around two million transgender people in the US alone.

I'll again recommend searching out the most talented people who share your core values and vision for the company. This means looking outside your close-knit scope of people. You may find the best matches for your business come from any walk of life, gender, age, political leaning, or sexual identity around the globe. Go go go!

Organizational F*ckup #8:

Firing Phobia

Fearful to fire an employee? Fear not. Startups need all hands on deck and if someone isn't the right fit, founders need to face their fear and fire.

There are two reasons why you should fire someone:

1.   They're not the right fit.
2.   You can't afford them.

Even when one of those problems is indisputable, many founders drag their feet and delay firing the lousy fit. It's understandable, of course. Unless we're psychopaths, we dread the idea of causing another pain. What's more, if we're a self-reflective leader, we realize that it's our fault that this bad hire was made in the first place. This double-whammy can be a lot to face. But all the same, the Firing Phobia Failure is just plain bad business. We need to get over our dread and rip off the Band-Aid as quickly as possible.

I still vividly remember the first time I had to fire someone. It shouldn't have been as difficult as it was for me: the guy I was firing had been dishonest and needed to go. But all the same, I woke at the crack of dawn that morning with a pit in my stomach. Even after a lot of coaching from my girlfriend, I barely managed to get through that conversation and deliver my message.

One experienced CEO I know hates firing people so much that he can't help but couch the bad news in platitudes. "You've done a fantastic job organizing the weekly meetings," he'll say. "But . . ."

This approach may seem like a kind way to couch the blow, but it leaves the door open for misinterpretation, and I don't recommend it. Of course, you need to be intelligent, polite, and human when you deliver the bad news. But, just as importantly, you need to be direct. The very first thing that needs to happen in this meeting is you firing the person.

Just ask the platitude-wielding CEO I mentioned above: One employee this CEO thought he'd fired face-to-face walked away from the same meeting with a very different impression.

"How'd it go?" asked a colleague.

"Great! I just got a raise," said the guy.

Thanks to his "nice" approach, the CEO was forced to fire the employee a second time the next day. That's just awful.

Unfortunately, I've fired a lot of people. I fired a lot in my time with Shockwaved and later with TBWA, and as COO at Aller Media I learned about firing at scale. I really hated that part, but at least I learned the most painless and efficient way to do the deed:

"This meeting is not going to be pleasant," I'll say right off the bat to the person I'm firing, "because I have to let you go." After a pause, I'll repeat myself, just to make sure the news has sunk in. Sometimes the person on the other side of the table can respond aggressively. Sometimes they might cry. Some just sit silently in their chair.

Once I've firmly established why we're there, I spend the rest of the meeting explaining the decision and building the person back up again. I'll offer any positive feedback I have, and normally (assuming they're a good employee who was simply not a good fit or too expensive), I'll offer to help them find another role elsewhere.

One thing that helps me to get through the unpleasant firing process is that I have a rule: I will never fire someone who hasn't seen it coming. The person should always have received warning that all was not well and know this outcome is on the radar.

If an employee is let go for poor performance, I will always first present an opportunity for improvement. For example, I might say: "We're having a problem in terms of your productivity. Last year you were at index one hundred, and now you're at index sixty. What's going on? If we can't improve that together over the next month or two, then we'll have to consider what to do with your role."

If the employee is being fired because we can't afford them, they will have previously been told something like: "It's looking as if we can't afford to have five people in this department anymore and will need to cut down to four." The point is to show the person the writing on the wall before a final decision has been made. I think this is the most humane thing to do.

Of course, if you need to cut down due to cost, then do it all in one go, so the remaining team knows they are safe. Working someplace where people are sacked every quarter means the talented colleagues will be looking for work elsewhere, leaving you stuck with those less so. That's the recipe for a downward spiral—and not in a Nine Inch Nails awesome kind of way.

The Fix: Ground Zero Exercise—Four Steps to Firing Everyone Frequently

Every six to twelve months, I run what I call a Ground Zero Exercise on my company.
Basically, the task goes like this:

1. (Imagine!) that you fire everyone and identify what is left of value. Imagine you're just starting the company today—with your current bank account, software package, general knowledge, connections, and so on—but with none of the people on board (apart from co-founders, who you will, of course, do this exercise with).

2. Define the ideal but realistic roles/employees for your startup. You then make a Post-it for each role you want in the company—under ideal circumstances, but with the realism of your current financial situation—and possibly add a few keywords on each Post-it Note. For example, if you wanted the lead singer Dave Grohl from Foo Fighters as a receptionist (What? Yes, the man is a fierce creative force and undoubtedly too sympathetic—why on earth would you want him to run your reception?) then skip that thought as you probably could not afford it. There is a severe risk that he would decline your kind offer. Anyway, add the realistic (and descriptive) roles you now know you want in your startup to each Post-it Note.

3. Compare the final fiction to fact. Next, you will build your organizational structure up again, still on paper, using your new Post-it

colleagues—they won't object. Once done, and you are confident that this fictional organization is ideal for your company at this stage, you then compare this to the current harsh realities of your startup.

4. Implement—go go go! Perhaps you have redundant resources in your company? Sorry, but they have to go. Maybe you are missing a vital role as head of customer support? Go hire! I still doubt that Dave Grohl is interested, but it does not hurt to try. Perhaps everything is 1:1 the same as it should be. Great, move on and pat yourself on the shoulders for not firing anyone. Next, pat your colleagues on the shoulders and compliment them for being such a good fit for this adventure!

C'est tout. You now have a trimmed and talented startup without having to consider all interim accounting and mental arithmetic of moving a few resources back and forth.

A Final Word on Firing

If you're in doubt as to whether someone should be fired or not, then they should be fired. That's always the rule, whether the person in question is an assistant, a manager, or a CFO. There's simply no room for doubt in a startup. Eighty percent equals 100 percent, remember?

Awful Accountability

Startups tend to be lean when it comes to employees. Ignoring accountability can lead a startup straight to failure city.

If you're running a small company, then you should be extra aware of the importance of building accountability and a strong culture with your employees, especially with those working remotely. In my current company, we have twenty people working outside of our principal office space. Some are situated in teams, and others work solo. This presents a challenge when it comes to building a strong company culture. It can be challenging to convey nuances to remote workers.

Maybe the ad copy text isn't singing to you. Perhaps the website colors need more "swish." When you're talking to someone in the same room, it's much easier to convey these subtle requests. But if you're working with someone who lives on the other side of the planet in a different time zone and who might be more comfortable speaking a foreign language, it can get tricky. The smaller the team and the startup, the less likely it is that you'll have project managers to help you manage these small details that can really make a difference.

If you're your own boss, it's easy to "allow yourself" to miss a deadline. You need a plan to ensure you're forced into a deadline. You can achieve this by promising something to a customer, getting a colleague involved, and setting up deadlines.

This is even worse for your employees if they don't feel management has the same level of commitment to the business.

I've seen examples from larger organizations where people "did their work" without doing it. One company I worked with needed to get a credit card system up and running for a Christmas campaign. A couple of weeks before the launch, management decided to skip this solution and find another. Why? Because the system we planned to put in place took four to six weeks to get up and running.

The failures here were in two places.

1. The business needed credit cards to make any revenue. Without it, we would lose 50 percent of the turnover.
2. They did not understand what the payment gateway had said (and did not brief them correctly). Had they instead asked, "What can

we do to be live in one to two weeks? What solution should we then select?" then they would have been able to find the right solution. It only took one phone call to have a resolution.

I was pretty irritated with the person in charge, and we had the system up and running a few days later.

If you don't see the task as yours and aren't ready to take full responsibility for outcomes, you aren't accountable. Accountability isn't something you do for someone else. It's your company. You should always be motivated to go in-depth with solutions. Fostering that same dedication in your employees will go a long way to building a strong team.

Take The Players' Tribune as an example. Co-founded by Derek Jeter, the athlete-focused media company aimed to compete with established sports media outlets by having a more direct relationship with the players. Initially, they offered great content focused on the sports talent they had access to based on the relationships already established by Jeter and his friends. Dedicated to quality over quantity, the startup struggled to compete in the noisy sports news marketplace. Staffers claimed a low urgency from the editors for fresh content. Stories took a month at times before going live. Whereas other competitors had regular content, The Players' Tribune would have dry spells more often than not. The lack of accountability was ultimately driving them into obscurity.

The Fix: What Gets Measured Gets Done

I know several founders who hold daily morning meetings, or "standups," with their remote teams. For me, a weekly video meeting with my crews in India and Albania is sufficient. This is my chance to look my employees in the eye and ask: Where are you spending the most resources? What trouble spots have you run into since last week? What are the one or two most important things you hope to accomplish this week? Then each team member reports on whether or not they met last week's commitments. Before signing off, we go over the week's schedule in detail, making it nearly impossible for my remote teams to waste time instead of meeting their deadlines.

Not only do I measure performance at these meetings, but I also measure time. I start the meetings at 9:15 a.m. rather than on the hour, to instill the ethos that we don't work in hour intervals—every minute counts. To that end, I want to make sure that we're getting real value out of our meetings. To determine this, I keep track of the amount of time spent, multiplied by the employees' hourly rates in attendance. If ten people attend the meeting, I do a quick and dirty calculation of the wages spent while in the meeting and ensure that the meeting's value justifies that expense. In startups, every penny and minute counts. If you can't justify the expense of having ten people in a meeting for forty minutes, reevaluate the goal of the meeting and the needed attendees. More importantly, it helps us fight mental laziness by just accepting meeting invites, because it's easier than thinking for ourselves—Mindless Acceptance Syndrome as David Grady hilariously named it.

This removes the tendency to invite nonessential employees to attend "just because." If we're not discussing marketing, then Jim from marketing gets a pass on the meeting.

My cost calculations also help me to remember to be superefficient with everyone's time. We skip the "What did you do over the weekend?" chitchat and get straight to the heart of things. Isn't that what everyone wants, anyway?

Go Easy on the Rules (For Your Employees)

You'll notice that all of the accountability rules I mentioned in my anecdote are around my behavior. As a founder, it's your job to set strict guidelines for yourself to follow.

If you've hired the right people, the same is true for your staff.

Why are you founding a startup?

I value being my boss, pouring my creative energy into a project with no clearly defined path or guarantee of success. Rules are suffocating for me, and the same is likely valid for anyone who signs up to work with a startup. Why are you going to hire energetic, creative, and smart people and then tie them down with rules upon rules?

Michael Seibel, managing director at Y Combinator, said, "My answer to why you should start a startup is simple: there is a certain type of person who only works at their peak capacity when there is no predictable path to follow, the odds of success are low, and they have to take personal responsibility for failure (the opposite of most jobs at a large company)."

He talked about founders, but the same is true of the kind of person who's attracted to working at startups. They *don't* want to be tied down to a rule book heavy enough to beat a man to death with, or at least the good ones don't.

Ironically, giving your team as few rules as possible will help them stay accountable.

The more rules you add, the fewer people will follow. So try implementing five core rules instead of, say, twenty. Personally, I can't remember more than five items on any list I make, anyway! So that's my golden number. After all, what's the point of creating a rule that people won't remember? And trust me, if they have to look it up, they won't.

Organizational F*ckup #10:

The Forever CEO

Your startup is your baby. Initially it needs near-constant love and attention. Over time, it may no longer need you. Plan ahead.

Right now, you probably imagine that you, as the founder, will be your company's CEO for the rest of this company's life. Most founders are used to thinking that they need to be a forever CEO like Bill Gates to be successful. But the harsh reality is that even though you might be an excellent CEO for your company in its early years, you might not be the best person to lead the company at a later point in time. Even Bill Gates realized that.

This is precisely what happened to Rahul Yadav, the founder and CEO of Housing.com, a startup out of India. Although the company did well under his leadership, commanding a huge valuation and a giant seed round, Yadav was suddenly fired just three years into the company's life. Now Housing.com was in a situation where they needed to find a new CEO on the spot. But with the banishment of the only person who knew every corner of the company, the search didn't go well. Unable to find an adequate replacement for Yadav, Housing.com's investors sold it to another company called PropTiger. Without a leader at its helm, the company sold for far less than it should have. This was a double loss for Yadav, who not only lost his job but millions of dollars in stock.

The reality is, no CEO is guaranteed a seat at the helm forever. Even if you're performing well, there's always a chance you'll be given the boot.

The Fix: Self-Fire—When the Time Is Right

Conventional approach: this happens all the time—it even happened to Steve Jobs! So the intelligent founder should recognize that it's possible and plan to self-fire when the time is right. The point is that you and your legacy will be better off hand-crowning the next great leader of your company than leaving this monumental decision to the members of your board at some later date.

This is exactly the approach taken by David Helgason, the founder of Unity, a game development platform. After a strong start in the gaming space, Unity hit a rocky patch. Seeing the writing on the wall,

Helgason realized that he wasn't the best person to lead Unity to safety as a computer game geek. The platform needed a leader with a strong marketing and sales background, which were not his strong suits. So Helgason decided to self-fire before things got any worse and his board did the job for him. This gave Unity's remaining leaders some time to find and hire a new CEO, which they did within seven months. As a result, Unity never lost a cent of its value. Today, the company is a huge success. Helgason can hold his head up high as the founder, board member, and majority stakeholder of one of the world's most successful gaming companies.

The truth is, as with everything in startups, you have to exercise discretion and good judgment. Silicon Valley VC Andreessen Horowitz overwhelmingly favors investing in startups with founder CEOs. They note that some of the greatest startups of all time were run by founders for most of their history, including Facebook, Twitter, Microsoft, and Amazon.

They also note that "founding CEOs consistently beat the professional CEOs on a broad range of metrics ranging from capital efficiency [amount of funding raised], time to exit, exit valuations, and return on investment."

Moreover, they believe that founders bring a degree of innovation, company knowledge, commitment, and moral authority that is tough to beat with a professional CEO.

If the conventional wisdom says one thing and research and numerous heavyweight VCs say another, then what's the real answer here?

In short, you're going to need some serious self-awareness and critical self-examination (qualities you better have in the first place if you want to create a successful startup).

But how do you recognize that the thing holding a startup back is its CEO—you?

When we've nursed our baby from infancy, it can be challenging to let go. Even the best CEO is subject to a host of cognitive biases, which will cloud your judgment when it comes to the project you've poured heart and soul into.

Back to Andreessen Horowitz. They observe that "being CEO requires a tremendous amount of skill. The larger the company becomes, the more skill that's required."

But few founders start with the skills needed to manage a behemoth like Amazon or Twitter. The rest of us have to learn it on the job, and that can be a "miserable, debilitating experience."

Ben Horowitz notes there are two required characteristics:

1. Leadership, as defined by these three characteristics: the ability to articulate the vision, have the right kind of ambition, and the ability to achieve the vision.

2. Desire—not necessarily the desire to be CEO, but the burning, irrepressible urge to build something great and the willingness to do whatever it takes to get there.

To that, I'd add a third: the emotional and physical resilience to get the job done.

Leadership and desire are outstanding, but if you're burned out on the business, neglecting your health, life, and relationships, then it's probably time to step back. The marathon is an entirely different race from the sprint. Some founders excel in the sprint but can't handle the marathon, and that's fine. Just know yourself and be honest enough with yourself that you know when to throw in the towel.

A Final Word on Organizational Failures

We began this chapter with a seemingly simple statement that your team matters most. Whether it's the people you found the company with, your first employee, or the guy you had to sack last week because he created a toxic work environment, your business is only as good as the people in it.

The interesting thing here is that when it comes to teams in a startup, one particular team is either overvalued or continuously undervalued.

If you had to hazard a guess, what would it be? What segment of your new startup could be so important that I'd devote an entire chapter to it? Ah, no peeking. Take a guess. Any guesses?

Channel your inner Jerry Maguire and let's all grab hands, start jumping up and down, and yell it out: "SHOW ME THE MONEY!"

Yeah, baby! Let's talk about how you can fail in sales.

Chapter 7

Sales F*ckups

When things are going well with your company, and the money is flowing in, it can be tempting to take your eye off your sales program. But this is a huge mistake: you need a structured, proactive sales program at all times.

When I first started my online entertainment marketing company, with the terrible name Shockwaved, I didn't think much about sales. Or at least I did not do much about sales. As somewhat of an introvert, I'd always hated the idea of pursuing clients. Plus, it was the early aughts, and the dot-com boom was booming, so I thought there was no reason to chase more work than my several developers and I could even handle. Honestly, I was not too fond of sales, and as it was not strictly required, I skipped it. As a solo founder (see the Missing Co-Founder Failure in chapter 6), I was so busy running the company's day-to-day operations that I barely had time to answer the phone. When I did, there was often someone from one of the big marketing agencies I sub-supplied to on the other end of the line, asking me to build a campaign for one of their clients.

"Can you deliver for us by next month?" they'd ask.

"Yeah, sure!" I'd reply. I'd name the price and hang up the phone, pleased with myself. This was how it went when the agencies I worked for were thriving, in any case.

Then, in 2000, the bubble burst. All across the tech sector, businesses were hit hard, massive budgets pulled out from under them—and suddenly they had no projects for Shockwaved to solve.

As a sub-supplier with no structured sales process, customer relationship management (CRM) system, or sales funnel in place, my work dried up surprisingly fast. That's as close to certain death as you will get as a business.

If there aren't any sales, there isn't any money, and there's no business left to do. That's it. So, of course, sales are at the very heart of any business.

And, of course, as the proverb goes, necessity is the mother of invention. We Danish put our spin on that idea, with the politically incorrect expression "*nød lærer nøgen kvinde at spinde*," which loosely translates to "necessity teaches the naked woman to spin." In other words, when it's cold outside,[1] and you're naked, you'd better learn how to make some clothes! In my case, I needed to start getting serious about sales. I went online and bought a ton of books on the topic, and began to study. At the same time, my girlfriend had started working as the digital division manager at an advertising agency—although she had no sales experience either. Despite lacking sales experience, she is still my girlfriend today and mother of our two beautiful (and most annoying) kids. Because we were both complete newbies in this field, we decided we'd take two afternoons off a week and learn how to make sales calls. We'd sit at the kitchen table and take turns cold-calling potential customers. Yes, that was romantic, right there. I jest because we both look back and laugh at those early days of learning those crucial skills. Both of us hated it. But, lo and behold, after a couple of dozen hours of practice, it got easier for us. And I even managed to entice a few new clients to hire Shockwaved for their marketing campaigns.

Today, I enjoy making sales calls, and I'm happy to tell you that I now make sure all my companies have robust sales and marketing divisions—because you never know what's around the corner. In this chapter, we'll look at the critical components of any successful sales program and the failures that can and will ensue when companies attempt to go without them. Let's start with the biggest failure I made before I got serious about my sales.

---

1. The average temperature in Denmark is 8.3°C, and while Denmark was the first country on the planet to legitimize pornographic literature back in 1967, we usually do not walk around naked. On July 1, 1969, Denmark had another first by legalizing "pictorial and audiovisual" porn—yep—and then, true to human nature, a few months after, the world's first pornography trade show business was about to kick off. Andy Warhol did his *Blue Movie* the same year, but this was, of course, art—and not porn.

Lacking Sales Talent

Early to bed, early to rise—and in between, you sell and advertise. No sales means no cash flow or product validation. Sales people are the lifeblood of startups. Choose them wisely.

The first significant failure that often occurs in the sales department is lacking a sales department altogether. While some industries don't have a designated sales force, knowing how to make a sale is as important as knowing how to work in your industry. If you haven't had any formal sales training, there are excellent resources available. Go find some books that fit your target group and situation, such as the classics like *SPIN Selling* by Neil Rackham, *Secrets to Closing the Sale* by Zig Ziglar, or Chet Holmes's book, *The Ultimate Sales Machine*.

If your startup is more extensive, it may be tempting to have your project manager, customer support people, CEO, or some other idiot make the sales. While these people are likely very good at their intended jobs, they are not trained salespeople. In essence, don't have people who do not know what they're talking about making your sales. There is always a chance to eke out a deal or five, but not knowing sales means the CPO (Cost Per Order) will be too high. The product will likely become too customized because of the misguided goal of getting to "yes" on a sale. Getting a "yes" mentality vs. a salesperson can include the product becoming too custom and expensive to produce. No matter what, it's not scalable.

Sales should be at the core of the business. If you step back and see sales isn't your primary focus, you need to reprioritize. If your company has no way of bringing in revenue with sales of some type, you don't have a business.

The Fix: Hire a Salesperson

I bet you never saw that one coming. Taking your business seriously includes the sales department. If you don't have at least one trained salesperson, you need to hire one. As you grow and scale, you'll want to have different people for all the differing aspects within your sales cycle. This will make the process more seamless and create less redundancy in task assignments. We'll get more into this as we go in the chapter, but you can't sell anything without a salesperson. At least not reliably.

Missing Sales Metrics

Sales metrics are the health-check of startups. Not measuring what is important means that it cannot be improved. What gets measured gets done.

It's crucial that you measure all conversions in your sales funnel. What's your conversion on cold calls? In-person meetings? Direct email campaigns? How many unique users visit your website, what's their average session length, and how many of them convert to signups? Measure all of it, not just the one or two areas where you put most of your energy.

MobileIgniter was a tech hardware startup that closed its doors in 2016. One of their primary mistakes was to set their target sales goals too far in the future. Along the way, they didn't track their progress toward achieving those far-flung goals.

Had they tracked their three-, six-, and twelve-month sales cycles, perhaps MobileIgniter would have been able to correctly match their production to the market demand.

The Fix: Track Your Data

As a startup founder, you can't afford to operate your business at arm's length. You can't leave anything unexamined, un-measured, or to chance. To know your business well, you need to understand how it's doing now, at this very moment. This is true for both brick-and-mortar and online businesses, but the former typically do less tracking than the latter for obvious reasons. Understandably so. It takes no extra workforce for a website owner to monitor how many customers come through their door each day, hour, and minute. For a flower-shop owner, however, this level of tracking takes more work. But it can be done.

Years ago, I co-owned a tea store with a partner. I would spend some of my days drinking tea and taking detailed notes on how many people visited, how many asked for help, how many requested gift-wrapping, how many asked questions, you name it.

Other days, I'd park myself with a sandwich outside our competitor's store and note how many people went in, how long they spent inside, how many (if any) shopping bags they came out with, and even estimated the amount of their purchase based on the size of those bags or just plain asking them. The data I gathered from these missions was invaluable—plus, the activity felt very James Bond, which is always fun.

Non-Structured Sales

Not having a well-established sales structure leaves the results both unpredictable and completely random, which hurts the company infrastructure. Plan your sales, or plan to fail.

Every organization needs a sales process or structure. Many terms encompass this idea, but it boils down to a few significant ideas. You should create a sales funnel, which is the design metrics for how you woo a potential new client until they either naturally drop off or you end your company. You should also have a customer relationship management (CRM) tool. But before either of those come into play, you need a plan.

Without a plan, businesses sometimes fall into the trap of yo-yo sales. This can look like a few different things depending on the industry you're in, but they all amount to unpredictable revenue cycles. For example, if you are a freelancer or gig worker, you will likely spend a ton of time trying to gain your clients. Once you have work, you spend less time working on attracting new clients because you're "busy." Fair enough. What happens when you complete all your work for your initial clients? You shift focus back to selling yourself and gaining more new clients. During this time, you aren't working for clients, so you have no income. This is a vicious repeating cycle, and it happens in a lot of industries. Even when you have work to do for your customers, you need to carve out time daily to bring in new business.

Other businesses fall into seasonal traps. For example, an ice cream shop may need to close when the weather gets cold because their sales drop due to the weather. They may also want to consider adding a component of their business that can appeal to their customers during the cold weather.

And our dear friends with the flower shop see sales spike around the major holidays. They either need to expand their sales efforts during non-holiday times or diversify and offer other goods. Perhaps chocolate, cards, handmade jewelry, or other types of small gifts—the list can go on. If a florist offers excellent gifts for women in one place, men (and women) will more likely make that shop their primary locale to purchase gifts for the women in their life.

Related to yo-yo sales is the less discussed separation of sales functions. If you have a company that needs to make sales "calls" appointments, you should have a team for that. Those people have the core responsibility of making cold calls and following up on warm leads. The people who meet with your potential new customer do not need to include the person who called to set up the meeting. As Nick Baum, TBWA's VP for Europe, always told me: those making the PowerPoint are not necessarily the best at presenting it. In many technology companies, there is even a position for the tech person on the sales team called a pre-sales engineer. These individuals typically accompany the salesperson to the second sales meeting to answer all the high-level "tech" questions. They also address implementation timelines. They don't sell anything other than their knowledge as an expert. Once a sale has been made, there is room for another position dedicated to post-sales. Not only do they follow up on the customer after the product is delivered, but they also look for add-on sales opportunities.

I can hear you already telling me you don't need all that. And you might be right. But if you have the same person calling ten companies to book ten meetings, then going to those ten meetings and writing ten proposals, isn't that overwhelming? The person would deliberately be messing up their own schedule. Wait. We aren't done yet. Add to it closing those ten deals, delivering and implementing products for ten customers, following up to ensure everything is working, and seeing if they need more product. When is there a break? How will that person have time (and feel motivated) to call ten more people to ensure your sales force doesn't stop because you have work? My rule is to have one person (at least) responsible for one action in your cycle. This keeps it moving and creates more availability for you to meet with more potential customers. Think of it as a stress reducer that opens you up for more consistent revenue.

As mentioned, the two main components of a sales structure should be a customer relationship management system and a sales funnel. The statistics on CRM systems may surprise you. Only around 50 percent of startups and companies with fewer than ten employees use a CRM system. The figures jump once a company adds one additional person, though. Statistics show that 91 percent of companies with eleven or more employees use a CRM system. It is of course unlikely that a single person is the catalyst of CRM investments; such investments are more a sign of sales and organizational maturity. However, CRM tools aren't costly. Implementing them as soon as possible will give you a leg up on the competition for your sales. Skipping this solution early on will cause more headaches in the future as you grow.

When it comes to the sales funnel, most companies do have a structure in place designed to lead a potential new customer through the stages from initial exposure to the product all the way through to an action or purchase stage. The outstanding ones have a plan to help create a need for these clients to return to do more business and become repeat or higher value customers and a plan for how to reengage customers that may have fallen by the wayside over time.

A significant number of startups do put time and energy into creating the sales funnel but don't spend the money on a CRM system to support it. It's kind of like having a great sales plan but keeping all your potential new clients in an old paper Rolodex. It may sound cool and retro, but you lose a ton of efficiency and potentially a host of missed sales opportunities as well as organizational red flags.

A prime example of how not having both can go wrong has to be Unify. Founded in 2008 as a relationship management tool for business professionals, the company created six products, made six pivots, and still missed the mark. Focusing squarely on the user experience in the CRM world, they aimed to create a highly automated system. Their goal was to answer CRM solutions seeming clunky to users because of low user acceptance, training, and implementation issues that churned out insufficient or inaccurate data. After two years of underestimating the sales cycles and their target audience, they realized that while they were passionate about the consumer and building a great end-user experience, no one in their organization of seven people had either the experience in sales or the passion for it.

After three and a half years, they were out of money and time. So, while producing a CRM product, they didn't understand the CRM for their own business, nor had the sales expertise (or enterprise sales funnel) to make it work.

Another fine example is MobileIgniter; a startup focused on the Internet of Things (IoT) in the business market. Dominic DiMarco, the co-founder, stated, "Most people don't need their refrigerator connected to the internet. But the people who manufacture that refrigerator are putting sensors and intelligence all along through their assembly and distribution channels that are making that refrigerator cheaper and more reliable." The company estimated the sales cycle between three and six months working with manufacturers but later had to adjust to nine to twelve months. Founded in 2011, the company eked along until 2015, when they finally launched a marketing campaign designed to appeal to their manufacturing client base. Unfortunately, after a year without any sales, the company gave up the ghost. Being a small, lean company targeting big, established clients who have long sales cycles, they couldn't meet their goals.

Enterprise software is complex and can take some time to implement, which can cause business processes to slow for a while. When it came to the upgrade and implementation of a CRM system, one of the most famous cases of misunderstanding is The Hershey Company. Most famous for its chocolate kisses and bars, the American chocolate manufacturer is a staple in the US. In 1999, as technologies were improving and customer relation needs were on the rise, the company purchased a CRM system from Siebel for the low, low price of $112 million. If you were to think of the worst timing for a chocolate manufacturer to install a new ordering and customer management system, you'd likely guess Halloween. Due to its production of fan favorites like Reese's Peanut Butter Cups, Jolly Ranchers, Hershey's Kisses, and Twizzlers, Halloween accounts for at least 10 percent of The Hershey Company's yearly revenue. When I say they couldn't have picked a worse time to install the new system, the number speaks for itself. The new system was cumbersome and took time to set up across all of the necessary platforms, leaving over $100 million in candies on the table and not in the hands of eager costume-clad kids. Thankfully, once they got the kinks ironed out, they were back at the top of the chocolate game. It shows that choosing the wrong system or not having a system in place can be a considerable detriment even to an established and successful company.

The Fix: Get a Structured Sales Approach and Start Using a CRM

Customer relationship management software is essential for any business. It's your all-in-one tool for managing your interactions with current and potential customers to drive sales growth. Essentially, CRM is a big, pro-active database of customer data, reminding you of everything you need to know in order to serve your consumers and grow your business effectively.

When looking at sales to see potentials for growth, you'll hear buzz words. The terms *sales funnel* and *sales pipeline* are often used interchangeably, but it's essential to understand they are entirely different.

A sales pipeline is the process a salesperson uses to brainstorm, organize, manage, and keep an eye on each stage of the sales process with each customer. Every business has its interpretation of the sales pipeline. Still, they basically boil down to the same five steps:

- Target a potential client.
- Prospect their qualifications to make sure your product is a good solution (including the budget).
- Entertain a sales meeting.
- Send a proposal.
- Close the deal.

If in the back of your mind, you heard "coffee is for closers," you already have a good understanding of the last step.

While used by the sales team, sales funnels are typically designed by the marketing team. They are a visual representation of the steps a customer takes from when they are first introduced to your product or company. These funnels are used to illustrate clients' total volume in each of the previous five stages and can be an easy-to-understand tool to show conversion and drop-off. This valuable tool can show any potholes in the pipeline that may be leading to greater drop-offs, and it can also reveal potential new avenues for conversion.

Okay, disclaimer: I have started Simply CRM platform as one of my startups, where our value proposition is to be full-featured, fully configurable, simple to use, and cost effective. But as you have hopefully noticed, this has not been the core story here, so my purpose is not to lure you in as a customer at Simply CRM. I'm not even giving you the web address. I've been building CRMs in different forms most of my startup life—either as Excel sheets (stupid, yes, I know, but that's how many start), custom coding, or today, a full-fledged does-everything-including-coffee platform.

There are several CRM platforms out there, and you should use what works for you. Make sure it is a consistent way to manage your customer data, that they will support you, and that the platform can notify you as required.

Your CRM is designed to support your sales funnel, which is the multi-step process that turns prospective customers into paying customers. Like a real-world funnel, the sales funnel is wide open at the top. While many of the visitors who enter here won't end up being the right fit for your business, the ones who are will come out at the other end of the process as buyers. As the visitor moves from top-funnel (ToFu) to middle-funnel (MoFu) to bottom-funnel (BoFu), they become increasingly valuable to your company.

You need to have activity in all levels of the funnel to ensure that your business will thrive in the near and long term at all times. This means that you need to keep feeding your sales funnel—moving those sales opportunities through the five phases.

Without customer relationship management, there's no way to sustain that ongoing flow into your funnel. You become vulnerable to what I call stop-go sales: fits and starts of intense work punctuated by dry spells that last months or even years. Whichever side of this pendulum you swing to, you'll be stressed—either overworked or fretting—and you'll go bankrupt. This is no way to run a business or live a life.

I firmly believe that CRM is essential for evaluating how your funnel is performing at every phase. So much so that when I couldn't find a simple, adaptable CRM to suit the needs of various companies I was working with, I built my own CRM company to help myself and other entrepreneurs fill that need. While it's technically possible to manage customer relationships on paper, most founders are too busy juggling a million things for that. They need automated analysis, updates, and reminders to help them keep those sales flowing.

A sound system will keep track of which organizations you've approached, who you've talked to at each one, and which services were proposed to them. It will prompt you to follow up in six months or a year and estimate the likelihood of successfully converting a client at any stage of your funnel.

The CRM system should not only keep the sales funnel flowing, it should keep every department of your company on track and on schedule. After all, as IT people are fond of saying, a deadline is missed one day at a time.

Another invaluable function of a CRM is to help you with twinning—finding similar customers to approach.

For example, say you had a great meeting with LEGO. You pitched some ideas, and they liked a few of them but asked you to check back in a year. Once you've recorded this information in your CRM system, it can give you an overview saying something to the effect of: "LEGO was interested in these five sales opportunities. Send them a Christmas card on December 15, then follow up with a call to the HR representative on January 4. Other clients who might like your LEGO pitch are Disney and Epic. Here's who to contact at those companies."

Good CRM systems are not only good at micromanagement, they're able to look at the big picture of your business too. This makes them precious tools for young companies lacking experienced teams. For example, your CRM might remind your newbie sales manager to step back and reevaluate a client relationship that's been undervalued. "Ooh, what's going on here?" the CRM might say (though probably not in those exact words). "You categorized this client as a type-B customer, yet their company spends $200,000 a year on similar services to the ones you proposed. I suggest bumping them up to type-A and having the CEO follow up directly."

The Flawed Product-Market Fit

The simplest business advice is to make a good product that a good market wants. Scratching where it does not itch will only get you a bloody mess.

It can be all too tempting for founders to rush to sell their product to the first interested customer. But keep in mind that not all buyers are created equal. Keying into the right audience for your product is everything, and neglecting to do so practically guarantees failure. Marc Andreesen, the famed venture capitalist, says the product-market fit is one of the top factors he weighs when considering a startup investment. Without a doubt, this is a fundamental failure to watch out for. And you may not be surprised to hear that I know this from personal experience.

One way to commit the Flawed Fit Failure is to target mass-market customers with a high-end product. Another way is to target high-end customers with a reasonably inexpensive offering. That's what my partners and I did with a company we launched in 2014, Boardmeter, a web-based tool for companies to evaluate the efficacy of their boards by tracking and scoring the outcome of board meetings: Were people coming prepared? Were the meetings frequent enough, the right length, focused on the right topics? How did each member of the board perform?

A great example of a flawed fit can be seen with dating app Swipes, a Danish company co-founded by three friends. In interviews, they all laughingly agree they knew nothing about dating. But they did know how to work well together, and they each had a strength that lent itself to creating a beautiful app with an excellent user experience. They took their talents and pivoted their way from the dating sector to personal productivity. While other companies were setting to-do lists, their app focused on goals and achieving results. However, over six years, they could not find a really good product fit to create the demand they needed to stay in the black. Even with almost $1 million in fundraising, they wound up closing up shop. This shows that even if you have a great product, if you can't find your fit with the market, you'll sadly lose out to the competition even if their product isn't as aesthetically pleasing as yours.

The Fix: Reinvent or Retool

There are two ways to go about correcting a Flawed Fit Failure if you're prepared to spend the time and money to do so. Either the product can be remade from the ground up to fit the needs of a new target audience, or it can be enhanced and re-priced to better satisfy the needs and financial considerations of its current, flawed-fit audience.

In the case of Boardmeter, my partners and I could one day start from scratch and create a super-simple product that's better suited to small businesses with small budgets.

Or we could stick with the existing product and add more value with packaged consultancy services for our high-end customers. The price, of course, would rise accordingly.

The reality is that founders tend to get excited about those very first customers and sales and sometimes overlook a customer that isn't a good fit for the product. I know, we've all heard people talk about laughing all the way to the bank, but for startups, selling to a bad-fit customer or flawed-fit customer is ultimately bad for business.

Case in point, a customer that isn't a good fit for your product won't be able to give you the valuable feedback a startup needs in those early days. They won't see the value in your product and will likely waste a great deal of your time needing assistance to make the product fit for them or asking for discounts. Spending a ton on servicing this customer isn't worth the sale. Nor is discounting your product. Besides, these customers will be onetime customers or low-value customers. All expenses going into acquiring them will be a waste because they won't be returning for another purchase, therefore increasing your churn rate. Someone once said that people with a bad experience would tell ten people about it, while people with a good one may only tell one person. These flawed fits are going to hurt your business in ways you can't even see.

Holding out for high-value customers can feel daunting, but these are the customers that will appreciate your product, use it often, expand to other products as you develop them, and keep coming back for more. These customers tend to need less follow-up care in the customer service area. They are great at providing valuable product feedback and insight because they are (almost) as invested in the product as you are! These customers make you and your staff happy to come to work and create more awesomeness.

To make sure your customers are a good fit for your product, I suggest putting them to this simple test:

1. Determine who is your target audience. Don't say "everyone," because everyone is no one's target market. Be clear and identify the people your product will most help.
2. Outline the criteria for your targeted people. Consider things like demographics, beliefs, education, income, opinions, and so on, so you can target your marketing to the right people for you.
3. Know what your customers want from you more than anything else. Putting yourself in the shoes of your ideal clients helps put any potential weaknesses front and center and allows you to see what component of your product most addresses their pain points.
4. Determine where your audience hangs out. If you are going to reach them with your marketing efforts, you need to know where to

market. Sure, Facebook might be a great place to market to online entrepreneurs looking for coaching services, but they would be hard-pressed for freelance gig workers to find clients advertising on the social networking giant.

5. Examine the data. After running a marketing campaign, it's essential to look at the sales and customer data to make sure you not only found your people but that they made a purchase. If you landed on a market that bought nothing, it's time to go back to step one and reevaluate your target audience.

Sales F*ckup #5:

Product Pleasing

Any idiot can get his hands on a half-bad product. It takes a real genius to keep your hands off a half-good one. Create good stuff.

It's not uncommon for young businesses to bend over backward trying to accommodate picky customers on a case-by-case basis. When a customer says to a hungry young founder, "I'll give you $100,000 to tailor your product to my exact specifications," it's understandably tempting for that founder to please the customer, oblige, and take the money. But— unless your core business model is customization—this will cause problems down the road. As a founder, your first priority is always your core product. It's much better to help all of your target customers by building a standard product that can work across the board than to tweak that product on a case-by-case basis.

With several of my companies, I've made the mistake of taking the money and customizing. There was a nice short-term cash influx, sure, but we probably lost three times the amount we earned in the big picture— money that could have been made by perfecting the product we already had to sell it more widely.

But don't just take it from my experience. Take it from Gary Swart, VP of Intellibank, a Dropbox-like platform that launched in 2002 and closed in 2013. Reflecting on his company's failure, Swart summed up the Selling What's Not on Your Shelves Failure beautifully in a postmortem: "At Intellibank, we did not achieve product-market fit. Every customer was asking for something different and we gave it to them. We had six markets with forty different types of customers, and in hindsight, we should have developed just one product. We couldn't be all things to all people—and by failing to declare our major, we created a world of chaos for our sales, product, and marketing teams."

The Fix: Validate the Business You Have

Avoiding this failure starts with an awareness that there is a right and a wrong kind of customer (see the Flawed Fit Failure, page 258). For example, say your startup is a shoe store specializing in imported Italian footwear. In walks a rich person who says, "I want you to customize a pair of shoes for me." Your response might be, "I'd be happy to meet your needs, and I'm sure I can do so with our current selection." This is also the perfect opportunity to sell your subscription service, if you have one, by adding: "You would probably love our subscription service, which sends you a perfectly suited new pair of shoes every month."

When you sell what's on your shelves, you're validating the business that you have. In the process, you get motivated employees and happy clients who know exactly what they're getting. Because that's ultimately what's most important: pleasing the customer. Pleasing investors is nice, of course. But sometimes, in your desperation to do so, you can lose sight of why you created your startup in the first place: to solve your customer's pain point—not your investors', right? As Intellibank's Swart put it perfectly: "Think about the product you're selling and think about where you see it going. Now, take a step back and ask yourself the most important question of all: When your customers are using the product, how will they feel? And what will keep them coming back?"

Building Sales on a Weak Product

Some products go to market without a significant consumer base or purpose. Even with a great sales force, they will fail.

If your product isn't there yet, and you start building sales around it anyway, then that's another way to f*ck up.

Take the case of EventVue, a social network designed to help people have better experiences at real-world conferences. The pain point they aimed to address was that of the frequent conference attendee who traveled to conferences worldwide but didn't know how to interact with fellow attendees before and after the event. I would call this a mosquito-bite problem. A mosquito-bite problem is annoying, but it's not painful, which means it's not a big enough problem to build a company around. A severe problem that customers are desperate to solve is what I call a shark-bite problem. Think headache pills, not vitamin pills, as we've discussed earlier. The fundamental flaw of EventVue was that it picked the wrong problem to solve.

From its launch in 2007, the product didn't catch on. While it worked well in terms of connectivity and interaction, event organizers could take it or leave it. Why pay for a service that didn't reduce their expenses or provide additional revenue?

Even when EventVue failed to live up to their early assumptions, its founders, Josh Fraser and Rob Johnson, didn't pause to reevaluate; instead, they added a useless widget or two and pushed forward with their sales efforts. But the founders were merely adding more wet cement to a foundation that wasn't even dry yet. After three years, the entire house collapsed, and EventVue became another failed startup statistic.

Ah, this section wouldn't be complete without addressing the exploding-batteries Samsung Galaxy Note 7. The phablet (terrible portmanteau of phone and tablet, typically associated with Galaxy Note) was announced in early August 2016, with pre-release sales soaring. By the time it was released two weeks later, it had broken pre-release sales records in parts of the world and stunted distribution to others. Less than a month later, Samsung suspended sales and issued a recall on the device, saying a manufacturing defect in the batteries caused the devices to overheat and catch fire. They replaced the batteries with ones from a new supplier. However, the replacement phablets also caught fire. A worldwide recall was issued, and they stopped production of the device permanently. They lost over $14.7 billion in revenue, and the blow to their brand reputation cost them even more.

Sadly, once they determined the batteries were problematic, they should have halted sales and gone back to the research and development stage rather than re-releasing the products with a simple battery replacement. Despite two different suppliers, the battery component of this device was ultimately the point of failure.

The Fix: Don't Jump the Gun

You created a product that basic testing says is passable enough, so you want to grab some of that pre-sale money you believe is headed your way. Differing from our "F*ck It, Ship It" fix, this failure is one based more on impatience and arrogance than anything else. If founders fear they're going to run out of money before the product goes out for sale, it can be tempting to try to release an early version of the product even if it's not ready. But doing so, in the long run, you hurt not only your reputation as a business but also the reputation of the product you're trying to bring to market.

Besides, when you start selling an incomplete product, there's a greater likelihood that, due to lower volume as a new product in a new company, you'll fall victim to other already-discussed failures. The Messed-Up MVP and A Poor Business Plan failures are two. Any time you customize your product for each customer just to make a sale, it's evident that you don't have a core product. Without a core product, you can't create a repeatable sales model, and lastly, you run the greater risk of a single point of failure situation.

It may feel a bit like I'm playing a broken record here. Still, test until you are sure your product is market-ready, don't sell what you don't have on the shelf ready to go, and value your quality over quantity (at the beginning, at least) to build your reputation from those early sales. So many clichés could be lobbied at this failure point, truly.

Bottom line: have your timeline for release as accurate as possible, and don't put an exploding product on the market, then double down on it to cover your losses like Samsung.

Pricing Predicaments

Pricing and value go hand in hand. Pricing mistakes come at a cost. You'll either eat into your reputation or your profits.

Ah, the crux of sales failures hinges on one point we haven't yet addressed: your actual pricing strategy. We've already seen a couple of examples where the ultimate failure was something other than pricing, but I'd be remiss if I didn't point out Juicero once more with their outrageously priced machine and packets. Going to the local juicer down on the corner was considerably more cost-conscious to any consumer.

Let's take a look at another pricing failure that led to a major US retailer's downturn back in 2012. Selling everything from clothing to housewares to furniture, JCPenney was a household name akin to Kohl's, Sears, and Macy's. Back when Target and Walmart began to have stores popping up everywhere, offering many of the same products without needing to go to an actual mall, the retailer decided to run an experiment. They stopped running ads, offering coupons, and got rid of all deals. Their pricing slogan went something like, "JCPenney, everyday low pricing."

In a momentous attempt to rewire decades of deal-loving behaviors in their clients, they offered the lowest prices possible on all items. Mind you, these were the prices a buyer would get when using a coupon or shopping a sale, but this was now the new item price all the time, every day. Unfortunately, their customers were not ready to give up decades' worth of price conditioning that sent them into the store to urgently save 15 percent if they shopped on a particular weekend with a store coupon. After a year, they gave up on this experiment and returned to their old pricing structure.

There are, of course, retailers who never offer sales and do just fine. What makes them different? Take Apple, for instance. How often do you see an ad to get an iMac or MacBook on sale? As an Apple user, I can say, "rarely, very rarely." But they sell well, right? Yes. But they also set a precedent long ago, at inception, that you were paying for quality, and whatever the tag said was the fair price for the quality you received. And knowing that the price is unlikely to change until they launch the next product iteration means that there is no rational reason for me to delay the purchase a few months.

The Fix: Create a Pricing Strategy Aimed at Profit

Sounds simple, right? It really is. There are a few ways to create a pricing strategy that will set you up for success.

- Understand your market and what motivates your customers. This information will help you determine your customer's threshold for paying for your product. If they already are used to coupons and discounts, build them into your pricing structure. If they are used to paying a set price for high-end items, you know what to do.

- Know whether your industry and market use cost-plus pricing (this has an added margin to your breakeven cost and is typically a percentage of that breakeven cost) or value-based pricing (this pricing is strictly set by the threshold of your market and not by the actual cost to produce an item). This should be determined before setting your strategy in motion.

- Know your actual costs. Take the costs of developing the product or service, your variable costs (materials, packaging, etc.), fixed costs (salaries, rent, etc.), and any other costs your product needs to cover, then take this sum and divide it by the volume to learn your breakeven cost for the product.

- Consider whether you will offer payment options, potentially have late payments, or any other factors that might affect your profit structure.

- Stay alert. Markets fluctuate all the time and therefore so does pricing. Staying current on trends will make sure you are keeping your prices acceptable to your market's expectations.

Over-Promise, Under-Deliver

Making promises and delivering on them is a great way to build a startup. Over-promising or under-delivering are the fastest ways to ruin one.

Commonly in new businesses, founders tend to over-promise on their deliverables to get people excited and gain their buy-in. But what happens when you can't deliver?

You guessed it: people get pissed. In 2015, The Grid, a startup promising to change the web development market completely, raided $5 million in funding from investors on the promise that their solution used AI (artificial intelligence, not Air India, although they might have had more success) to create custom websites on what was uploaded. Pictures, videos, text, nothing was too much of a challenge for the supposed AI developer.

Great at promotion and promise, but lacking in follow-through, The Grid came under harsh scrutiny when the product was buggy, produced barely stylized websites, and took too long to render upon loading. And as for that AI component they had raved about, yeah, it was essentially a WordPress integrated with social media and e-commerce, then auto-resized for different screen sizes. Their underwhelming performance left users and investors pretty upset and posed many questions related to the founders' ethics. Not the kind of impression a new founder wants to make.

When it comes to over-promising and under-delivering, the case of Fyre Media needs to be included. As discussed earlier, Fyre Media, founded by Billy McFarland, was set to be an app where anyone who had the funds could book a celebrity, music act, or model for an event they were hosting. Partnered with rapper Ja Rule, the initial scope of the project seemed reasonable: connect people "in the industry" with people looking to hire professionals for events. The concept was well thought out, the app looked good, so investors backed the company. All seemed to be looking good for the company until they decided to host the most exclusive "launch party" ever seen in the startup world. With tickets selling at anything from $500–$12,000, people were promised an exclusive event on a private island in the Bahamas, entertainment from some of the artists available for booking on their app, private jet transportation to the event, luxury accommodations, and top-rate celebrity chefs.

What ensued was nothing of the sort. Some people were left waiting at the airport for planes that never arrived, those who did make it to the festival were greeted with a tent city of accommodations, cold cheese sandwiches, and headliners who dropped out days before the event and were too polite to bash the company on social when they realized things were not on the up-and-up. Needless to say, as the date of the first of two festival weekends approached, funding fell through, and McFarland defaulted on a $3 million loan. In an effort to still make the event happen, he cut corners, stiffed vendors, and overall left everyone in the lurch. McFarland was later brought up on fraud charges, was sentenced to six years in prison, and was ordered to repay investors and customers more than $26 million in restitution.

It's worth mentioning the Paige Compositor as well in the over-promise, under-deliver category. Developed by James Paige, it was supposed to replace human typesetters with a mechanical arm. Unfortunately, it needed constant human intervention and adjustments, making it inefficient. Lest we forget to mention, it also wound up costing three times more than the initial estimates to produce. Mark Twain overinvested in this machine and lost a fortune. Some people credit this product as the catalyst for the author's fall into depression and financial decline.

The Fix: Under-promise and Over-deliver

Getting people and investors excited about your product is a good thing. Just check your ethics and values when you start making promises. Any time you under-deliver on a core promise, you run the risk of alienating your customers and investors, and losing the faith your staff has in the business.

Drum up the excitement, by all means, but keep the expectations reasonable and possible to exceed. People much prefer when you can over-deliver on your claims than the sour taste of deceit. To set the proper expectations, you need to know your data. Understanding your industry is key. Suppose you are creating a physical product that needs to be shipped to the customer. In that case, it's essential to understand the expectations of the product's market and the shipping market that will deliver your product.

The more you can educate yourself on any potential hazards, the more prepared you can be, and the more reasonable the expectations you set. Customers who see that you consistently set realistic expectations and deliver on your promises will keep coming back time and time again. They will choose you over the competition to get that dependability.

Do yourself a favor and research to make sure you wind up on the right side of this all-too-often-seen failure.

Rejecting Revenue

While revenue from day one is unlikely, ignoring it while focusing on building a potentially fantastic product can be lethal. Profitability is a startup's ultimate goal.

It sounds unbelievable, but there are countless examples of founders thinking that their businesses can somehow survive without revenue. They imagine that revenue will magically appear at some later point in time, even if there are no signs of it now. One such company was Alt-School, an edtech (education technology) startup founded by a former Google executive, Max Ventilla.

Ventilla's idea was to disrupt the status quo school system through a private network of schools with a personalized learning approach that would let students work at their own pace. When it came to fundraising, Ventilla was a superb evangelist for his vision. And with $174 million in funding from Silicon Valley billionaires like Mark Zuckerberg, Priscilla Chan, and Peter Thiel, Ventilla left Google to launch AltSchool in 2013.

AltSchool would be centered around a software platform and would require around $30 million per year to run. The price for students to join AltSchool was $150 a year, which sounded fair on paper but soon proved to be prohibitively more than families wanted to pay for an online learning platform, given that others were available at a fraction of the price—or even for free.

Even as early sales proved disappointing, Ventilla unapologetically pressed on with expensive improvements to the platform. "Our whole strategy," as he put it back in 2019, "is to spend more than we make." Yep. His reasoning? Ventilla simply had a good feeling that the losses he was incurring in the present would be turned into, as he said, "steep profits, once AltSchool redefines the products and lands enough customers."

And get this: Ventilla didn't just expect that magic would result from his flagrant spending. He even went so far as to admit: "We're measuring our business on our burn rates."

Granted, those were the good old dot-com days, when the burn rate was an actual KPI that you would measure. The prevailing mentality was if you're not burning enough, then you're not building business. Needless to say, it was a terrible way to do business.

It was only after burning through many millions of his investors' money and discovering that his price point was too high that Ventilla began to seriously consider how to bring in the revenue he needed to survive. What he realized, of course, was that he had a sales problem. He hadn't prioritized sales by investing in a first-rate sales team. He'd been too busy building his empire to put sales on the agenda.

Just to be clear, I'm not saying that you need to be in the black your first year, because most startups can't do that. But if you're not focusing as much on sales as you are on building your world-changing product, then you're not validating your business case. The road to success starts with survival.

Jeff Orr, a product designer, joined together with two friends to create Gulp, an app to pay bar cover charges by credit card. Students by day, entrepreneurs the rest of the time, the threesome saw the problem of having to stop by an ATM for cash to pay the $5–$10 bar covers as an inconvenience the town's thirty thousand students could do without. They added a convenience fee of ninety-nine cents to each cover but lost about forty-seven cents on each transaction due to the credit card companies. With little know-how on ad placement in the app, their marginal earnings weren't enough to cover operating costs. Jeff and his team also learned that while "If you build it, they will come" might sound cool, it's clearly exaggerated. While Gulp didn't last, the lessons learned set the three founders off on new (and better) adventures.

The Fix: Money Makes the World Go 'Round

Every startup needs a revenue model—you know, that plan that outlines all the ways you will bring profits into the business. Once this model is created, it should be regularly evaluated and revised to meet your business's actualities as the product goes to market. It's also the touchstone you will use to determine whether you have your marketing strategy on target, if your sales are where you need to keep the lights on for another month, or if you need to pivot your product placement or ideal client profile.

There are many resources available to help you build your revenue model, but I like to keep it simple (precisely like my business plans).

These steps will help you create the revenue plan you need to identify, track accurately, and evaluate your revenue plan data:

- Choose the revenue model that fits your company. Perhaps you should start with a revenue projection template, then decide if it should be linear or exponential.
- Show what makes you valuable to your customers. For example, do you offer a subscription model or a unique service? What do your customers think is valuable about your business or product?
- Are there potential investors based on your revenue model? If so, identify them here.
- Project your foreseeable future. I usually recommend twelve months out as more easily projectable than, say, three years.
- Your revenue model will be flexible. If you pivot focus, it will change. If the world suffers an economic shutdown, it will change. Be open to the changes.
- Identify any key variables that will affect your revenue. Think back to the earlier Hershey situation with new software that could not process orders installed at their busiest revenue time of year.
- Plan to mitigate those variables. If-Then statements work great here. You don't need a whole action plan, but some simple way of acknowledging the potential foreseeable variables and what you see as a fix for it goes a long way to being prepared.

Indeed, this document will serve you well when properly compiled. You'll find it easier to identify trends, predict the future (aka forecast), and be prepared when that storm of cats and dogs comes raining down from the sky one day.

Final Thoughts on Sales Failures

We've spent quite a bit of time talking about great deals and how to deliver the optimal experience to your customers for a value the market expects while having a profit plan. I'm going to let you in on a little secret: if your business makes it to this stage and avoids the failures listed, you stand a good chance of making it. You stand a better chance than the people who aren't using CRM tools and sales funnels properly or are over-promising on a weak product.

With this level of understanding and success at your feet, the next logical step for your business is to grow. So let's jog onward to the next chapter and see what awaits us in the way of growth failures. You may be surprised by just how epic these failures can be.

Chapter 8

Growth F*ckups

Congratulations! You've secured your funding, elevated your team-building, and solidified your sales operations. Now it's time to run your business. Markets and customers aside, your success at running and growing your company will mainly come down to how you handle yourself—day in and day out. To be successful, a founder must have confidence, sure. But more importantly, they must also be introspective, willing to ask over and over again: "Is this the right decision? How will I get through this really shitty day without blowing up at someone on my team? Am I focusing on the right tasks? Staying true to my mission?" Also: "How's my mental health?"

Returning once again to my running analogy, your startup's growth phase is a marathon, not a sprint. And as any runner knows, marathons are, above all, a mental game.

I learned a profound lesson about the importance of mental stamina when I ran my first Ironman Triathlon. It is a grueling race consisting of a 2.4-mile swim, a 112-mile bicycle ride, and a marathon 26-mile run. After more than a year of intense training, I admittedly still doubted whether I had what it took to complete one of the most challenging single-day sporting competitions in the world. It didn't help my mindset knowing that a triathlete died of a heart attack the year prior. It wasn't just my physical stamina I worried about. I worried about mental fatigue—being able to keep my head in the game long enough to finish.

On the morning of the race, I wrote this on the back of my hand with a felt-tip pen:

"Don't give up."

And under that, I wrote:

"Don't die."

It sounds stupid, but I can't tell you how many times, over the next almost twelve hours, I looked down at that message on my hand. I can tell you that whenever my brain started looking for possible excuses to stop, I'd read those words. And then I'd keep pedaling, or I'd take another stroke, or I'd run another step. And then another. And then another.

That silly little note kept me going.

As I forged on, I occasionally passed people who'd given up, dropped to the ground in sheer exhaustion. But mostly, I passed people who'd slowed down to give themselves a break. These people weren't quitting. They were recalibrating, just as a founder must regularly do. At the end of the day, I was exhausted, but pleased. I'd survived. I'd overcome all the obstacles in my way. One more minefield in my life was behind me and I'd stuck to my Rule Zero and worked hard to find success. It's the same method I apply in business.

Growth F*ckup #1:

Poor Pivoting

If Plan A doesn't work, the alphabet has plenty more letters. Just keep the alphabetical order, and remember that P, as in Pivoting, comes in at 16th place.

Other than *disrupt,* *pivot* might be the most overused word in the startup world. Pivoting, or drastically shifting the direction of your company, might also be the most overrated tactic. And also underutilized. Poor Pivoting is a double-edged sword that can harm you in multiple ways: pivoting typically for young startups is far from a golden ticket to success. In the majority of situations, in fact, to pivot is to f*ck up. But not pivoting (typically seen with more mature companies) can be equally bad.

Take Wanful, an online gift-giving service that launched in 2011. Answering a few simple questions would suggest gift ideas to a user for their friend, family member, co-worker, and so on. This customized gift-shopping experience sent their growth rate soaring until they decided to pivot into a more generalized e-commerce shop. Unable to compete with other giants already in the market and having now lost their personalized approach, the company closed in 2013.

Let's not forget Toys "R" Us. For years, they were the go-to toy store in the US. But when online sales became more of a household staple, they brokered a ten-year exclusive partnership with Amazon. When sales shot through the roof, Amazon began allowing other vendors to sell toys on their platform. It was too late for Toys "R" Us to compete with the pricing other online retailers offered. They filed for bankruptcy in 2017.

Another large business destroyed due to *lack* of pivoting is Blockbuster. When Netflix came into the market space in 2000 and offered online movie rentals, Blockbuster's CEO dismissed them. Now, many years later, we all know what happened. Netflix was adaptable to the market and demand for online streaming content, while Blockbuster held out for its brick-and-mortar approach. We all have seen the Blockbuster memes and jokes. They couldn't pivot to keep up with their too-easily-dismissed competition.

The Fix: Spin Slowly

I'm not saying that you shouldn't pivot if you have legitimate reasons to do so. For example, maybe your product is a three-legged chair, and your product testing tells you that people don't trust or want to sit in three-legged chairs, no matter how sturdy. Then you might want to do a small pivot, try a chair with four legs. Okay, fair enough. You're basing this pivot on solid market research, sticking to your core competencies, and targeting the same audience. That's a good start.

Just remember that building a company takes *years*. So give yours the time that it requires. This starts with the planning phase—specifically with creating a realistic timeline for development and an adequate sales budget. For example, say you're making a SaaS (Software as a Service). Typically, it takes two to four years for a startup to begin operating in the black, but longer for a SaaS-type business. Now, say you're some years in, revenue is still profoundly red, and you want to pivot. The first thing I'd advise you to do would be to go back in this book to chapter 3 and brush up on market research failures. Did you complete your MVP successfully? Are you focusing on your key value proposition?

Ultimately, you can't just ignore everything that you've done until now and then one day say, "I'm done with making X. I want to make Y." You need to follow the same process as you hopefully did with your original product: do your market research, test your prototype, consult with your advisors and board members, and so on. To pivot may sound like a quick act, but it should be done with great deliberation.

Here are a few things to consider before pivoting:

- Encourage employee ideas. Allow them to build products on the side and offer up new ideas. This can lead to significant breakthroughs.
- Build a basic prototype or MVP *before* pivoting. This way, you can test it and determine if it answers the problem you're facing or if there might be another, better option to consider.
- Keep communication open. Marketing, development, sales, investors, everybody should be communicating regularly about the product, state of affairs, and problems.

Pivoting can be the difference between staying relevant and becoming obsolete. Take Yelp as an example. Users pushed them to pivot from an email system for requesting recommendations to one where they could post reviews. Thankfully, they listened to their customers and pivoted within a year of launching. Users have written over 115 million reviews. I cannot only find a good recommendation for a plumber but also know which eateries to avoid.

YouTube is another pivoting success. Launched initially as a video dating site with the slogan "Tune in. Hook up," the founders realized no one wanted to watch dating profile videos. A year later, they opened it up to any video content. One of the co-founders posted their first video titled "Me at the zoo" and featured himself and elephants at the zoo. It was a hit with users. They now have almost one billion users.

PayPal is another positive pivot. In the late 1990s, PayPal was established by Max Levchin, Peter Thiel, and Luke Nosek as Confinity, and was used to send money to people via a PalmPilot. Confinity eventually merged with Elon Musk's X.com, shifted gears, changed its name to PayPal, and began handling online sales transactions for eBay, who acquired them. Now their service is almost everywhere, online and in apps for payment options. Currently, they have 179 million active accounts.

Tote was a way to shop online and save items to be notified when they went on sale. When they realized people were just curating and preserving the images to share in collections, they shifted gears. Welcome to the world, Pinterest.

So if doubt creeps in when it feels like you might need to pivot, turn to those who've gone before you and found success.

Wrong-Work Distractions

Founders have a lot of things vying for their attention. Not knowing where to focus time and energy and how to differentiate distractions from necessities is deadly.

Ah, Delicious definitely belongs to wrong-work distractions. Initially a social bookmarking platform, the company was bought by AVOS, the company owned by YouTube founders Chad Hurley and Steven Chen. As the relaunch date loomed, users were advised to complete a transfer process believed to keep all the bookmarks tagged and organized as the original version of the platform allowed. However, it quickly became apparent upon relaunch that something was rotten. People who completed the transfer process lost data, bookmark tagging methodologies that users loved were gone, and for the users who didn't do the transfer, their accounts were gone.

At the core, it appeared to end-users that they had been duped. In reality, it was more likely that AVOS didn't understand how people were using the platform or the API. Messing with an already live product presents a unique set of challenges they weren't prepared to manage. The legacy Delicious had built was long gone by the time they finished their redesign, so in essence, they bought a brand name and user base but didn't bother to focus on how the users who interacted with the platform get value from it.

The Fix: Provide Instant Gratification

There are a few identified distractions that often indicate a failure is right around the corner. If you see that you have one or more of these distracting you from your startup's actual business, it's essential to make a change before you find yourself in an avoidable failure.

- Clingy clients. We spoke about the quality of your customers. If you have mostly clingy, needy clients who waste a ton of your time but present little return, you could be in trouble. Always aim for high-value clients even when the low-hanging fruit is tempting.
- Lost in learning land. Founders need to dedicate time each week to learn about their market, trends, business, and so on, but if

you spend all your time with your nose in a proverbial book and no time acting on what you're learning, you're setting yourself up for failure. This is another form of analysis paralysis. Don't let learning keep you from accomplishing it.

- Neurotic logo and web design. Remember when I told you about my logo hang-ups for Shockwaved? And how we never created business cards? If you are hung up on creating the perfect website and logo, you aren't focused on the product. Using minor details as a distraction from the product can and will hurt your business. Product is a priority.
- Meaningless meetings. We've all seen the memes. You know the ones I'm talking about. The ones where there's a meeting to discuss another meeting or when there's a meeting to say what could've been done in an email. Sure, sometimes you need to meet to work through issues, but you lose money every time you take people away from doing their jobs. Remember, I try to justify how a meeting can net me the salary paid while hosting it. It keeps the people count to the minimum necessary as well as the time spent.

I'm going to be as blunt as possible here. Only focus on the jobs and responsibilities that matter. While it's great to want to adopt a way of managing like Steve Jobs, you aren't him. Concentrate on what *you* need to do to manage your team and get your company going. The better you get at ignoring distractions, the better your company will be.

Bad Decisions

Decisions are hard, and rank high on the list of reasons for failed startups. Even a correct decision is wrong when made at the wrong time.

If you've read this far, you're undoubtedly well aware that bad decisions come in all shapes and sizes. You've probably also noted that most startup failures come down to a founder's poor choices.

Salorix, a now-bankrupt ad agency that offered an online networking platform for brands, illustrates one such case. In 2000 in Bangalore, India, the company had $3.5 million in funding and a cutting-edge feature called MFI. This AI-based service would listen in on ongoing social discussions and rank them to distinguish the most relevant to the client's brand.

By 2009, the much-buzzed-about Salorix was fielding regular acquisition offers. Google tried to buy the company in 2012 and again in 2013.

This was a tremendous business opportunity for Salorix, and Google's offer was more than fair. But it's widely thought that the company's founder, Santanu Bhattacharya, quibbled with the price to the point that he killed the deal. Furious with Bhattacharya for screwing up an opportunity they'd seen as golden, Salorix's investors stopped funding the company, eventually forcing it into the ground.

You know the adage about there being no stupid questions, only stupid answers? That's pretty much what happens in the startup world to equate to Bad Decisions.

The case of Everpix illustrates my point. In 2009, founder Pierre-Olivier Latour traveled throughout Asia and became frustrated with the limited ability to sort and store his digital pictures. Upon returning home, he teamed up with a friend and built Everpix, a product that sorted your photos, stored them online, and utilized an algorithm to highlight the best shots taken at any time. By 2012, they had 55,000 users and financing.

The app itself was brilliant. Easy to use, clean design, and a ton of user-friendly features, but it was missing one thing. The duo behind the app weren't salespeople. They focused so much on creating a perfect product with a fantastic experience, but they did nothing to sell the product. It wasn't in their scope, and they never brought someone on to do it for them. They expected (insert my sigh here) their super excellent app to be cool enough to sell itself. I think we all know what happened. Within a year, they were broke.

The Fix: Mental Models for Better Decision-Making

Over the years, I've found it greatly helps to keep a storehouse of what I call mental models to draw upon when I'm at a professional crossroads. Biases. Heuristics. Same thing. All of the following models have been useful at various times when I've needed to make a clearheaded business decision or to sell others on my company's offerings.

Loss Aversion

Loss aversion can affect any business when the thought of losing in one area of the business overshadows the potential gains that could be made elsewhere. Unlike being scared of taking a risk, loss aversion plays a psychological role in decision-making when it stops forward movement at any stage to avoid losing either real or perceived ground financially.

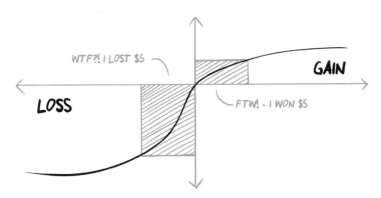

When you're making business decisions, you might think that you've arrived at a conclusion due to common sense or data that you've collected over some time. But the truth is a bit more complicated than that. There are unseen forces at work that influence your decisions as much or more than any research you may have done. One of those forces is loss aversion.

A famous theory in behavioral economics posits that humans have a stronger tendency to prefer avoiding loss over acquiring gains. To put a finer point on it, if someone hands you $5, you may receive a satisfaction boost of 50 percent. But if you lose $5, the negative consequences will be much greater than any happiness you received from finding the money in the first place. And this, in return, affects people's decision-making. As long as you're aware that loss aversion could be a factor in your decision-making, you can avoid acting out of fear and instead allow yourself to take calculated risks, strive for what you want, and dream big.

Availability Heuristics

This concept's idea is simple and something most of us employ daily: that whatever we're hearing about, thinking about, or seeing in the news must be important, prevalent, and widespread.

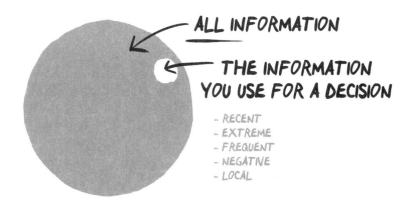

Availability heuristics is the mistaken belief that whatever happens to be at the top of our minds is more relevant or common than the things we're not hearing about. Remember "Summer of the Shark"? In the summer of

2001, shark bites were being reported in the news daily for no apparent reason. Although shark attacks had not become more prevalent—bites were on the decline from previous summers—the widespread discussion and media reports about the phenomenon led people to believe that they were at greater risk of being attacked by a shark if they swam in the ocean. There were more "available" stories about shark bites, so people believed they were more common—when, in fact, they continued to be rare.

Why is this an important, even helpful, mental model for business owners? Because sometimes we are offered so much information, making a decision can feel overwhelming. Availability heuristics allows us to grab the available information and make a decision, for better or worse. Let me give you an example using yours truly.

When I was the CEO of TBWA Denmark, I remember sitting down with our creative director Paul "Clem" Clements (a creative prodigy whom I've carefully dragged with me since the Shockwaved days) and a substantial client whose business we were trying to win. We came up with a PowerPoint presentation offering ten objective points of value by which the client could evaluate our agency. One was about our financial stability, another was about budget, another was about our creative output, and so on. I chose which data points I wanted to bring into the light— or make "available" to them—by which they could make their decision. Naturally, I only chose data points that showed our agency better than that of the competition. Once everyone got settled, I suggested they write down the other companies' names that were pitching to them and make a little checkmark next to the name they preferred to work with when comparing this specific set of data. If I was lucky, by the end of the day, they'd crossed all of the other companies off their list.

Anchoring

Anchoring creates an arbitrary bias that, once established, becomes the focal point—or anchor—of all discussions. Any prices set or decisions that are made are made in relation to the value of the anchor, even though the value is, once again, an arbitrary one.

In Copenhagen, there's a district known for its bars. Okay, several districts actually, as we're the country in the Nordic region with the highest per capita alcohol consumption. Anyhow, when you enter one of these bars, you're offered a choice of three different sizes of beers: one is labeled "very small," one is considered normal, and one is large. The truth is that the "very small" beer is the size of a regular bottle. But no one is going to order that beer, whether you're ordering for a colleague, a girlfriend/ boyfriend/spouse, or buying a round for friends, because that would be embarrassing. So most people go for the "normal-sized" beer as a minimum, which is helpful for sales. That's the anchor, an arbitrary value that has been set for the customer. The same thing happens if a store sets a limit on the number of items a customer can purchase. Consider what happens when you enter a store and see a sign that reads: "Only two items per customer." What are you likely to do? Buy two items, even if you only intended to buy one. That's anchoring. The customer is no longer entirely in charge of his or her buying decisions.

There are more subtle forms of anchoring, as well. Say you approach a salesperson in a vintage clothing store and ask about an unmarked item you're coveting. They won't tell you that it's $500; they'll say it's $493, a number that doesn't sound made up on the spot. This item comes at a very precise price. You might be able to bargain it down by a few dollars. But if they set the price at $500, you're more likely to ask for $100 off, not $10 off. Make sense?

Confirmation Bias

Confirmation bias means that we tend to search for knowledge, facts, and information that support our existing beliefs. If I believe in climate change, I'll look for facts, news reports, and anecdotes that offer proof that temperatures are rising, the ice caps are melting, and the rain forest is disappearing. I will not change my existing beliefs; I'm merely looking for data that will confirm those beliefs.

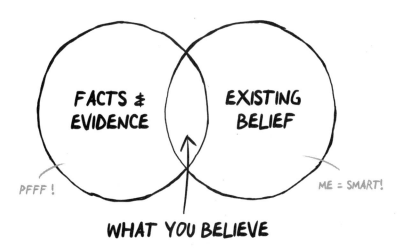

When making decisions, it's essential to be aware of confirmation bias because it won't make you smarter or make your decisions better to confirm what you already believe. In fact, I even have a friend who always looks for the opposite of what he believes in because, as he puts it, "This is not a man-made problem."

Survivorship Bias

Forgive the sense of déjà vu you might feel when you see survivorship bias listed a second time in the book. I hope we can all agree that ignoring it here would be a detriment to the fix for poor decision-making. So not only is it important to consider when looking at potential f*ckups in general but also when studying decision-making setbacks. Keep in mind, survivorship bias is the flip side of confirmation bias. Every day, we are bombarded with articles about the "12 Things Incredibly Successful People Do Every Day," or "The Best Workouts from the World's Top 10 Trainers." These articles might be true for their subjects: maybe this is how LeBron James trains in his off-season, or how Richard Branson turned his company into an empire. We tend to look at the winners, hoping to learn their secrets, instead of looking at the people who failed to do the same thing. And that's what survivorship bias is: focusing on the winners while ignoring the losers. Many people have used the same strategy as Warren Buffett without becoming successful for a variety of reasons.

It's the premise of this book that we mistakenly overvalue the tactics of the people who survived. It's true about business, and it's true about life: we want to hear about the people who are doing well, not the failures. But I believe the opposite is true: it's the failure stories that will save us in the end.

Over-complicating Operations

Complexity is often in direct opposition to growth. If you find a problem, just fix it—don't appoint a committee on problems.

When I was finishing my MBA and starting my first business, Shock-waved, I bought a big fat book by Robert N. Anthony and Vijay Govin-darajan called *Management Control Systems*, which, running comfortably over eight hundred pages, was chock-full of formulas and strategies for running a business. And I'm admittedly still a fanboy. One management tool that particularly intrigued me was the Balanced Scorecard, which allowed large companies to improve their strategy performance by keeping track of how various staff execute various activities and monitor these. Though I only had fifteen employees, I thought this was a supercool idea, and I decided to try it out. Instead of spending my time focusing on my budget, sales funnel, and KPIs, I set out to quantify my company's "strategic objectives," "financial dimensions," "customer dimensions," and more with my Balanced Scorecard. Truly a misuse of my time, making me a sucker for a fancy and new (at the time) tool rather than focusing on the tasks at hand.

Learning the ins and outs of the Balanced Scorecard was some undertaking. I spent countless hours educating myself and my employees—all young creative types who mostly just wanted to draw logos—on how to use it. Though I didn't realize it at the time, my obsession with mastering the Balanced Scorecard was confusing to my colleagues. Why was I trying to get them to learn about something utterly irrelevant to their expertise? In my eyes, it seemed imminently worthwhile for us to understand how long our various tasks took us to complete to give our clients more realistic budgets. Another purported benefit of the scorecard was that it would help me facilitate the automation of many processes that I found arduous and time-consuming if correctly filled out. How could it not be worthwhile, in the long run, to spend countless hours hounding my employees to account for how they spent every minute of their days?

Maybe you can see where this is going: my efforts to make things run more smoothly with the Balanced Scorecard did just the opposite. The problem, of course, was not the Balanced Scorecard. The main problem was that I was trying to shoehorn a process built to be used in a corporate setting into my small startup. I was overcomplicating things, alienating my colleagues, and wasting everyone's time introducing fifty different measures that didn't need to be measured. Keep your operations ~~simple, simple,~~ simple.

The Fix: From Super-Complicated to Supercell

Later we'll briefly visit Rovio, the Finnish company that launched the smash-hit *Angry Birds*. One of their arch competitors is another Finnish gaming studio, Supercell. Valued at around $1.6 billion today, Supercell, the maker of games like *Brawl Stars*, *Clash of Clans*, and *Clash Royale*, was once hamstrung by the Overcomplicating Operations Failure. Supercell's CEO, Ilkka Paananen, had admitted to wasting countless hours on building management structures before he finally stepped back and took an approach more conducive to his company's creative nature.

Once an admitted top-down micromanager, Paananen had a well-known problem with keeping good talent on board. Then he had the epiphany that his company could be more productive if it took a cue from its name and organized itself into different cells. Each cell was allowed to work freely and independently. Management's role wasn't to control and micromanage. It was to support these cells. Once given their independence and the simple mandate to create cool games, Supercell's independent teams flourished. Their hours weren't being counted, and their output wasn't being micro-measured, but all the same, the teams worked long hours and got more done than ever. Morale lifted. And when a product didn't meet the team's expectations, they looked to themselves to find the solution, instead of complaining that their boss had hamstrung them from the beginning and giving up.

Growing Too Fast

Growing pains are a real thing in the rollercoaster of startups. Too fast, too furious will have you crashing and burning in no time.

A delicious example of a small company that grew too fast: Crumbs Bake Shop, a cupcake retailer that expanded aggressively in the early aughts, then crashed hard when the cupcake craze died down. Opening their first shop in NYC in 2003, they rode the sugar rush, growing to over seventy stores across ten states in less than ten years. Unfortunately, even Wall Street could see the icing on the cake for the company that expanded beyond its wrapper. Until 2010, the company was widely successful and profitable thanks to a boom in the cupcake pastry industry. In 2011, they went public. This prompted an aggressive expansion plan into new, expensive markets with high-end locations. But as they expanded, each new store and market began sucking their accounts dry. By 2014, they no longer met the NASDAQ requirements for a public company and were filing for bankruptcy.

Most notably, when we talk about companies that grew too fast, Zynga comes to mind. Founded in 2007, Zynga is an online gaming platform that launched its best-known game, *FarmVille*, in 2009. At the time, Zynga offered its games on Facebook. (Do you already see a warning sign? If you say "SPOF," I agree.) Within six weeks, the game had ten million daily users, and within six months, the game had more than eighty million players (that's a lot of people farming digital corn). During this time, they were creating and releasing other games, which meant they needed more developers. To get new talent, they opted to hire mainly recent grads willing to work for lower salaries who were hungry to learn and dedicated to the team. These initial hires were promoted before they had matured into leaders, causing the new hires behind them to miss out on sound leadership, training, and onboarding. At each level of the organization, burnout was the norm. By 2011, the company had two thousand employees. Teams were still stretched thin and short-staffed, so they grew again with another one thousand employees and built their own data centers rather than continuing to use Amazon Cloud services. By 2015, the company could not maintain the costly expenses of the data centers. CEO Mark Pincus admitted the leap to running their own data centers was not a good strategic scaling option. Unfortunately, this rush to grow before they were ready resulted in the closure of the data centers and a workforce reduction of nearly 18 percent. By the end of 2015, the final staffing numbers for the company were only 1,600 employees down from their all-time high of 3,600. What did the company learn from this? Growth should be strategic while innovation should be free flowing. Once the company began to return their focus to innovation and creative pursuits, they began to regain their foothold in the online gaming market.

The Fix: Make Haste Slowly

When it comes to growth, the phrase *festina lente* always comes to mind. The phrase was initially recorded in Greek, but this Latin translation is the most known: "Make haste slowly." "Hurry up and wait" also might make sense in this case. No matter what, focus on natural growth, be thinking about expansion and development, but wait for it to happen naturally. Don't rush.

Kemar Newell's company, Flip, has all the hallmarks of a company making haste slowly. He's spent time understanding his market, his customers, and the product. With sneakers being a hot item, his platform offers people a place to sell in-demand shoes in less than ninety minutes, or Flip will buy them. With these principles in mind, he's making it work:

- No holding inventory.
- Offer the best product possible.
- Cash is king. Make it last.

But most of all, he works hard. Like many other successful entrepreneurs, he isn't scaling fast. In the meantime, he's putting in the extra time and effort to make sure the business can tolerate any new expansions or employees.

For founders, the idea of growth is exciting and rightfully so. It validates the idea that once only lived in your head and shows, so far, at least, you haven't had any significant failures divert your path. But much like parents tell their kids who want to stay up past midnight on a school night, you have time for that when you're older. Don't rush it. There will be a time when you'll be up working past midnight three or four times a week and wish you could go to bed early. But how do you know at what rate you should grow your startup?

I always suggest remembering your core values and focus. Offer an excellent product to an eager market and make sure your customers are the focus of your mission statement.

While growing, often founders lose sight of the "customer first" mentality. Instead, they focus on the business, the product, the financials, the marketing, everything besides the customers. In doing so, it's easy to miss warning signs customers give when service slips, product failures occur, or they see delivery dates become obscure guesstimates. These warnings indicate that your growing pains are negatively affecting your most important asset, your customers.

Since we know mindset is vital at every stage of your startup, it's worth mentioning here. If you focus on scaling, it typically becomes forced. By changing your mindset from "needing" to scale to seeing scaling as a natural outcome for consistent growth and customer acquisition, it will occur naturally. With your leadership at the helm, you will find yourself on course for successful growth without really trying.

My next piece of advice will sound a bit like bootstrapping. Mainly because it is, but instead of using your own money, it's keeping your eye closely on your finances and your staffing needs. Landing a VC can make it tempting to overstaff and overspend. But having the funds available doesn't mean you should take your eye off what the business truly needs. Leave the funds sitting in reserves for the more logical and natural progression growth. You can continue to see a little go a long way.

On the same topic of VC funding, with great funding comes great pressure to fill funnels, make the numbers dance, and essentially answer regularly to the powers that be. You spend more time validating that you still deserve the money they gave you and that you are as concerned about them making it back as they are. Back in our discussion on funding failures, we talked about letting the VCs get in your head and take you away from your core mission: delivering a great product and excellent service to your customers. This is not me saying you shouldn't take the money when offered, but it reminds you that using that money to grow too fast will bite you and those investors in the @ss. Keep your finger on the pulse of the customer experience, and you'll stay more strategically focused than those founders focused on filling their funnels to appease the VCs.

Honestly, though, the easiest key factor in whether or not you're growing too fast comes from the office's energy. Every startup has that buzz of excitement coupled with healthy anxiety, but if you're growing too fast, you'll feel the shift into tension, frustration, and abandonment. If you walk in your office only to see fewer and fewer people occupying the desks from a month ago, it's not only you feeling the strain; your people are, too, and they aren't sticking around.

Remember, it's all about your core mission. Trust the mission and growth will occur naturally at a reasonable pace.

Growth F*ckup #6:

Giving Up Too Soon

Great companies are built from sweat, tears, and perseverance. Even if everything around you seems to be exploding, keep moving forward.

Over the past decade, several startup founders have tragically ended their own lives. Unequipped or emotionally unable to adapt to the stress, setbacks, and sky-high expectations that come with entrepreneurialism, they caved to the pressure. These bright, talented people gave up on themselves and their dreams too soon. Each time I read news of another such case, I'm reminded of how important it is for me to take care of my mental health—not only for the sake of my businesses, but for the sake of my family, and of course, for my own sake.

Back in 2008, Chris Hill-Scott founded SwiftKey, a company that designed the AI for predictive text, with friends Jon Reynolds and Ben Medlock. Just two months later, Hill-Scott found himself at a loss. The pay was low, the time demand was high, and startup life's stress wasn't for him. He resigned and sold his shares, and purchased a bike. Years later, Microsoft purchased SwiftKey, and the remaining two founders walked away with about $50 million each.

The Fix: Stay on Target

Now that I've told you a sad story, I'll share a happy one. Finnish entrepreneur Pekka Rantala founded his company in 2003 and released fifty-one games in the company's first six years. None of them took off. Despite

Rantala's prodigious output of high-quality games, the company was near bankruptcy in 2009.

Then they released game number fifty-two, *Angry Birds*.

Rantala's company, Rovio, is one of the biggest gaming success stories ever. But as you can see, things didn't always look so rosy for the startup.

One of my favorite movie quotes is also the one I've probably known the longest, stretching back to a film released the same year I was born: "Stay on target."

Uttered during a spectacular space opera battle by "Gold Five," leading the rebels toward their final target. Perhaps you even recognize the quote and remember the scene. Being born in the same year, I still cling to the undeniable and eternal fact that the very first *Star Wars* movie (Yay! You guessed it!) never gets old.

This same line of "stay on target" has followed me through many entrepreneurial hardships, and my modest hope is this reminder would do the same for you.[1]

Rising to the stars, Rovio in 2013 even released *Angry Birds Star Wars*, a launch title on PlayStation 4 and Xbox One. And yes, those were hot gaming consoles back then.

Today, thanks to that stubbornness and runaway success, Rovio has over five hundred employees and reaps hundreds of millions in yearly revenue. All because Rantala stayed on target with the program: no customizing for flawed-fit customers, no pivoting when the going got rough (see the earlier failure, Poor Pivoting), and most importantly, no giving up. Rantala and his team stayed with the program, kept improving with each game they released, and eventually earned some hard-won success.

---

1. Yes, I admit that there are a few motivational issues with the quote, as both Gold Five and Gold Leader died mere seconds after—but it still stays with me. Add to this the controversy that the rebels were basically terrorists, trying to overthrow the existing government and implement a completely useless governmental system: The Galactic Senate. Yikes.

Thanks to *Angry Birds'* massive profitability, Rovio was able to invest in making the transition from gaming to other entertainment channels, such as their *Angry Birds* television series and movies, where the first grossed an impressive $350 million worldwide. Anyhow, the lesson we can all take from their story: every startup deserves a fair shot. If you're creating quality products and have a solid business plan and good marketing and sales teams, it's probably worth giving your business ample time to find its footing. How long? That's unique for every business. But research shows that three years is the average amount of time it takes a startup to show significant revenue.

Remember:

- There are tons of successful individuals who failed before eventually becoming a hit.
- Charles Schultz, creator of the comic *Peanuts*, was rejected by his high school yearbook staff for every cartoon he submitted.
- Walt Disney supposedly got turned down 302 times before getting the financing to create Walt Disney World.
- Twelve publishing houses rejected J. K. Rowling's first Harry Potter manuscript.
- KFC founder Colonel Sanders was allegedly rejected 1,009 times before someone bought his now-famous chicken recipe.

To be fair to Hill-Scott, the startup life isn't for everyone. And most founders have a moment (or twenty-seven) where they think about quitting. Some do, others don't, and others still just pro-con list themselves into early gray hair. Before pulling the rip cord, ask yourself these questions:

- Is your business what you initially set out to build? Have you had to pivot so far from where you first began that you can't even remember why you started this business in the first place?
- Is it financially feasible to keep going? If you're a few years in, not making a profit, and depleting your personal savings to keep living, then is it worth it? Is an end in sight?

- Can your product become the basis for your business? Let's revisit whether you have an actual business or a product that you are trying to pass off as a business.
- Have you really given your startup a fair shot? Or have you set a line in the sand that no business could succeed in?
- Is all the stress worth it? The initial years will be challenging and lean. Is the stress of that worth the investment of your time, energy, and maybe your sanity?
- Is your personality suited for stubbornness or conservative realism?

You did not come this far only to come this far.

Not Knowing When to Quit

A fate worse than failing: not quitting. There is a difference between giving up too soon, and rationally knowing that you'll never arrive.

"**Whatever you do, don't** quit! Just hang in there!" You've probably heard this before. It's almost what I've just said a few pages back.

It's a common refrain in the startup world. And for a good reason! As we discussed at the top of this chapter, one of the most significant risks founders run is that they'll succumb to mental fatigue and throw in the towel before their company has a chance to prove itself.

So, of course, I'm fully supportive of founders encouraging and lifting one another up. We all need it from time to time. At the same time, there is such a thing as not knowing when to quit.

Suppose you're stuck in limbo between making a meager profit and going bankrupt. If you're pouring all of your energy into this thing but never really going anywhere, you may have what I call a "stale startup." And if this is the case—sorry—it may be time to quit. In fact, I'll go so far as to say that not quitting will be worse for you, in the end, than bankruptcy.

This brings me to the case of the German company DaWanda. Co-founded in 2006 by the well-respected entrepreneur Claudia Helming, DaWanda quickly rose to become the leading online marketplace for homemade goods in Germany, Austria, and Switzerland—basically the German Etsy.

In its heyday, DaWanda hosted the online shops of about 380,000 artisans from around Europe. With an average of over six million products for sale, it averaged a decent 140 million euros in yearly revenue. Still, DaWanda struggled for years to scale up. One problem was the difficulty of internationalizing a German-language site. To truly broaden its horizons, DaWanda's offerings would need to be auto-translated into English, one of many costly technical overhauls that the company neglected to make. As its North American competitor, Etsy, grew in leaps and bounds, Helming tried in vain to find a partner to help lift her now stale startup out of its rut. After years of holding on, Helming finally threw in the towel in 2018.

Another fantastic example turns a spotlight on RadioShack, an American company notorious for offering any electronic gadget you might need or want. In 2015, after ninety-four years in business, the company announced it would be filing for bankruptcy. Sadly, even with online retailers becoming worthy adversaries for their customer base, RadioShack refused to pivot. Their freestanding stores still ordered parts you needed (that weren't in stock), but it took longer than Amazon to come in, let alone be delivered right to your door. With the gift of hindsight, we can see the writing on the wall, but RadioShack didn't waver. Until eleven consecutive quarterly losses. Not quitting when realizing that their business model, marketing strategy, and inventory mix were no longer competitive was worse than filing for bankruptcy.

The Fix: Goals and Deadlines

How do you avoid wasting years of your life committing the sad Not Knowing When to Quit Failure? How do you know that you won't be committing Growth Failure #6: Giving Up Too Soon by closing your company? It's basic stuff: set yourself some goals and deadlines. If your company repeatedly fails to meet them, then you'll know that, by quitting, you won't be succumbing to mental fatigue, but in fact making the wise choice to get on with your life and career. On the other hand, if you're making measurable good progress toward your goals, you might indeed be giving up too soon.

In fairness, if you're at the point where you're unsure if you should keep going or quit, ask yourself this: "Am I still passionate about this product, and do I feel like it's gaining ground?" If you say yes, of course, then stay the course. If you're a hard no way, Jose, then it's time to walk. If you're a mixture of half yes, half no, then you still have some options.

- You can stay the course and keep moving forward. But if you don't think the business is taking off, this might be a no-brainer way of realizing it's time to say "adios."
- If passion is your issue (and remember all we learned about passion in chapter 1), it might be worth considering an option to pivot in a direction that brings you more joy.
- You can always change your mind and leave the company. We make very few decisions throughout our lifetime that we can't decide to change our mind on. Starting a business is one of them. If the company isn't serving your needs any longer, you may need to put in your notice.
- Selling isn't a bad thing. If you aren't feeling it anymore, there's always the option to entertain bids to buy the business. Sell it for whatever they are offering and move on to something new.
- File for chapter 7 and shut down. It's not the same as filing chapter 11 bankruptcy, but all assets are distributed to creditors first, then remaining assets trickle to preferred shareholders, and lastly to the common shareholders.

No matter what option you choose, know that I understand the pain you might be feeling. Walking away from something you poured so much time, energy, and money into can hurt. It may even have you questioning your abilities and yourself. But hear me loud and clear when I say this: "Failure is a stepping-stone to success. Each failure is a course in future success as long as you learn something." Imagine, if you will, me patting you on the shoulder in commiseration. So many that came before you have walked in your shoes, and many will behind you. Take time to care for yourself, your family, and those you love. Let them surround you with their love and support until you are ready to square your shoulders and start fresh.

A Final Thought on Growth Failures

Growth failures are probably the hardest to swallow in the whole book. I know. I saved it for last intentionally. Once you've laid all the groundwork to get your company up and running, circumvented a whole host of potential other pitfalls, once you get to the point of growing, you've already tasted some measure of success.

We all remember that 90 percent of businesses potentially fail. The statistic haunts us even when we're awake. But when you have made it "this far" only to take a wrong turn in growth planning and decision-making, seeing yourself as one of the lucky 10 percent can change overnight and feel horribly defeating.

I said it before, and I'll repeat it, if you make a failure here that you cannot correct, know you've learned a valuable lesson, and you will find success again. Probably even more than you thought you had now. But if you see one of these failures approaching in the distance, you can still make some changes to course-correct and keep moving forward.

Ultimately, the decision is yours. Only you know how much energy and passion you have left. Tolerance testing people, especially startup founders, isn't like testing metals. Each one of us has an entirely different and variable threshold for pain tolerance. There's nothing wrong with tapping out if the going gets too tough.

And if you made it through this chapter and felt the overwhelming sense that you're doing everything right and you're sure to be in the famed 10 percent, congratulations! However, I will pause here for a moment to let you know there's still one more chapter left.

It's a doozy.

Brace yourself for all the failures you never saw coming.

Chapter 9

All the F*ckups You Never Saw Coming

Until this point, each of the f*ckups we discussed were tangible and based on analysis of those thousands upon thousands of actual startup failures and their historical statistics of failure. Which makes getting this far without significant incident commendable. There are a few last potential points of failure coming your way if you aren't careful though. And while these two major future failures are deserving of their own chapter, they also can potentially be seen in some capacity in other failures we already discussed. Simply put, one occurs when a founder doesn't consider far enough into the future, the other when a founder looks too far in one hyper-focused direction and misses the obvious points of failure littering the pathway before them.

Claiming that I have the tools for you to accurately predict the future would either sound completely bonkers or above-founder-average arrogant (which can admittedly be massive compared to ordinary people). So I won't make that claim. But that does not mean we can't get reasonably close to the target. I've worked with many companies on scenario planning and positioning as an advisor. I've also worked for several years with the Copenhagen Institute for Futures Studies, and their associate director Thomas Geuken, who is not only a skilled strategic futurist but also a speaker and accomplished author.

Long story short, I do believe most of the hurdles that come our way can be predicted to some degree.

Not Believing the Future Is Predictable

Failing to fundamentally believe it's possible to predict the future is the cause of a torrent of failures. Not even trying is just plain stupid.

The brilliant theoretical physicist Stephen Hawking once said, "God plays dice and sometimes throws them where they cannot be seen." It's a fitting example of the unpredictability of the future, especially if you don't even look for the clues.

Funnily enough, the Magic 8-Ball, a Mattel toy, was inspired by the inventor's clairvoyant mother. The toy, shaped like an 8 ball, is filled with water and a twenty-sided dice. While this toy has ranked as one of the top one hundred greatest toys, still selling about a million units each year, it's not a viable future prediction method.

Too often, companies use little more than this Magic 8-Ball approach to plan for the future outside their next budget year. While the toy is entertaining, it shouldn't be the go-to method for planning your company's future.

Failures in this category are plenty. They also have other failure components that are often given more attention in the media than future prediction. However, companies like Kodak and Xerox are great examples of businesses that failed to look to the future despite having products that could shape the landscape of their industry. They feared making strides outside of their target existing marketplace.

Perhaps this sounds a bit like the fear of failure component of attitude failures to you. If so, you'd be correct. That is one of the issues they faced when it came to believing the future wasn't predictable.

Kodak definitely deserves a spot in the Great Hall of Failures. Founded in 1888, they once held 85–90 percent of camera and film sales in the US. With that command of the market, they had nothing to gain but a lot left to lose.

Which, unfortunately, they did—sadly, to the advent of digital photography. Interestingly enough, Kodak gets credit for inventing the first handheld digital camera in 1975. Yes. 1975. However, they did not have the passion or talent for the category and neglected it in all imaginable ways until it was impossible to ignore any longer. And by then, of course, it was far too late to recover.

At the same time, Kodak underwent an intense rivalry with Japanese Fuji, who had entered the US market with increasing success.

Kodak failed to anticipate the future. It would not be accurate to claim that Kodak only failed from being a mulish manufacturer, but they went far to avoid any predictions. Their once-successful strategy deprived them of their share of the future. They continued to steer their ship with the horizon planted firmly on photographic film rather than digital.

Enjoying their version of a Kodak moment, Xerox is another example of a company being both sizable and silly. Similarly, Xerox invented a ton of brilliant stuff, including the personal computer, a graphical user interface (GUI), the computer mouse, laser printers, object-oriented programming (a big thing if you're a geek), ethernet, and so much more. All in their Palo Alto Research Center (Xerox PARC).

Long story short, the initial models of their otherwise revolutionary computer developments were too expensive for the mass market. Instead of further developing them, Xerox abandoned them to focus on what was then considered their core business.

Perhaps cut a bit short, as their story contains a few fun anecdotes from the company that could have been Apple, Adobe, and Pixar—just to mention a few:

Their computer, the Xerox Alto, was admired throughout Silicon Valley. The GUI was even touted as the future of computing by most in the industry. In 1979, a CEO named Steve from a company called Apple even bought access (via stock options) for his engineers to receive demonstrations of the Xerox computer technology. This inspired the Apple Lisa and Macintosh systems, while the rest is, as they say, history.

Not only did Xerox quite literally sell what could have been a bright future, but this and other decisions frustrated many of their talented employees. One of them, John Warnock, left the company, and, with PARC colleague Charles Geschke, founded what we all know of as Adobe (yes, Photoshop and all that jazz).

Pixar, you ask? Yes, Alvy Ray Smith and David DiFrancesco also left Xerox. They later became founding members of that impressive company that brought us box office blockbusters like *Toy Story*, *Finding Nemo*, and *Cars*, to mention a few, which have been running in our living rooms ad nauseam.

Similar stories could be told about Charles Simonyi and Richard Brodie, who made the programs that later became Microsoft Word, Excel, and Access.

Both Kodak and Xerox are classic cases of incumbents ignoring the innovations presented right in front of them. Had either of these companies taken a more systematic look into the future, they could have had a completely different ending.

Granted, the gift of hindsight does wonders for a business after it has failed. Instead, imagine taking hindsight and seeing the warnings and changing trends early. That is future prediction.

The Fix: Look Through the Johari Window at the 3 Ps of the Future

A key component in predicting anything is simple awareness of potential futures. This awareness can be achieved in different ways. For our purpose, I like to work with two sets of building blocks: a slightly modified version of the Johari window and three different futures.

The Johari window—named after its inventors, psychologists Joseph Luft and Harrington Ingham back in 1955—is a way for people to understand their relationship with themselves and others but is equally valid as a tool to uncover blind spots in businesses. Yours included.

The technique became quite famous thanks to Donald Rumsfeld when he used the phrase the "known unknowns" when addressing a connection between Baghdad and terrorist groups in 2002. At the time, the concept was hard to understand. It took years until the idea took on a deeper meaning for me.

This classification of uncertainty and predictions leaves us with a window of four quadrants: Known/Knowns (things we are aware of and understand), Known/Unknowns (things we're aware of but don't understand), Unknown/Knowns (which we understand but are not aware of), and Unknown/Unknowns (those nasties we're neither cognizant of nor understand). Despite writing it, I even have to read that line once more myself.

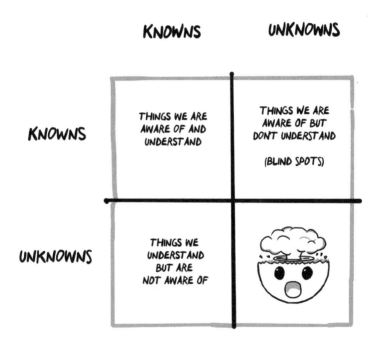

So in the Known/Knowns, everything is good. Still, in the Unknown/Knowns, we meet a Black Swan (as in the book by Nassim Nicholas Taleb, not the otherwise awesome song by Thom Yorke, the lead singer of Radiohead) of highly unexpected events of massive consequence. Stuff we probably did not predict, despite our best effort.

To employ our slightly adjusted version of the Johari window, you can use the illustration above. As seen in the image, there are four quadrants.

You can either understand an outcome or impact or know the threat or concern in all but one quadrant. That leaves one lonely quadrant, which is the Unknown/Unknowns. That 25 percent is a risk. If you apply anything in the Johari window and land in any of the three quadrants with at least one known factor, you can pretty accurately predict a situation. However, if you land in the fourth, you're likely in alien territory as crazy, unfathomable situations commonly land a person there. This simple way of evaluating predictable outcomes can really help you plan ahead, reduce risk, and forecast with greater accuracy.

Okay, so, with our ability to see through the Johari window, we can move on to the different futures. When it comes to predicting the future in the simplest terms, I use a framework of three possibilities: the Provable future, the Probable future, and the Possible future.

- **Provable** addresses events you can predict with "certainty." For example, we know technology will continue to improve globally, and we will see more AI built into our everyday life.

- **Probable** speaks to the "likely" things in the future. Based on what we know currently, what will likely happen in the future. This includes the idea of self-driving cars with AI. Based on the provable growth in the AI market, this is a probability likely to come to fruition.

- **Possible** is the stuff that "might" happen based on what we currently know to be true. Sticking with our AI vehicle, a possible outcome is that those self-driving future cars might also fly.

The point in looking at these three possible futures is you should start from the certain and build onward from there. Most people do take a backward approach to this prediction methodology to their detriment. If you begin with uncertain items, it's easy to spiral into a world of unknowns and find yourself stuck, unable to make a decision. Understanding this means that when you begin with areas of certainty, you can then take a step further by asking, "Now that we know this to be true, then what is certain to happen next in this area?"

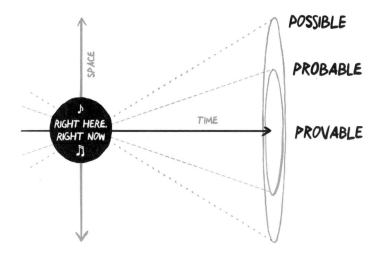

Typically, I recommend using this predictive method for not only the short-term future but also for longer-term projecting as well. Obviously, at the cost of less accuracy, but still adding perspective. While I often end up with three-year predictions, you can, of course, do shorter and longer forecasts when making decisions based on your situation, market, industry, quality of data, and so on.

When evaluating different options as you move through your startup and make decisions, there are two main reasoning options: reasoning by analogy and reasoning from First Principle.

- **Reasoning by analogy** is a quick and simple tool to use in decision-making depending on your industry and decision. Simply put, comparing your situation to another, similar situation with similar parameters another company has faced and seeing their outcome can provide you a reasonable analogy comparison.

The most important thing to keep in mind when using this reasoning technique is that the parameters of the decision you're considering must match a similar situation in another business. It should be an apples-to-apples-style comparison.

- **Reasoning by First Principle** can be traced back to Aristotle but has recently experienced a popularity surge, thanks to, among others, the Tesla and SpaceX captain, Elon Musk. The First Principle is essentially digging down to the smallest known true component of a situation and building up from that point. So start with what is proven to be true and build from there. This reasoning methodology works best for complicated frameworks where the analogy cases may not exist or be relevant to the decision.

I find both approaches valid under their specific circumstances, but it's important to be aware of what approach you select.

The Future Is Certain but Unwritten

Every morning when you wake up, you are picking up the pen of life and beginning a new page. What you write is somewhat predictable.

Failure also comes in the form of people who complete some basic future predictions but just completely miss the target or sometimes fail to follow up on what they discover. These can also be people who formulate future analysis for a set period (perhaps a year or two) and then never reevaluate as time moves on. Realistically, looking to the future should be as routine as any other regular operating procedures of your business. To stay on top of new trends, world events, and market movers, regular evaluation and assessment must occur.

The most commonly cited failures in this area come from stock market crashes. Take the Great Depression, for example. Irving Fisher was an economics professor at Yale University, a statistician, and an inventor, known for his pioneering research and significant contributions to the field. He was perhaps the world's first celebrity economist and definitely a clever guy. What most people remember him for is his October 1929 quote in the pages of the *New York Times*: "Stocks have reached what looks like a permanently high plateau." He was an expert, and he was firm in his analysis.

Nine days later, the market crashed, leading to the Great Depression. Following the subsequent "black days," he (and many others) continued with optimistic predictions. For months after the crash, Fisher continued arguing that recovery was just around the corner.

Talk about educated incapacity; Fisher was an expert in his field, but it was, in fact, his detailed knowledge of the market that made him miss the bigger picture.

Fisher and his peers made it easy to think that stock analysts were invented only to make weather forecasters look good.

Another famous example comes from William Orton, the president of Western Union, when he was quoted as saying, "The telephone has too many shortcomings to be seriously considered as a form of communication." Intent on the notion that telegraphs would stay the communication method of choice, Western Union dismissed Alexander Graham Bell's invention rather than finding a way to embrace the new technology. This shortsighted refusal to follow up as the communication industry began to change left them in the dust fighting with Bell Telephone and losing. Failure to acknowledge what you see as the future or to reevaluate the market due to new conditions, inventions, and so on will only result in a lot of heartache and pain for a business. Worry not. There are three great ways to look at future predictions more in-depth to get a reasonable evaluation that can be rinsed and repeated as often as you'd like to ensure your company stays ahead of, or at least on top of, new trends.

The Fix: Stick to Reason

When it comes to techniques to think about the future, there are some interesting tools available. The US military used the phrase VUCA more than thirty years ago as a way to talk about our environment, drawing on the ideas of American scholars Warren Bennis and Burt Nanus. The term is still widespread today, as it's a reasonably easy-to-remember and straightforward framework. It stands for Volatility, Uncertainty, Complexity, and Ambiguity:

- **Volatility:** You know that we're seeing an exponential change in technology and many other areas, but also the cycles are shortening. Changes that earlier took decades now take years.
- **Uncertainty:** We might lack information, and it's increasingly difficult to predict how events will unfold. And consider how we talked earlier regarding Irving Fisher about the stock market. Similarly, Ken Olsen is known for his contribution to the basis of modern-day computers. Both men were experts in their fields, and today entirely off target. An illusion of certainty.
- **Complexity:** Complexity is just there—with more coming. And actually, that creates more options. It's that simple.

- **Ambiguity:** This is the Unknown/Unknowns of our Johari window. Not only do we not know the outcome, but we also don't even know what parameters are available or the game we're playing.

If you're with the in-crowd, then you can also use TUNA (Rafael Ramirez and Angela Wilkinson's more recent take on VUCA, developed at the University of Oxford: Turbulent, Uncertain, Novel, Ambiguous), as VUCA to a degree is redundant: *Complex* already involves volatility, uncertainty, and ambiguity. On the other hand, *novel* also seems a bit irrelevant. Anyway, as this is not a competition and we're here for a practical purpose, I will stick with the more well-known VUCA.

It is important to note here that while both VUCA and TUNA are shorthand for "Weird stuff coming up!" they're also a bit misleading, in the sense that it sounds impossible to plan for. Lucky for us, we're not intellectually lazy people, so we can plan. It's also possible to notice the connection VUCA offers to our earlier-discussed 3 Ps (Provable, Probable, Possible). When comparing the two, VUCA essentially takes the opposite approach and begins with the most uncertain aspect, working backward until you land in a more certain territory.

So, with this understanding of VUCA, we are now getting very practical. To make a more focused prediction for your company, applying a (oldie but goldie, developed in a simpler form as ETPS by Francis J. Aguilar all the way back in 1965) PESTLE framework gives you a broader scope of what is on the horizon. It allows you to make decisions with intelligent and actionable data. Keep in mind, we don't want to get stuck in analysis paralysis when completing this evaluation tool.

- **Political:** What is the current political climate in your industry? Does anything major politically affect your company?
- **Economic:** Do factors like exchange rates, inflation, interest rates, or economic growth affect your business?

- **Social:** Social factors include population growth, demographics, education, career attitudes, safety concerns, cultural accommodations, and health consciousness.

- **Technological:** Are there any tech issues that might impede your ability to enter a marketplace? Is your industry affected by the rate of technology improvements, or are you limited by R & D?

- **Legal:** Are there any laws on the books or currently being reviewed that might affect your industry? What about employment law, consumer laws, antitrust laws, and so on?

- **Environmental:** Are there any environmental aspects that may affect your place in the industry? Are you impacted by weather, climate, or natural disasters due to your geographic region?

As shown in the illustration, PESTLE takes into account factors such as Political, Economic, Social, Technological, Legal, and Environmental to help you make an accurate prediction for the future of your company. On my website, kimhvidkjaer.com, you can download this canvas and input information for your startup to see how relatively simple it is to generate actionable intelligence and foresight for your three-year future. Stay open and alert and, as the facts change, make sure to also change your mind.

POLITICAL

GOVERNMENT
LEGISLATION
REGULATION
TAX

ECONOMIC

MONETARY POLICY
GROWTH
LABOR
INFLATION

LEGAL

REGIONAL LAW
LAW ENFORCEMENT
INDUSTRY REGULATIONS
COURT SYSTEM

COMPANY

SOCIAL

EMPLOYMENT
DEMOGRAPHIC
CULTURAL NORMS
INCOME DISTRIBUTION

CLIMATE CHANGE
WORKFORCE HEALTH
ENERGY AVAILABILITY
RESOURCE MANAGEMENT

ENVIRONMENTAL

NEW TECH
TAKE-UP RATES
R&D EFFORTS
COMMUNICATION

TECHNOLOGY

A Final Word on Future Prediction

With all of this in place, you will end up with different plausible scenarios of the future. Your task is then to maximize your future freedom of action so you avoid getting trapped somewhere unpleasant. This is also the definition of intelligence Dr. Alex Wissner-Gross (also an accomplished entrepreneur) explained to me. Alex has developed an equation for this: $F = T \nabla S\tau^1$, explaining how intelligence can be viewed as a physical process, trying to maximize future freedom of action and avoid constraints in its own future. This is the goal for our startups when predicting possible futures.

And as with most other things in life, practice also moves you closer to perfect in the world of predictions.

Predictions also relate to loss aversion—the fear of losing a buck is greater than the joy of gaining one. At the same time, we're more likely to buy into an optimistic prediction than a negative one. So try inverting the picture—ideally, combining forecasts from several independent sources can give you a more accurate image of the future reality.

Like some of our previous chapters, the fixes for future prediction failures boil down to planning ahead. Sure, it sounds simple when you read it in this book, but the idea may seem overwhelming in practice. The good news is that plenty of people have been studying the science behind future prediction for a very long time. Their hard work is to our benefit.

When it comes to risk, I'm often told that people see me as a risk-taker. My life as an entrepreneur seems like I'm opposed to having a "real job" or something. It boggles my mind. While it's improbable I would consider a position working for someone else, I wouldn't rule it out *entirely* if the right opportunity came my way. But knowing I have the ultimate

---

1. Intelligence is a force (F) trying to maximize future freedom of action (keeping options open), with some strength (T), with the diversity of possible accessible futures (S), up to some future time horizon (τ—tau). In short, intelligence doesn't like to get trapped.

control over my earning potential, employment, and career future makes me (at least in my mind) super low-risk oriented and risk-averse. Sure, I've had some devastating failures along the way in my career. But they were always calculated and, to some extent, within my control. Without question, the fantastic highs achieved consistently outweighed the lows.

In fairness, going back to the chapter 8 introduction, I've always stayed true to what I call "Rule Zero: Don't die." It's elegant in its simplicity, but it is still the rule that guides me in this world of startups. What doesn't kill me makes me stronger. Choosing to found a startup isn't risky if you do the work. It's gratifying and will provide a learning experience as nothing else can. So if you worry that you're gambling with your future if you get into the startup game, it's not true. Unless, of course, you ignore everything I've shared with you in this book. Therefore, if you were to ask my opinion on what is riskier, being a freelancer or an employee, I'd have to say the employee. I realize startup life isn't for everyone, and I believe everyone needs to find their path to happiness and success. But if the startup life is for you, then let's talk about how to spot those hidden mines along your marathon's path.

No matter what you do, always make a decision. Don't let analysis paralysis hold you hostage. The worst decision you make is not making one at all. As long as you take at least a moment to consider the provable outcomes and build from there, you will likely make a decision you won't regret. So don't get stuck worrying about the decision and living in a place of indecision. Be bold. Run the provables. Look at sound reasoning principles and affecting factors. Make a decision. Then make another. And another.

Thus gifted with foresight, I predict you, my esteemed reader, to the degree of provable, will continue reading the following sentence. And yes, it seems that we were right. Next, I predict to the degree of probable that you will continue to the next page!

CONCLUSION
(Okay, So You Still F*cked Up. Now What?)

Here we find ourselves at the end of the book. We've learned not only how to spot the mines along the course of our marathon to create a startup but also how to detonate them. We've learned how to fix the attitude, business model, market research, funding, product development, organizational, sales, and growth f*ckups of your startup. Heck, we've even gone so far as to learn how to predict with a good degree of certainty where the unknown future f*ckups might occur on the horizon. But before we part ways, I want us to take a minute to remember something we've mentioned multiple times throughout the book—Rule Zero: Don't die.

One of my favorite startup stories of all time comes by way of a little startup started by two high school friends in Seattle, Washington. The two pals belonged to The Lakeside Programmers Group at school, which was provided free computer time in exchange for writing new computer programs. Traffic usage calculated using pneumatic road tubes and counters that mechanically count the puffs of air generated by tires rolling over the tubes on paper tape need manual computation. Those paper tapes are translated by large firms into data the local and state governments use to determine road usage, traffic patterns, and roadway conditions.

The two boys believed they could process the data cheaper and faster than the firms manually processing the information. Together with their classmates, they began to translate the punch tapes into computer codes. With the assistance of a computer at the University of Washington, the pair was able to produce traffic flow charts in faster time than the manual firms.

This code began their company. Their next goal was to build a device to read the tapes automatically without the manual labor required. They set out to build a custom computer that could read the manual data and create the reports. Amazingly enough, the students were able to win bids and sell their services—until it became known they were still under the age of eighteen. Then, sales became harder to come by. Despite their age, and an ad-hoc computer built from spare parts, the company lasted for three years, but never really made it big. Unfortunately, the state began offering an automated service free to local towns and cities making private contractors, and their company, Traf-O-Data, obsolete—thus earning them the merit of their first startup failure.

The two founders of Traf-O-Data took a beat to regroup after the closure and went on to found a company we all know: Microsoft.

You read that right. The two friends in high school that created Traf-O-Data were the same two guys that later dropped out of prestigious universities (Paul Allen had a perfect 1600 SAT score and attended Washington State University, and Bill Gates was enrolled at Harvard) and founded Microsoft. We don't have to discuss how wildly successful that venture was.

So if you fail, don't give up. Had Bill Gates and Paul Allen given up, so many products we use daily wouldn't exist.

Whether you picked up this book to see if the startup life might be for you, or if you're experiencing some failures along the way, or if you are on the other side of a significant failure that ended your startup, you need to remember Rule Zero: Don't die.

Write it on your hand. Post a note on your computer screen. Set a reminder on your phone. If you get it as a tattoo, then please send me a photo!

Whatever it takes to remind yourself. Rule Zero stands above all else. Even if your startup fails, you didn't fail. I've known founders who filed for bankruptcy only to begin anew and become hugely successful. I've known founders to sell their company for a life-changing profit, only to be broke five years later.

"Don't give up. Don't die." Those were the words I wrote on my hand the day of my Ironman in Copenhagen, as you might remember from chapter 8. It might sound a bit melodramatic (okay, it *was* a bit melodramatic), but I had decent reasoning. I'd suffered a couple of blackouts while training, and a triathlete died from a heart attack in the half Ironman a year prior. The news story seemed to play a loop in my mind some days. So I figured it was nice to have my priorities straight on race day.

DON'T GIVE UP
DON'T DIE

I wrote it in the order of how I felt I might need to remember it that day, but it applies to every startup I've had too.

There are two levels at which you should apply Rule Zero: Don't die.

Don't die. I mean physically this time. Even if you *did* go personally bankrupt (I just told you not to, so I'm then assuming it happened before you read this book), don't lose hope. There are people who love you and need you. There are people whose lives you can affect in a positive way. If everything seems like crap right now, then know it will be better. There are a surprisingly large number of founders that commit suicide. Even if it feels like *everything* is lost, hold on. You'll see later it's not the case. A feeling of hopelessness will distort your idea of how things really are, and affect your decision-making capabilities.

If you are experiencing hopelessness, reach out to a close friend or loved one, or a doctor or mental health specialist—anyone who would have your best interests at heart. As you now know, plenty of people messed up completely—in relation to business, friends, family, reputation, and everything else—and bounced back with great success. So hold on. There is so much good to come. And so much more you have to offer the world. I promise.

Don't risk everything. Don't bet the farm. Avoid personal bankruptcy if at all possible. Don't run around to loan sharks (I did; it didn't work), as this is as close to pissing your pants for warmth as it gets. Don't sacrifice family, friends, or your household. Avoid getting in debt above both ears if at all possible. Seriously. It's better to come back and start again later than risk everything you have on this one venture. You have more startups in you; I promise that too.

Know your limits. I'm not saying that you should always obey them—but definitely know them.

You didn't fail if you are here to tell the tale. You have done something remarkable, and you should be proud of yourself. I know I'm proud of you. So please hop on over to my website and celebrate with us. There's nothing so freeing as failure. All the pressure is gone. You can take a breath of fresh air and reconnect with everything that sat on the back burner while you tried to manage your startup and learned valuable lessons along the way. Now it's time to reset your mind, body, and spirit. Throw yourself a party, spend time outside, spend time with your loved ones, and when you're ready, do a postmortem on the business. I'm sure you'll learn even more with the fresh eyes and the gift of hindsight.

You didn't fail; you progressed.

If your startup failed or is failing, then it is easy to dismiss what you've done as "just failing with your startup." That would be wrong—and also a gross oversimplification.

You did not "just" throw a basketball and miss the basket at the buzzer during the playoff game.

No. You did so much more:

- You engineered and produced the ball.
- You conceptualized, designed, created, and hung the basket.
- You studied and memorized all the rules.
- You trained and hit the basket plenty of times for an entire season, or two or three.

But somewhere in the game, you also missed the basket. This is an entirely different thing than failing.

It is the same case if you fail with your startup.

- You've developed an idea.
- You created a business model.
- You probably developed a product, solution, or a store.
- You perhaps had funding (yay!), or you bootstrapped and did it yourself (double yay!).
- You probably sold to customers.
- Maybe you had partners or employees.

All of these are successes. They are mines you avoided in the minefield. Then, somewhere, you perhaps also had a severe failure—a f*ckup—that was enough to halt your startup. That is nothing to be ashamed of. It is something to be proud of.

~~F*CK UP~~

LEVEL UP!

While it may feel like a failure, it wasn't. You've just leveled up in the great game of startups. I challenge you to go back to the parts of the book that spoke most to you and replace "f*ck up" with "level up."

Inhale the future, exhale the past.

What happens next, you ask?

After a f*ckup comes another start(up).

Know this: Next time, your likelihood of going all the way is much, much greater. So make sure there is a next time.

~~START OVER~~

STARTUP AGAIN

What you've done is complete several levels.

If you've leveled up, head on over to my website at www.kimhvid kjaer.com and take our "Leveled Up" pledge. Print that bad boy out and hold it high with pride! Feel free to share it with me and on social media, so together we all can celebrate the learning process, the new-found knowledge that is bound to make you a greater success next time around, and the courage you have to start up again. Remember, there is no shame in failing. It is the by-product of actually doing something. As long as you've learned something and are better prepared for the next time around, you've succeeded.

Many of the founders mentioned throughout this book have gone through these very same steps. They failed. Licked their wounds. Learned from their mistakes. And then started again. Remember Paul Biggar who failed with NewsTilt? He later founded the very successful Circle CI and Dark. EventVue founded by Josh Fraser? He co-founded PriceSlash and Origin. Or what about Gary Swart from Intellibank? He became the

CEO of oDesk, now Upwork, the largest freelancer marketplace in the world. And the list goes on and on and on. Each new project reaches a greater level of success than their previous venture. Learn from these giants. Learn from my mistakes. Learn from your mistakes. Keep learning and working toward your startup success.

I look forward to hearing all about your startup experiences. Feel free to share them and select the category where you leveled up with your company on the website in our f*ckup database. Join me and other entrepreneurs as we share where things went wrong, how we fixed it (if we could), and everything else in between.

As they say, it's like déjà vu all over again.

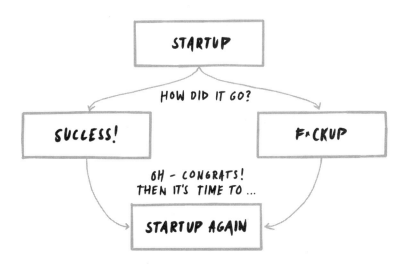

PS: I've compiled *The F*ckup Toolkit* to support the book. It includes a list of all the f*ckups discussed in this book, the models and tools as downloadable files, a f*ckup test, an overview of the most common cognitive biases, and several other resources.

Find the toolkit at www.kimhvidkjaer.com/startup, or send an email to startup@kimhvidkjaer.com to request it.

ACKNOWLEDGMENTS

First off, thank you, dearest reader, for actually buying this book.

It took years to write, much longer to conceptualize, and would *definitely* not be possible without the help of a very long list of people. A list long enough that it could fill up a chapter of its own. Acknowledging that only *they* would even read such a chapter, my editor asked me to skip it—so I'll keep it brief. The ideas presented here are obviously not mine alone. They are instead a synthesis of thoughts I've collected over the years from a myriad of sources.

Most importantly, I sincerely want to thank all the noble founders who have shared their stories and honest analyses of their failures, allowing the rest of us to learn from them. They are the heroes of this book. Without their candid descriptions, compiling the advice in this book would not have been possible. From my own adventures, both failed and fruitful, I also greatly appreciate all the customers who have supported me over the years and even the many competitors I've encountered— most of whom are irritatingly sympathetic and inventive. All the greater, the many partners, vendors, and mentors I've been blessed with over the years.

In addition to my many talks and interviews with founders, my more quantitative analysis of over 160,000 failed companies is a homemade, non-alcoholic cocktail mixed from a multitude of databases and compilations such as Dun & Bradstreet, Crunchbase, CB Insights, Failory, various European business registers, and several other ingredients. Without them, this would all be imaginary.

Credits to Austin Kleon, from whom I've stolen plenty, and so should you. Nods to Jimbo for creating Wikipedia, a source for countless hours of procrastination over longevity, philosophy, and quantum mechanics. An appreciative hat tip to the many members of both VL *and* Bongorama for a frequent flow of fresh ideas. Thanks to NIN and Radiohead for the playlists, and to tea, literally hundreds of gallons of Earl Grey, for keeping me awake.

Loving brownie points to all my friends and family—without you, I would have finished writing this much earlier. Ditto to all my former (and current) colleagues at great companies such as Shockwaved, TBWA, Natur-Energi, Boardmeter, Moranti, GAFFA, and Simply CRM—as you're also both friends and family. And unpaid therapists.

Thanks to the now-defunct Space Invaders for letting me in, and to Copenhagen Business School for letting me out.

A very warm high-five goes out to both the Royal Danish Academy of Fine Arts, School of Architecture and School of Design, for diligently dismissing all my applications, which, in return, forced me to start my own company.

INDEX

customer relationship
  management (CRM) systems,
  82, 249, 250–256. *See also* sales
customers. *See also* industry;
  market
  diversifying, 64–68
  feedback from, 102, 259, 260
  focus on, 100–103, 125, 307
  high-value, 260
  needy, 291
  number of, 68
  pivoting and, 289
  product fit and, 257–261, 311
  retaining, 98
  size of, 67–68
  in testing process, 110–111
  understanding, 271
customization, 68, 98

D
Daqri, 187
Dark, 31, 344
data, 109
DaWanda, 315
deadlines, 230
debt, 342
decisions
  anchoring and, 297–299
  availability heuristics and,
    296–297
  bad, 293–300
  confirmation bias and, 299
  importance of making, 338
  loss aversion and, 295–296
  not making, 108, 110
  reasoning by analogy, 329–330
  reasoning by First Principle,
    330
  survivorship bias and, 300
Delicious, 291

depression, 15
Descartes, René, 28, 32
desire, 237
details, minor, 292
Diaz, Ariel, 65
differentiation, 86, 87, 88, 91
DiFrancesco, David, 326
Digital Knowledge Assets, 179
dilution, accepting, 140
DiMarco, Dominic, 252
Disney, Walt, 312
disruption, 57
distractions, 290–292
diversity, 220–223
divorce, 208
Dixon, Rex, 65
Domino's Pizza, 207
doubt, 40, 228, 289
  impostor syndrome, 21–26
Dropbox, 170
drop-shipping, 129
Dru, Jean-Marie, 57
drug trade, 115
Dunn, Jeff, 60
Dunning-Kruger effect, 24, 38
Dunstone, Charles, 146, 147

E
eBay, 289
EBIDA (Earnings Before
  Interest, Depreciation, and
  Amortization), 53
economic climate, 334
80 percent = 100 percent rule, 177,
  189, 228
Einstein, Albert, 61
Einstein, Ben, 61
employees. *See also* organizations;
  teams
  bad, 218–219

ABOUT THE AUTHOR

Kim Hvidkjaer is an award-winning serial entrepreneur, keynote speaker, and angel investor, having built more companies from startup to exit than he has ever scored goals in soccer. He has admittedly also shattered several startups—and is downright terrible at any sports involving balls.

He started his first company at the tender age of 19, and as a 29-year-old millionaire, he was aptly named one of Denmark's "6 Rising Stars."

Two years later, after a cluster of f*ckups, he found himself broke—having lost more money than the average American earns in a lifetime.

Kim has since, through 25 years in business across a broad range of industries, rebuilt his fortune through several startups and become an expert in failure. Interviewing dozens of startup founders and studying thousands of collapsed startups, he has developed a comprehensive guide to failure—what it means, what it looks like, and how to avoid it.

As a surprise for some, failure was actually never something Kim aimed for, much less something he anticipated dedicating his life to. Today his interest in failure stretches well beyond startups, and into health, parenting, author bios, etc.

Kim has advised major brands from LEGO to PlayStation, Motorola, and Huawei, as well as enjoyed speaking engagements and board work for organizations around the world. He has also been nominated for myriad awards that he never won.

He yearns to take a year-long vacation with his family, write books and music, but some startup somehow always gets in the way of his yearning. Meanwhile, he lives in a beautiful home in Copenhagen with his partner, their two kids, dachshunds, rabbits, and obsessive collection of guitars.

TLDR: Kim has crashed a handful of his startups completely. Please buy his book.

If you want to know more about Kim's work and writing—or have your own stories of failure—please visit his website at www.kimhvidkjaer .com, or find him on social media.